THE WIZARD OF WASHINGTON

The Franklin and Eleanor Roosevelt Institute Series
on Diplomatic and Economic History

General Editors: Arthur M. Schlesinger, Jr., William J. vanden Heuvel, and Douglas Brinkley

THE WIZARD OF WASHINGTON

EMIL HURJA, FRANKLIN ROOSEVELT, AND THE BIRTH OF PUBLIC OPINION POLLING

MELVIN G. HOLLI

palgrave

THE WIZARD OF WASHINGTON
Copyright © Melvin G. Holli, 2002.
All rights reserved. No part of this book may be used or reproduced in any manner whatsoever without written permission except in the case of brief quotations embodied in critical articles or reviews.

First published 2002 by PALGRAVE™
175 Fifth Avenue, New York, N.Y. 10010 and
Houndmills, Basingstoke, Hampshire, England RG21 6XS.
Companies and representatives throughout the world.

PALGRAVE is the new global publishing imprint of St. Martin's Press LLC Scholarly and Reference Division and Palgrave Publishers Ltd. (formerly Macmillan Press Ltd.).

ISBN 0-312-29395-X

Library of Congress Cataloging-in-Publication Data
Holli, Melvin G.
The wizard of Washington : Emil Hurja, Franklin Roosevelt, and the birth of public
opinion polling / by Melvin G. Holli.
        p.   cm.—(Franklin and Eleanor Roosevelt Institute series on diplomatic and economic history)
    Includes bibliographical references and index.
    ISBN 0–312–29395–X (hardcover)
    1. Public opinion—United States.   2 Public opinion polls.   3. Hurja, Emil.   4. United States—Politics and government—1933–1945.
I. Title.   II. Series.

HN90.P8 H63   2002
303.3'8.0973—dc21   2001053166

A catalogue record for this book is available from the British Library.

Design by Letra Libre, Inc.

First edition: February 2002
10 9 8 7 6 5 4 3 2 1

Printed in the United States of America.

CONTENTS

Dedicated to
Dr. James Ojala and
Professor Betsy B. Holli.

Acknowledgments

My interest in the first pollster to work for an American president dates back to my graduate school days when I worked as a research assistant and then curator of manuscripts at the University of Michigan's Bentley Library cataloging the papers of Mayor, Governor, U.S. Attorney General, and Supreme Court Justice Frank Murphy. My mentor, Professor Sidney Fine, was then researching what would become a multivolume biography of Murphy. While cataloging the papers I came across correspondence from the Democratic National Committee's executive director, Emil Hurja, discussing a Hurja-directed poll of Michigan voters: the poll persuaded President Roosevelt to ask Murphy to resign his post as high commissioner of the Philippines and to come back to run for governor of Michigan. The sampling of Michigan voters that Hurja collected with Donald Kennedy in 1936 indicated that FDR would need the popular Murphy to carry Michigan in the presidential election. Murphy complied and returned to run successfully for governor, and Roosevelt carried Michigan.

The fact that President Roosevelt had been quietly using a pollster to guide his campaigns and to secretly test the popularity of his New Deal programs was not then generally known. In fact, most polling studies credit John F. Kennedy and Louis Harris as the first presidential poll team in history. It seemed to me that the United States' first presidential pollster deserved a scholarly study. Although this was the natal period in scientific polling as applied to politics, Hurja from his engineering and mineral analysis background understood scientific sampling, probability theory, and how to use quotas to get representative samples. Perhaps equally important, he knew how to reweight and correct mega–straw polls such as those of the *Literary Digest* and make political sense of them.

Although Hurja is sometimes mentioned by New Deal political historians and FDR biographers, the comment is generally limited to Hurja's 1935 "secret" poll measuring the damage challenger Huey Long might do to FDR's reelection campaign. The full extent of Emil Hurja's polling for FDR has not been generally known. Emil Hurja was the first presidential pollster to apply the newly developing science of polling to election campaigns and governing. Only recently have a few political writers recognized the importance of Hurja's polling to FDR's presidency.

I began researching and collecting materials on Emil Hurja and polling a good many years ago, researching in presidential and other library archives. When I left Michigan for my first job, however, it was teaching urban and ethnic History at the University of Illinois at Chicago, and this required me to shelve the Hurja polling project for some time. I then concentrated my efforts on my first book, *Reform in Detroit: Hazen S. Pingree and Urban Politics,* which was published by Oxford in Richard Wade's Urban Life in America series. For the next two decades I focused on urban, ethnic and political history and turned out a dozen books.

As we moved into the fin de siècle decade, I realized that *tempus fugit* and I had better bring the Hurja project to a close. Assisting in the process, the University of Illinois provided a sabbatical leave and the campus's Humanities Institute grants-in-aid to help cover travel to various archives. I am grateful for the assistance and cooperation I have received from several different archives and their fine professional staffs. These include the Franklin D. Roosevelt Library; other presidential repositories, such as the Hoover, Truman, and Eisenhower libraries; the Tennessee State Library and Archives and related archival holdings at the University of Michigan's Bentley, Notre Dame and Finlandia University libraries; the Library of Congress Manuscripts Division; and the National Archives in Helsinki, Finland. I am also thankful for research assistance from local repositories, such as the Iron County Historical Museum and the Harbour House collections in Emil Hurja's home state of Michigan.

I also wish to acknowledge the assistance of several individuals: Emil Hurja's sister Lillian Ojala, and nephew Dr. James Ojala (both of whom were helpful in locating Hurja manuscripts); the Reverend Olaf Rankinen and Lorraine Uitto Richards of the Finnish-American Heritage Center; Marcia Bernhardt of the Iron County Museum; Raymond Teichman of the FDR Library; Dr. Viekko Litzen of the Finnish National Archives; and Dr. Robert Warner, former national archivist and director of the Bentley Library. Finally, Dr. Betsy Holli was a superb research assistant on many of our archival visits. This brief acknowledgment is of course inadequate, and that reminds me of an old rural saying that Emil Hurja sometimes repeated: "We have all drunk from wells we didn't dig and been warmed by fires we didn't build."

CHAPTER 1

GROWING UP IN A FRONTIER BOOM TOWN

THE LIFE AND TIMES OF THE HURJAS

FROM HUMBLE BEGINNINGS IN A FRONTIER TOWN IN THE UPPER PENINSULA of Michigan, Emil Edward Hurja vaulted to national prominence in the Franklin D. Roosevelt administration. One of 12 children, he was born on January 22, 1892, in Crystal Falls, Michigan. He was the second child of Matti and Anna Hurja, who were Finnish immigrants.

Hurja's father was born Matti Pitkakangas in a *torppa,* or tenant-farm house, near the village of Evijarvi in west-central Finland on March 31, 1863. One of 11 children in a poor family, Matti gained notoriety for his unrestrained, carefree ways and for his readiness to fight. According to his nephew, Dr. James Ojala, Matti grew adept at wielding the Finnish *puukko*—a long, curved knife and a working tool used by farmers, fishermen, and foresters, but sometimes used for combat—which was worn at the waist behind one's back. Recognizing his wilder side, Matti's friends dubbed him *hurjamatti.* A Finnish word with many meanings, *hurja* can be understood as meaning "strong," "brave," and "unbending," as well as "crazy," "wild," and "happy-go-lucky."[1]

The population of Finland more than tripled in the nineteenth century, and the rural economy did not provide land for everyone. Small farm units could not be subdivided easily to create farms for the children of operators, and children could not always save enough money to buy a farm. Landless rural classes, including male laborers and women servants, immigrated to the United States. Some planned to save money and then return to the homeland, so they saw no reason to learn English for a temporary stay. In fact, about 20 percent returned to Finland, while others became permanent residents with the passage of years.[2]

Besides economic conditions, others left Finland to avoid compulsory military service in the Russian army. Finland had been part of the Swedish kingdom for six centuries when Russia attacked in 1809 and defeated Sweden, putting Finland under Russian control until 1917. The ethnic, cultural, and religious chasm between Lutheran Finland and Orthodox czarist Russia placed a heavy burden on Finnish men who had no desire to be conscripted into the Russian army. Six centuries of close association with Catholic and then Lutheran Sweden had created a westward and not eastward outlook in what became a "Grand Duchy" of Russia in 1809.[3]

Another internal problem for emigrants was that the Finnish establishment opposed emigration. Leaving the homeland was roundly denounced as unpatriotic throughout Scandinavia by the clergy and government officials. Undeterred, Finnish immigrants were enticed by appeals from steamship companies of the promise of a better life, as well as by glowing accounts in letters from family and friends already in the United States. Immigrants often arrived penniless, and their first concern was work, no matter the kind. Most were unskilled workers.[4]

As a middle son in a large family, Matti had no prospect of making an adequate living from his family's small land holdings. With annual per-capita earnings in the Vaasa province averaging 1,500 marks ($300 US), a wage-earner's life offered him a meager alternative, assuming that he could find a cash-paying job in an economy that offered few. Accordingly, Matti came to the United States at the death of his parents in 1886.[5]

Like people from many other nations, Matti Pitkakangas saw America as a land of opportunity and came in quest of a better life. He heard the entreaties of agents recruiting workers for mines and read praise-filled letters from friends already there. To counteract the grass-roots image of America as a land of opportunity, a vigorous propaganda campaign was conducted in Finland by clergymen, publishers, officials, prosperous farmers, and other spokesmen against emigration. Clergymen and editors regarded emigration as responsible for immoral conditions, in which some married men left wives and children behind to become public charges. However, the vast majority of emigrants were unmarried and between and ages of 16 and 30.[6]

The mass migration to North America was channeled initially through Swedish and Norwegian ports. Pitkakangas left home a bachelor in 1886 and traveled to Sweden, where he boarded a ship bound for the United States by way of Liverpool, England. Once at sea, he resolved to start his new life in the New World with a new name. Emigrants generally traveled third class, and many brought along their own food. When Matti emigrated, the fare to America averaged $20, a figure within reach of many of the *torppari,* or tenant, farmers. For those who borrowed the cost of passage, it did not take long to pay it back once they began working in the United States.[7] The major destination was New York harbor. A soon-to-be-christened Statue of Liberty greeted Matti's arrival there.

Although Finnish immigrants were among those with the highest literacy rates, like most immigrants they were unable to read or write English. Finns who emigrated often changed or shortened their names, and Pitkakangas followed suit. Anglicized, "Pitkakangas" translates as "Longfield." Matti chose to become Matt Hurja (pronounced Hur-ya), no doubt preferring the word's more admirable meanings. His offspring later insisted that the term meant "strong, like a mighty oak tree that stands unyielding before a powerful wind." They viewed it as a euphemism for another Finnish term, *sisu,* which translates roughly as "guts," "determination," "stubbornness," or "never-say-die," and is considered, at least by the Finns themselves, to be that people's singular character trait. The Finnish self-image is that they are as determined and iron-willed as the granite that lies beneath the Finnish subsoil. Whatever his interpretation of the name, the new Matt Hurja enjoyed his reputation as a free spirit and wanted sole proprietorship of his new name. Once, while hospitalized in Chicago, Matti Hurja came across another Finnish immigrant who had also planned to change his long, multisyllabic name to "Hurja." According to family members, Matti paid off the other man who agreed not to use that patronymic in the new land.[8]

Many Finns settled in Michigan, Minnesota, Montana, Oregon, Washington, and Wisconsin, especially in copper- and iron-ore mining locations. Hurja ventured west to Michigan's lower peninsula, working for a short time in a lumber mill in White Cloud, north of Grand Rapids. He soon grew restless and, responding to the urgings of friends who were there already, left for Crystal Falls, Michigan, in 1886.[9]

Michigan's Upper Peninsula was a land filled with adventurers conducting fur trade with Indians, scouts, and explorers. Catholic missionaries from France came as early as the 1600s. For centuries it had remained the province of Menominee and Chippewa (Ojibway) Indians. In 1800, Congress established the Indiana Territory, which included the greater portion of Michigan's Upper Peninsula. Michigan was granted territorial status on June 30, 1805. During the War of 1812, the United States lost forts at Detroit, Dearborn, and Mackinaw, which were held by the British for two years before being reoccupied. Congress admitted Michigan to the Union in 1837, and thus the current boundaries of the Upper Peninsula were formed. The mineral rich Upper Peninsula only fell to Michigan as a consolation prize for losing a strip of land near Toledo, which was ceded to the state of Ohio. The full knowledge of the large, hidden bodies of copper and iron ore in Michigan was not yet realized in 1837.[10]

Explorers and missionaries knew about native copper of the Lake Superior area as early as the beginning of the sixteenth century. In 1843, there were three copper mining permits issued, but three years later, in 1846, over 900 leases were issued, each for one square mile of land. This expansion necessitated the completion of land surveys by the General Land Office.

Since no surveys were extant, land survey crews were dispatched to the Upper Peninsula to complete town and range lines. On September 18, 1844, as William A. Burt led surveyors running a line near Negaunee, the magnetic needle of the solar compass spun so crazily that work was halted. Burt had developed a solar compass to determine the true north, independent of the earth's magnetic field. Astonished and excited, Burt called out, "Boys, look around and see what you can find." When they did, the source of the problem turned out to be outcrops of magnetic iron ore, part of the Marquette Range.[11]

There was a growing demand for iron by railroads and building industries in the late nineteenth century. Of the six principal iron range areas in the United States, three are located primarily in Michigan—the Marquette, Menominee, and Gogebic Ranges. Michigan's iron and copper "locations" ranked for decades among the most profitable mines in the world.[12] Only in the twentieth century would Minnesota's Mesabi Range mines surpass the combined output of all the other ranges. Matt Hurja had settled in a land of boom towns.[13]

During the early years of the mining boom, primitive extraction methods and extreme remoteness hindered the growth of both the copper and the iron industries in upper Michigan. There were many problems in mining, but the greatest of them all, and the key to the ultimate success or failure of the whole peninsular enterprise, was transportation. The problem began at the mines and continued to the docks, where there were no ships designed to carry ore. Then there was a 19-foot falls at Sault Ste. Marie. To circumvent the falls, the state of Michigan obtained federal aid to build two locks, and the canal opened in 1855.[14]

Conditions in 1855 changed rapidly after construction of the canal to ford the rapids at Sault Ste. Marie. In early days, the ore went to the docks first by sled in winter; then by plank road, by mule-drawn tram cars on strap rails; and finally by steam railroad. Ore-producing companies eventually developed their own fleet of carriers, whose size and carrying capacities were steadily increased to ship to the steel industry markets in Ohio and Pennsylvania. During the Civil War, Upper Peninsula ore was a major source of iron for the manufacture of guns, cannon, and railroad rails. By 1897, about 12 million tons of ore passed through the Sault.[15]

Earlier, in 1853, the lands of the Menominee River watershed in Iron County, Michigan, were offered for public sale, and a few decades later a land buying rush occurred during the years 1870 to 1875. In the decades that followed, hundreds of land examiners, timber cruisers, and mineral seekers roamed the forests, transporting their provisions in canoes along the streams, rivers, and lakes, packing them on horses, or as man-packs over land. Miners, lumbermen, settlers, merchants, and others came to the Upper Peninsula in endless streams throughout the year. Many traveled east via the railroad, which ended in Florence, Wisconsin.[16]

Besides mining, timber production was a major source of employment in the Upper Peninsula for immigrants. Real estate and mines were inseparable. Companies needed land for offices, for roads to the mines, and (in the early period) for building plank roads to the ore docks. Mining and timber production were parts of a single operation. Houses had to be built for workers. Hardwood, hemlock, and tamrack were often harvested for "mining timber" to support the underground tunnels. Red and white pine and cedar were desired for manufacturing. When Michigan was heavily forested, white pine ranked first in importance, and Norway pine was also logged. Other timber in the Upper Peninsula included white oak, white and black ash, black walnut, cherry, hemlock, balsam, beech, elm, cedar, and maple. At its peak in 1890, Michigan led the states in lumbering activity, with over 2,000 sawmills.[17]

Two entrepreneurs arriving in Crystal Falls in 1880—Solomon D. Hollister from Sparta, Wisconsin, and George Runkel, who was born in Germany and lived in Florence, Wisconsin—formed the Crystal Falls Iron Company. They obtained the option on the area from the Malthy Brothers and Ephraim Coon. In 1880 prospectors uncovered "inconceivably rich" deposits of 65 percent pure red hematite ore along the Paint River. The mine was located on the west bank of the Paint River at the foot of the falls. Hollister and Runkel's objective was to enlist capital, explore for ore, and obtain leases. No attempts had been made toward the establishment of a settlement until early after 1879, when the Chicago and Northwestern Railroad reached the village of Florence, just 15 miles to the south of Crystal Falls and Iron County. A town quickly sprang up on a hillside west of the stream and was named Crystal Falls after a series of rapids nearby.[18]

Most of the early houses in the settlement were built of local logs, as cut lumber had to be transported over rough roads from Florence. In 1881 the village of Crystal Falls was centered around a sawmill built by the Crystal Falls Iron Company. Around the company office were shops; a store where people called for their mail, which was brought by teams from Florence; and a mill, shanties serving as dwellings, a stable, a blacksmith shop, and boarding houses for approximately five-hundred local miners, millhands, and railroad construction workers. The need for a permanent town site was recognized and the Crystal Falls Company purchased land for that purpose. After platting it, they proceeded with the sale of lots.

A railroad was needed to transport the Iron County ore to market. Most of the work of constructing the grade of the Menominee River Railroad was done in 1881 from Iron River Junction, where a branch of the Chicago and Northwestern Railroad was constructed. The desire of mine officials to ship their stocks of ore hastened completion of the railroad. To reach the objective, all mine employees were pressed to the task of grade construction and the laying of rails to the mine in late summer 1882. The first train arrived in April 1882, and regular service was inaugurated on May 22, when the station opened.[19]

According to the Lake Superior Mining Association Directory, in 1882 there were seven mines operating in Crystal Falls, collectively employing more than 500 men. In 1882 the Crystal Falls Mining Company shipped 1,341 tons of iron ore, and the Mastodon mine 3,477 tons. Crystal Falls ore was taken by rail to the outlet port in Escanaba, Michigan, and then shipped by water to lower lakes steel makers.[20] Crystal Falls was just beginning to grow and had, in 1882, four commercial buildings—the William Doncett Opera House, the D. Bannerman House, the Martin Rogan building, and the early Stephenson House. Some homes had also been completed. After the sawmill opened, wooden frame buildings began to slowly replace log cabins. The school district was established July 5, 1882, as a census of children showed 210 eligible for school. Classes were scheduled from October to May, and in 1883 a contract was signed for construction of a school.

The town expanded rapidly. The four commercial buildings in 1882 expanded by 1885 to 25 business establishments, including 3 hotels, 2 drugstores, 2 dry goods stores, 1 hardware store, 1 bakery, 3 grocery stores, 1 restaurant, 1 barber shop, 1 jeweler, 2 public halls, and a number of saloons trading with lumberjacks and miners. In addition, there were 3 blacksmith shops specializing in wagon repair and 1 saddlery. The population grew to 3,231 shortly thereafter. It was possible for some to replace their kerosene lamps and candles for lighting when a hydroelectric power plant and water system were constructed in 1891. It was more than a decade later, in 1902, before Crystal Falls had streetlights and a sewer system. Crystal Falls was incorporated as a village in 1889. It became the seat of Iron County the same year, and a courthouse was built the following year.[21]

Matt Hurja found work in the Dunn iron mine in late 1886. In the 1880s, miners received $2.00 to $2.25 per ten-hour day, had a six-day week, and worked one week on day shift and the next week on night shift. Contract miners received $2.50 to $3.50 and surface laborers $1.70 to $2.00, the latter being Matt's wage scale. The Dunn mine was a large producer, shipping every year through 1915 except 1900–01 and 1904. A total of 2,208,511 tons of ore were shipped in the years the Dunn mine operated.[22] The ore was a soft, reddish brown ore of high-phosphorus, non-Bessemer hematite. The soft, crumbling nature of hematite ore added further to the danger of tunnels collapsing. Matt made his living in a hazardous occupation.

The Dunn mine had 15 levels. The main shaft went down 13 levels, and a second shaft went even deeper to levels 14 and 15. Lighting was limited and candles gleamed in the darkness. The miners wore a candle on a hat or drove the holder onto a post or a timber to give them light. A piece of tin served as a shade on the hat so that dripping water would not extinguish the flame. It was especially difficult in drafty places, and sometimes the men had to walk backwards down the horizontal tunnels or "drifts" so that wind would not blow out the light. A miner burned six to seven candles each shift.[23]

Unlike the "predominantly personal, folk-agrarian milieu" of Matt Hurja's homeland, the mining environment was a highly structured, company-corporate environment, complete with a well defined occupational hierarchy, inflexible working hours, established salary scales, regimentation, and hazardous working conditions. Eighty percent of the Finns were employed by the mining companies as semi-skilled and unskilled laborers, and as such, they occupied the very lowest levels of the entire occupational hierarchy. With the exception of the Finns who came from Norway, they had agrarian but not mining skills. Skilled and supervisory positions were held mostly by the English, particularly the Cornish, known locally as "cousin Jacks," because every time there was a job opening, supervisors seemed to have a "cousin Jack" qualified to fill it. Cornwall, England, had long been an exporter of tin miners to the copper and iron ranges of Michigan and later Minnesota.[24]

Matt Hurja became a "trammer." "Tramming" involved conveying the ore or waste rock in cars from the ore chute, along the drift or tunnel, to the mine shaft. An ore car held 2.5 tons of ore, and trammers had to push the cars by hand and shoulder several thousand feet to the shaft. During one working day a trammer might load 20 tons of rock and make 8 to 10 trips to the shaft. Cave-ins and loose rock slides were a daily hazard. There were different types of iron ore. The "hard" ores, hematite and magnetite, were "dense and compact," thus hard to drill and break. The "soft" ores, most of that mined in Crystal Falls, were more porous, but equally high in grade, principally hematite with some geothite.[25]

In some mines, mules pulled the tram cars and a mule barn was built underground. Mules were led back and forth in tunnels to be trained before attaching them to tram cars. In some mines, mules taken down were never brought back to the surface, but in others they were taken up once a month. At the mine shaft the ore was transferred to the "skip" or large hoisting basket used to raise ore from the lower levels of the mine to the surface.

At the end of the work shift, Matt Hurja and his fellow miners changed their clothes at the mine in the "dry." The dry was a building where miners prepared to go to work, or washed to go home at the end of the day. As they came up from the mine, they would be soaking wet and red with iron ore water. Hooks hung from the ceiling by chains. Miners hung wet clothes on them and pulled the chain, hand over hand, until the mining clothes were hung to dry near the ceiling. It was said that you could identify a miner's house because of the red underwear on the clothesline. It started out white, but was dyed permanently the color of hematite ore, a reddish-brown.[26]

Those working underground took lunch in a tin bucket, eating it while the smoke cleared after the blasting at noon. The oval tin pails held coffee or tea in the bottom and on a tray on top of the liquid, a sandwich with meat or double sandwich made with boiled egg. A piece of pie, cookies, or cake completed the meal. Sometimes the men would build a little fire to warm themselves, and they would use a shovel as a stovetop to warm their pasties (a Cornish pastry filled with meat and potato) or to boil tea. Upper Peninsula Scandinavians rapidly adopted the pasty and made it their own, to the point where many visitors mistook it for a Nordic instead of a Cornish delicacy. Finns and Swedes sometimes modified the ingredients, substituting venison for beef or Lake Superior trout for red meat, the latter which became known in some circles as the "kala pasty" or fish pasty.

By 1880 many Finns found employment in the iron ore mines of Marquette and Menominee Counties of the Upper Peninsula, in Michigan's copper mines, and in mines in other states. The growing size of American business—characterized by an increasing economic and social gap between employees and employers—created a labor relations crisis. Between 1889 and 1900 the United States suffered 23,000 strikes. Many corporations turned to paternalism. In the mining regions, however, paternalism was a business necessity rather than a way to quiet discontent and combat unionism. In the Upper Peninsula wilderness areas, with few roads and primitive conditions, mining companies had to provide basic necessities until larger communities were developed. Companies provided housing through boarding houses: the typical boarding house was a two-story frame building with common areas on the first floor and several small rooms with double bed or double bunks on the second. Housing 20 to 30 men, they slept in rotation. Each evening men on the day shift used beds the night shift workers had just left, increasing the number of men who could be housed.[27] The mine owners also provided company stores, and company-employed physicians. The Oliver Mining Company established a hospital in Crystal Falls in 1901.[28]

Matt Hurja and approximately five-hundred other Finns worked in Crystal Falls mines in 1889. One out of nine Michigan miners hailed from Finland. As immigrants, many of the miners, including the Finns, did not speak English and could not communicate with people of other nationalities. Workers in the Upper Peninsula mines represented many nationalities including Irish, German, Russian, Swedish, Polish, English, Danish, French Canadian, Scotch, and Norwegian, although Scandinavians comprised the largest group. The unskilled, such as the Finns, were assigned the pick-and-shovel jobs and were subject to discrimination. They were called "roundheads," "flax heads," and "dumb Finlanders." "Dumb" was not a reference to a lack of intelligence but rather to the quiet, hard-working style of immigrants from Nordic Europe. One Cornish mining captain described the typical Finn miner: "All week he works like a damned ape, not saying a word. On Sunday all he wants to do is sweat in his bloody hot sauna."[29] It was probably natural for immigrants to cling together and to their native tongue and culture. Finnish miners in Crystal Falls enjoyed what was to them a higher standard of living than what they had experienced in their homeland.[30]

In the spring of 1889, Anna Liisa Keisari arrived by train at the Crystal Falls station. Anna's brother lived at the Dunn "location," and she came to America when she was 18 years old with her brother's fiancee. Born September 25, 1870, in Alavus, Finland, she immigrated from Jyvaskyla, a central Finnish city. Although most immigrants were men, approximately one-third of all immigrants from Finland were women. Settling in the nearby Dunn location, Anna found work as a housekeeper, which was a typical occupation for newly arrived immigrant women. Domestic work did not require speaking English, and many women spoke it poorly or not at all. In cities women worked as servants for the wealthy or in hotels or restaurants and were known to be hard workers. They learned household skills, cooking and keeping house American style, and learned English on the job. Work was hard and days were long. It was common to have off only half a day during the week and half a day on Sunday.

At the Dunn location, Anna soon met Matt Hurja, seven years her elder. Matt and Anna described their meeting to their children as a case of love at first sight. They enjoyed a November 1889 wedding before an itinerant Methodist minister.[31]

Newlywed Matt Hurja, after four years as a miner, sustained serious injuries in an 1890 accident. While working as a trammer in the Dunn Mine, Matt Hurja suffered a crushed left leg beneath a cascade of falling rock. Lacking proper medical attention at the time, his injuries never fully healed and made him a semi-invalid the remainder of his life. Thereafter he relied on a cane and a specially built shoe to walk. There was no regularized workers' compensation in those days and Matt received a one-time payment of $1,000 compensation for the accident. Widows and children of dead miners usually received funeral expenses and one or two months' pay.[32]

Mining was dangerous work. Many men died from accidents. An Iron County record of mining fatalities from 1905, for example, listed those killed as 9 Finns, 1 Englishman, 1 Irishman, 1 German, 1 Italian, 1 Austrian, and 1 Swede. All worked underground. Two were laborers, 9 miners, 1 a trammer, 1 a trammer boss, 1 a powderman, 1 a pumpman, and 1 a skiptender.[33]

Fortunately trammer Matt Hurja was not killed in his accident. And not discouraged from working by his handicap, he gave up mining and moved the family to Crystal Falls. Although he had no business experience, Matt used the money to start a general merchandise store. According to his advertising in the *Diamond Drill*, the local weekly newspaper, he carried groceries, provisions, fresh smoked meats, crockery, glassware, and "miner's supplies." The sidewalks in front of the store were constructed of wooden planks on stringers, and Superior Street was not paved until 1910. There were no streetlights until 1902. When the Hurja children were old enough to work, they also contributed to the support of the family by working in the store. There were no supermarkets, and customers simply produced a list of items needed and let the grocery store clerk gather and weigh the foods to fill the order. In those days all meat was cut to order, pickles came in a barrel, dry foods such as beans and peas were in bulk bins, cookies and crackers were in bulk in large boxes, and flour and sugar came in large cloth bags. Peanut butter, lard, and candy came in large pails. Almost everything was doled out by the grocer, who collected on customers' bills monthly.[34]

Immigrants had access to other food sources as well. Although most land was owned and controlled by the many mining companies, it was accessible to everyone for hunting, fishing, berry picking, and cutting firewood. Matt Hurja's young son Emil saved his pennies to buy a rifle with which he would hunt. Prior to 1895, there was no limit on the take of deer and a hunter could shoot as many as he liked. Later the kill was limited to 5, then 3, then 2, and finally 1 in 1915. Many immigrant families supplemented their store-bought food with venison or what was called "Michigan beef." Fish was abundant in lakes and streams. There were trout and pike in the summer, burbot in the fall season, and smelt runs in the spring. Men netted carp or caught trout. Much was salted or smoked for winter meals. Sometimes maligned as "herring chokers" by the "cousin Jacks" (Cornishmen), Scandinavian immigrants put their pickling and preserving skills to good use on different New World species.

In the spring there was maple syrup, and in the summer wild berries, including blueberries and raspberries, to pick while battling the mosquitoes and sand flies. Women canned the berries for winter and kept them in a root cellar, if available, along with potatoes, carrots, rutabagas, cabbage, and other foods. In warm months, milk was kept cool by putting it in a bucket in a well or in a small crib alongside a cold spring. Families planted vegetable gardens and potatoes and some kept a cow and chickens. People used a horse and buggy in summer and a sleigh in winter, since there were no plows to clear the deep Upper Peninsula snows. Wood was used to make homemade skis, cooking spoons, ladles, sauna buckets, and the like.[35]

The mainstay of the Finnish diet was bread, and for the emigrants from coastal Finland or Norway's Finnmark, herring and potatoes. Fish, potatoes, dairy foods, and whole-grain cereals were popular. Finns were fond of soups and stews made with meat or fish with potatoes and onions, and sometimes made with milk and butter instead of water. In Finland the stew is called *keitto* but in America it is called *mojakka* and *soppa,* from the Ostrobothnian dialect.[36] When animals were slaughtered all parts were used. The blood was often made into puddings, pancakes, and sausage. Pressed and jellied meats, called "head cheese," were prepared along with herring, beet, and onion salads. Milk was served at every meal but the favorite drink was coffee. Almost all emigrant families made a home-made yogurt, which the Finns called *viilia* and the Swedes *viil,* eaten with a slight sprinkle of salt on top and with hardtack. They often took pride in having gotten the original germ from the homeland. Those with dairy animals, or cows, knew how to make an oven-baked cheese *juustoa,* generally at its best during the spring of the year, when cows carrying calves produced an extra-rich milk. Because of its somewhat rubbery texture, which made a slight sound when bitten into, non-Finns called it "squeaky cheese."[37]

Matt Hurja also knew how to harvest the bounty of nature to feed what would become a large family. In time, he and Anna brought forth their own with 12 children. They christened their second child Emil Edward Hurja, born January 22, 1892. At a time when hospitals were almost nonexistent, Finns had the ideal sanitary environment for childbirth, and that was the heated sauna, with its steam and abundant hot water. Experienced Finnish American midwives were always on hand for delivery. Doubtless a few of the Hurja dozen were birthed in such a setting. Of Emil's 11 brothers and sisters, 5 died young; including 2 at birth, 1 as an infant, and 2 in accidents while they were young adults.

The Hurja family life centered around Finnish institutions. Both parents were early founders of the Finnish Lutheran Church, led by the Reverend Jaakob Juhanpoika Hoikka. Hoikka was the first Finn educated and ordained a clergyman in the United States, and was originally a member of the Swedish Augustana Lutheran Synod, graduating from Augustana Seminary in 1883. First serving in Astoria, Oregon, he organized Finnish congregations in Washington, Oregon, and northern California. Called to a congregation in Republic, Michigan, in 1885, he organized congregations in Ishpeming, Negaunee, Palmer, Republic, Champion, and Newberry. He went to the congregation in Crystal Falls in 1900 and organized all the Finnish church work in Iron County, which included Crystal Falls, Amasa, Alpha, and Stambaugh. Before there were church buildings and local pastors, religious services were held in homes. Hoikka was unique in that he was fluent in three languages: Finnish, Swedish, and English. He was one of three founding fathers of the Suomi (the Finnish name for Finland) Synod.[38]

The Hurja children studied Lutheran catechism in Finnish and were taught and confirmed by Reverend Hoikka. Matt served as a deacon on the Finnish Lutheran Church board of control for over 30 years and was made an honorary director shortly before his death. He traveled in 1905, for example, to Eveleth, Minnesota, as a delegate from the local Finnish Lutheran Church.

Anna was active in the church sewing circle and in the Martha Society, whose purpose was raising funds for church work and paying off the debt. Anna was a loyal member of the society for over 50 years, serving as president when she died. She had previously served both as treasurer and vice president. The society also sent funds to missions in Finland[39]

The majority of Finns are Lutherans. The church grew slowly in the United States partly because many viewed their new life as free from the domination of religious life and from compulsory church tithes they had known in the homeland by the state-controlled Church of Finland. But the commitment of the temperance movement to Christian principles and the availability of Finn Halls as meeting places facilitated church expansion. In 1890 the Suomi Synod, or the Finnish Evangelical Lutheran Church of America, had 9 congregations with 4 ministers, but a decade later, in 1900, the synod claimed 49 congregations served by 11 pastors. Sunday Schools in early years were conducted entirely in Finnish. The Suomi Opisto (Suomi College and Theological Seminary, now renamed Finlandia University) was opened in Hancock, Michigan, in 1896 to prepare young people for preaching and teaching and to perpetuate the Finnish language and culture. Matt sent his oldest son Arthur to study at Suomi.[40]

Matt belonged to the local chapter of the Knights of the Kaleva and Anna to the Ladies of the Kaleva, both staunchly conservative fraternal societies devoted to preserving Finnish traditions as recorded in the *Kalevala* the national epic poem of Finland. The Knights of the Kaleva was organized by immigrant John Stone in 1898 in Belt, Montana. Six years later, in 1904, the Ladies of the Kaleva was formed. Patterned after American secret societies but adapted to the Finnish culture, it was organized into lodges locally. Each chapter adopted a name from the *Kalevala,* and meetings were conducted in Finnish.[41]

Matt and Anna also became charter members of the Hopeful Temperance Society (Toivola Raittius Seura), which built a Finn Hall in Crystal Falls. The temperance societies campaigned against the evils of drinking, card playing, and gambling, which they believed threatened the foundations of immigrant life. But they did much for their members besides battling the evils of alcohol. They sponsored history and language classes; athletic teams; choral and band groups, often featuring an accordion; plays; public speaking clubs; and other social activities. Meetings were limited to members and opened and closed with prayers. Members pledged abstinence from alcohol and committed themselves to mutual assistance. Some lodges banned social activities such as dancing, as well as festivities on the Sabbath. Other lodges were more liberal and permitted dancing.[42]

Temperance Halls (called Finn Halls) were built in almost every Finnish community from Massachusetts to Washington state and became centers of activity. They were used as meeting places for congregations lacking a church building, for clubs, and for mutual aid groups. They had modest mutual insurance plans for members who suffered unexpected accidents, illness, or death. Accident and burial funds were available. The Finn Hall served as an associational, political, and cultural center in the lives of immigrants and was their major recreational center. Controversy was created when later immigrants wanted to dance to Finnish *jenkkas,* polkas, and waltzes, and to play cards. To attract youth, compromises were sometimes made and dancing permitted. The Finn Halls also witnessed heated political discussions that sometimes divided the more conservative Finns from strong socialist activists.

Yet the main goal was sobriety or temperate use of alcoholic beverages. The more than 30 saloons that lined Superior Avenue, the main street in Crystal Falls, were a challenge to the temperance societies. "John Barleycorn" often triumphed among single bachelor men. Saloons became the chief centers of leisure activity and the general meeting places outside of the home. Private and public business was transacted there, and there were social activities such as dancing. When men immigrated before marriage or left a wife behind in Finland, they had no home life and the saloon was often the substitute. According to the *Diamond Drill,* miners celebrated on payday: "Last Saturday was pay day at the Dunn; many of the boys are celebrating the event yet." Some Finns, especially lumberjacks, were known for hard drinking and for fighting.[43]

To compete with the saloons for the attention of young people, the Raittius Seura (Crystal Falls temperance society) sponsored drama companies, choirs, bands, and gymnastic events, and taught self-improvement skills such as reading and sewing. The self-help and individual betterment activities met many of the needs of immigrants and were important social institutions for the 40 years before Prohibition in 1919. The majority of early immigrants were rural oriented, conservative, and centered on family. They came from a traditional folk society with predominantly agrarian values and lifestyles.

Native-born Americans often dichotomized Finns as a group, saying that Finns were either church or hall," "red or white," "wet or dry," or "morose or happy." The Hurjas, as nephew Jim Ojala put it, were "church, white, dry, and happy."[44]

Coming from a literate homeland, Finnish immigrants were believers in the importance of the best possible education as a route to a better life. A long tradition of literacy fostered by the Lutheran Church in Finland made Finns the most literate of European immigrants who came to the United States. More than 95 percent could read and write their own language. The Lutheran belief that every man should be literate enough to be "his own priest" (that is, to be able to read the Bible) accompanied even the agnostics who came from Suomi to the United States. Finns, for example, would be denied the rites of the church, including marriage, if they could not read and interpret the Lutheran catechism. Reflecting that tradition, all 12 Hurja children completed high school, and five of the seven who survived to adulthood completed college. The Hurja family spoke Finnish at home and the children studied it at the Finn Hall and in their church. As second son Emil recalled: "we learned to speak and read Finnish, albeit confined to religious topics for the custom in those Finnish-American homes was to compel the children to get their religious teachings in the mother tongue." Just as the Hurja children learned Finnish, Matt the store owner and autodidact taught himself to read, write, and speak English. His wife Anna, however, was primarily a housewife and confined her outside activities to Finnish fraternals and church work; she never mastered the English language.[45]

Nevertheless, Finnish American women, unlike other immigrant women, were generally not laggards when it came to asserting their political rights. Because women in Finland were the first in the Western world to gain full suffrage rights in 1906 (the right to vote as well as the right to hold elective office—several were elected to the national legislature in 1907), Finnish American women found it easy to join the United States suffrage movement. Among them were Aino Malberg, expelled from the Finnish Diet (parliament) by the Russians for her nationalist and feminist beliefs and who came to America to join Jane Addams in her campaigns for women's rights and to organize the Women's Peace Party. Although Finnish immigrant women were part of the Victorian culture that prescribed "separate spheres," the Finnish women's sphere was considerably larger than that of many of their immigrant counterparts. Finnish women exerted influence in church and fraternal circles, and as noted above even in politics, as well as in temperance and leftist drama circles.[46]

In houses lacking electricity, water heaters, and running hot water, bathing took place on Saturday night in a galvanized washtub or in the sauna. A sauna, or Finnish steam bath, has two rooms, a changing room (or cold room) and a hot room. The sauna building was often the first structure built on a property and was lived in until a homestead could be built. The sauna and bath actually performs two different functions. The sauna is not only a bath but a spiritual experience to a Finn. As a dipper of cold water is thrown on heated rocks on a wood-fired stove and steam rises, a *viihttaa*—or cedar or birch branch freshly cut with the leaves attached and tied together—is used to gently beat the body to open the pores, increase circulation, and induce a state of relaxation. Participants sit on tiered benches; the higher the bench, the hotter the sauna. The mind rests while the body sweats. If there is a lake nearby, a plunge into cold water closes the cleansed pores. Otherwise, one sits in the changing room to cool off. Not everyone had a sauna, so saunas were often shared. Following the sauna, welcome guests were served coffee, *nisua* (a cardamom flavored sweet bread), and dessert.[47]

Ethnic newspapers filled the immigrants' need for communication and information in their own language, keeping them in touch with both the old and the new world. Coming from a country that linked reading to religious salvation, Finnish immigrants were "exceptionally literate" and among the most literate immigrants to the United States. Between 1876 and 1913, eight Finnish newspapers were established. There were 20 in 1913, not counting biweeklies and periodicals. Poetry and prose reading were promoted, and those who could recite spiritual verse or ancient tone poems were highly regarded. The circulation of books from lending libraries satisfied a desire for self-education. Over 350 Finnish-language newspapers and periodicals have been published in the United States if one includes those of church bodies.[48]

Young Emil Hurja sold some of those Finnish-language newspapers, including the *Paivalehti* and *Suometar.* By the age of six, he worked as a newsboy hawking the Chicago *Tribune,* Milwaukee *Journal,* and two local newspapers called the *Diamond Drill* and the *People's Mail.* Next he moved from peddling to printing. When Matt purchased the store on Superior Avenue, he discovered an old hand-operated printing press and trays of lead type beneath debris in the loft. Cleaned and repaired, Emil used the press to print handbills for Crystal Falls businesses, circulars, envelopes, stationary, and business cards, becoming a small businessman and using his earnings to buy himself a typewriter and a Winchester repeating rifle for hunting. He also worked in his father's store. Emil was a workaholic like his immigrant parents and an exemplar of the Protestant work ethic, the powerful belief that one redeemed ones self daily with hard work. In Yooper (what downstaters called Upper Peninsulans) vernacular some people "work to live," but others "live to work."

Emil, or "Amiel" (a phonetic rendering of the Finnish pronunciation) as it was spelled at school, was a good student. In his Scholar's Report Book he noted, "God be Thanked for Books." Emil was an avid reader and had picked up his father's zeal for knowledge and the printed word. In second grade, from 1898 to 1899, he had perfect attendance all months but two, according to the record of his teacher Anna Koepeke. The message to the pupil in the Report Book encouraged students: "Tis an honor to do well. Aim to reach the highest mark for what is worth doing at all is worth doing well." "Strive to lay the foundation of a useful life by achieving excellence in your studies." Young Emil did just that.[49] The course of study was rigorous. rhetoricals, music, and drawing were required in all elementary grades, but languages were optional.

In Crystal Falls High School the first year of his education included a year of arithmetic, grammar, and U.S. history with a semester each of physiology and classics. Second-year students studied a year of general history, algebra, and English with a semester each of civil government and bookkeeping. In the third year, studies were a year of algebra and physics with a semester of rhetoric, botany, physical geography, and geometry. The fourth-year program had a year of geometry and literature with a review of history, U.S. history, grammar, and miscellaneous studies. Emil developed a passion for history and politics. He also took courses in the German language. Filled with energy and talent, Emil also appeared in theater productions and played varsity basketball and baseball.[50]

When schoolboy Emil was not studying, he stocked shelves in his father's store. Matt operated the grocery and general merchandise store for 12 years. A genial storekeeper, Matt extended credit liberally to his customers. But then an economic slowdown hampered bill payments by his credit customers and a cash flow problem of a serious nature forced him to close the store. A close-out sale of the stock in the store was held beginning in January 1904, and in August of that year the business was liquidated by a federal bankruptcy court.

During the next two decades, beginning in 1905, Matt opened a candy store, sold insurance, and worked as a local agent for a steamship line, selling prepaid tickets to bring Finnish immigrants to the Upper Peninsula. Most young Finns had only enough money to purchase one ticket, so they arrived alone. They left behind their families and friends, hoping that they would earn enough money to pay the cost of bringing over other family members from the old country later. A second reason many came alone was to see whether or not they liked the United States well enough to stay and pay to bring other family members. If not, it was less expensive for one individual to return to the homeland than a whole family. Tickets were purchased from Matt. In addition, he kept a boarding house for the contractors working for John Hassestrom in the wood and logging business. According to the local paper: "Mr. Hurja has the best success in supplying woodchoppers of anyone around here."[51]

Matt built a large home for his family on Third Street and lived there for 32 years. Immigrants from Finland and other Scandinavians who had bought tickets through Hurja sometimes stayed there. When family members from the old country arrived at the railroad station, their relative was often working and unable to meet them. Arrangements were made in advance to meet at the Hurja residence. Often Matt Hurja's home was the site of reunions between the ticket purchaser and arriving family members. Because he assisted so many Finns who came to this area, the name Matt Hurja became well known. A letter sent to him from Finland with only MATT HURJA, U.S.A., written on the envelope was received by him without delay, an astonishing feat that doubtless could not be repeated with today's Postal Service. He served as interpreter and advisor to newcomers to this strange country and guided them in business and other affairs. The coffee pot was always on and the welcome mat out at the Hurja home. Many clergy sent from the mother country also stayed at the Hurja home while in Crystal Falls. Church functions, such as baptisms and marriages, were also held there.[52]

Emil grew up in a teeming ethnic and varied political environment, and as a store delivery boy and job printer Emil made contact with the adults of many organizations, including the Cornish Sons of St. George, the Irish Order of Ancient Hibernians, the Italian Vittorio Emmanuel Society, the Swede-Finn Order of Runeberg, the Finnish Ladies and Knights of Kaleva, and the "Red" Finns who belonged to the Socialist Federation. Unlike his conservative parents, who were Republicans, Emil later become a Democrat. Finnish Americans generally voted Republican until the Great Depression. Part of the reason for that was the traditional values of the GOP, and part was due to the voting practices in the mining ranges. Emil recalled that on an election day in the 1890s immigrant miners were lounging around his father's store in Crystal Falls and Emil asked why: One miner, an immigrant from Finland, answered in Finnish, "It's election day, we have a holiday." Hurja responded, "Yes Peter, but you don't vote, you can't vote, why do they lay you off?" "Well," Peter replied," I don't know about that, but when I go to the dry, they told us to go to the time-keepers office. We went into one door, they handed us a folded slip of paper. We walked to another door and put the slip of paper in a box and went home." That's where the "big Republican majorities came from at that time," Hurja recalled, but things had changed by the time he was telling the story. There were several reasons why some Finns became Democrats, among them the fact that one of the best-known Finnish Americans, Emil Hurja, had a position in Franklin D. Roosevelt's inner circle. Second, the Republican party had been considered the party of "big business," which could offer little to poor Finnish immigrants. Finally, there were some Finns who had radical political beliefs and would be attracted to the New Deal reforms.[53]

An excellent student, Emil was active in school plays and served as class president his senior year, graduated and decided to seek his fortune elsewhere. By the time his last sibling was born in 1912, Emil was living in Alaska. Emil's early experiences on the frontier developed his self-reliance, independence, resourcefulness, and pragmatism.

Emil's father Matt Hurja succumbed to pneumonia April 30, 1930, at the age of 67. At the time, Emil was living in New York. His mother Anna suffered a heart attack at the age of 69 and died January 27, 1940.[54]

CHAPTER 2

COLLEGE DAYS
AND BEYOND

EMIL HURJA GRADUATED FROM THE CRYSTAL FALLS HIGH SCHOOL in 1909. Having decided to seek his fortune elsewhere, he followed Horace Greeley's advice. With the consent of his parents and the blessing of his pastor, he boarded a train in June for the West. His local Lutheran pastor gave young Emil a one-dollar gold piece to ease the travel discomfort for a penniless sojourner and a copy of the New Testament in Finnish. Although Emil spent the coin, he carried his ethnic identity with him for many years. Stopping in Ironwood, Michigan, to work, and later in Duluth, he spent most of his money and had to take a freight train for Butte, Montana, to look for work. He traveled by boxcar or by "riding the rods." Butte was also the home of many Finnish immigrants working as miners. He lived there for half a year, delivering groceries as he had done at his father's Michigan store.

Living frugally, because he was self-supporting for the remainder of his life, Hurja earned enough to continue his westward journey in early 1910. He rode the rods, and the last leg of the journey was in the hayrack of a cattle car. On train stops on side tracks, he ate mulligan stew in the "jungles" with other wayfarer workers and, according to one source, learned to sing the worker protest song "Pie in the Sky." All of this before he was age 18. But it should be added that this was not unusual for young men on the job hunt, for very few could afford passenger trains and coach rides.[1]

Upon reaching Seattle, he took a job as a printer's "devil" or apprentice, using skills he had learned as a typesetter in the back room of his father's store. Several months later, he decided to move on to Yakima, in eastern Washington. Chronically short of money, he hiked to the railroad yards and arrived there on a freight train, with a "battered valise and capital assets of one cent, a hungry stomach, and ambition." A hotel runner at the station took his valise as collateral for a night's lodging. He found work sweeping out a printer's office. Vowing not to remain an "ink-stained wretch," he later took an examination in the postal service, passed it, and became a mail sorter from September 1910 to June 1911.

Returning to Seattle periodically, Emil became friends with Richard Seelye Jones, one of the directors of the Alaska-Yukon-Pacific Exposition, an agency aimed at simulating economic development. When Emil was a boy, friends of his father engaged in Alaskan mining were frequent visitors and showed Emil gold-bearing rock and even nuggets. At age ten he had studied Alaskan maps, trying "to trace the course of adventures of my father's friends." With ample evidence of the opportunities in Alaska, Emil became interested in going there. He first completed a business degree at North Yakima College and then, on May 25, 1911, sailed for Alaska with a co-worker from the Yakima Post Office, Leslie D. Bennett.[2]

Steamers sailed along the Inside Passage, the local name applied to the coast and the sheltered waterways connecting Seattle and Skagway. After landing in Skagway, he traveled by rail and on several ships along the Yukon and Tanana Rivers to the town of Fairbanks, the largest town in Alaska, a trip totaling 21 days. The absence of sufficient roads made river transportation the practical method of travel. When roads were available, travel was by wagon in summer and by sled or sleigh in winter. Fairbanks had a summer population of about 10,000, but many left before winter, returning to look for work the following spring.

Founded only eight years earlier, Fairbanks was similar to Crystal Falls in its frontier orientation. Fairbanks would become the center of the road system of Alaska, as from there roads and trails led not only to adjacent mining districts, but also eastward to the Salcha Valley; northeastward to Circle, Eagle, and Dawson; and northwestward to Hot Springs. Fairbanks grew rapidly. Alaska surpassed all other equal areas of the United States in the variety, extent, and value of its natural resources, which included gold, silver, copper, tin, coal, lead, antimony, marble, gypsum, petroleum, oil, timber, furs, and fish. However, interior mining was done under the great disadvantages of a severe climate, a short season (about four months annually), costly transportation, insufficient water, expensive fuel, frozen ground, and uncertain labor. Because of the long winters, thousands of men left in autumn and returned the following year.[3]

Short of money, Emil took a job as a newspaper reporter. In a July 17, 1911, letter to his former Crystal Falls teacher Amanda Hamilton, he wrote: "After I had been here five days I happened to be in a receptive mood and landed the job as reporter for the Times. . . . Arriving here a perfect stranger, I considered myself exceedingly lucky, more so because there is a salary of about $200 a month attached to it. It is costing me about fifty or sixty dollars a month to live, and liking the work I think I am slated to become a sourdough, or in other words intend to remain throughout an Arctic winter." In his position he interviewed U.S. judges, notable mining engineers and owners, resource developers, and locals for articles. He was promoted to city editor of the Fairbanks *City Times* and held that position in 1912 and 1913. He learned about the Alaskan interior territory, mining and business conditions, and resources. At age 21, without any formal training in journalism, he began to sell stories about Alaska and the Yukon to newspapers throughout the country.[4]

In the spring of 1912, he became a legal citizen of the territory. As might be expected in an area of great open spaces and few people, club life served a social need. Emil joined the Arctic Brotherhood, which dominated the fraternal field. Founded as a means of passing the time on steamship trips to and from the United States, it grew so that there were local chapters in almost every town in Alaska. Teddy Roosevelt was a life honorary member. As an Alaskan citizen, Emil relinquished his Michigan residency, an act that later haunted him when he ran for Congress from Crystal Falls, Michigan, in 1946 and 1948. He worked hard and saved his money.

Ambitious, restless, and possessing his family's high regard for formal learning, Emil found that the frontier offered him limited opportunities. Seeing that educated mining engineers and others had a college education, he decided to pursue a degree. For Alaskans, this meant returning to the lower 48 states and enrolling at the University of Washington in Seattle, an institution with about 3,800 students.[5] During his freshman year, in September 1913, Emil participated in freshman hazing. Freshmen were thrown off the steps of Denny Hall. They also participated in "freshmen tie up," a battle with sophomores in which each class attempted to tie up members of the other class, along with tug-of-war.

Students from Alaska were a minority at the University of Washington, and Emil was instrumental in organizing a group for them. The Sourdough Club was founded on December 9, 1913, with 32 charter members, including all of the sourdoughs at the university. It was composed of students from Alaska and the Yukon who had lived there one whole year. "Sourdough" was a term for a prospector or pioneer, especially in Alaska or Canada, and one who had spent winters there, rather than returning to the lower 48, as many did. Emil was elected sourdough chief, or first president.

The purpose of the group was to unite the students of Alaska and the Yukon, to further the mutual interests of Alaska and the University of Washington, and to promote acquaintance between the university and prospective students in the north. On September 6, 1916, he described the club in Alaska and at the university in the Fairbanks *Times*. The old Alaska spirit showed itself, and thereafter, at regular intervals, the club held meetings, entertained prominent northerners, and enjoyed many a talk-fest about the "good old days in Alaska." One of his nicknames was "Sourdough" because of his propensity for reciting the wonders of Alaska.

With his background as a newspaper reporter, advertising man, and printer at several Alaskan newspapers, Emil joined the staff of the student newspaper. As a sophomore, he was managing editor, as well as a local representative for several Alaskan newspapers and a contributor to a number of monthly magazines. On April 28, 1915, he was elected without opposition editor-in-chief of the University of Washington *Daily*, garnering 1,299 votes. Emil published the paper with 44 student-assistants. As editor he received kudos, including complimentary letters from Roy D. Pinkerton, editor of the Tacoma *Times*.[6]

His academic career included courses in the liberal arts and in his major, journalism. During the fall semester of 1915, for example, he was enrolled in Journalism 5, Journalism 11, English 11, Philosophy 41, and History 33, while doing 25 hours of newspaper work a week. In 1915 he was elected to membership in the Oval Club, Washington's premier honor society of junior and senior men. On March 26, 1915 he was inducted into Sigma Delta Chi, the national honorary journalism fraternity, at the Hotel Butler. In subsequent semesters he continued his liberal arts and journalism studies, and met and heard a famous guest lecturer, Professor Frederick Jackson Turner, the author of the "frontier thesis" in American history. In addition to accompanying Turner and a group of students on a mountain hike, Emil read Turner's book on the *Significance of Sections in American History*, which pointed out the need for historians to use economic and statistical evidence in their studies. Always an avid student of mining, Emil also sat in as a student reporter on courses in mineral analysis and engineering. The university's School of Mines often invited in outside speaker-experts, including Donald Campbell, from the Guggenheim mining syndicate, who spoke on modern sampling techniques used to assay ore samples sent from Alaska mines. Turner's stress on the importance of statistics and Campbell's mineral and ore assaying made an impact. Hurja's auditing of such courses would serve him well when he later became the nation's first political consultant to apply the science of sampling and scientific polling to guiding political campaigns. As a New Deal pollster he continued to use mining metaphors and ore analysis examples to explain this new science to the press.

Emil met his future wife—blond, blue-eyed, Nordic beauty Gudrun "Goode" Cecelia Andersen, who became the belle of the campus—during freshman year. She was the "daughter of a Danish mining operator who had pioneered in the Klondike." Her parents and grandparents were early residents of Washington State and of the Yukon Territory and Alaska. Gudrun's father, Captain A. C. Andersen, was a Danish immigrant and former Canadian army lieutenant, who, upon hearing of the discovery of gold on the

Klondike River in the Yukon Territory, rushed to Dawson City and struck it rich. He brought his family with him from Chicago to the goldfields, and two-year-old Gudrun Cecelia was reportedly the first white child in the settlement. Musically inclined, by age five she played piano, sang, and danced at benefits for destitute miners. One of her standard numbers was "A Bird in a Gilded Cage." Gudrun also majored in journalism.[7]

Hailing from Fairbanks, Alaska, Gudrun was also a charter member of the Sourdough Club. A member of Tri-Delta sorority, she was active in the Dramatic Association, serving as secretary her senior year. During December of her sophomore year, she played Ida Taley in the University of Washington Dramatic Club's play *Ready Money.* In November 1916 she portrayed Tillie, an ingenue, in the Junior Review, a junior girls' vaudeville production she chaired, which was attended by Emil. According to the 1916 *Tyee* (the school yearbook), Gudrun "sang and smiled her way into the hearts of her audience as the dainty shop girl, who was a countess for a week." Later that month the Dramatic Association presented a comedy-drama, *A Gentleman of Leisure,* in which she performed the part of Miss Wolfe, a "house party guest." In a student comic opera, *The Little Tycoon,* she did not have a singing part, but was said to have had a delightful "stage presence" as Dot. She was on the University of Washington *Daily* staff for two years and inducted into Theta Sigma Phi, the honorary women's journalism society. She was a member of the Sacajawea Debating Club for women.

In an article published in the University of Washington *Daily* on November 7, 1916, the news staff compiled descriptions from men concerning their ideal college woman. Emil Hurja noted: "She must be broad, human, sympathetic, intellectual and ambitious." In answer to "What is your ideal college man?" Gudrun Andersen's quote reads: "He must be broad, be human, sympathetic and intellectual, and ambitious to a marked degree. I prefer one who is an idealist and yet withal a practical man. No, he doesn't have to be good looking exactly, but he must have a nice face." It sounds like they would be a perfect match. Or did Emil, as a *Daily* staff member, write his response after reading Goode's?[8]

Emil was inducted into Kappa Sigma fraternity on April 22, 1914. The "Chapter Letter," an annual booklet about chapter activities and featuring membership lists, gives Emil's nickname as "Funny" in May 1914. The 1915 "Chapter Letter" calls him "Hooge" and says of him: "eats blubber, talks Eskimo and says 'mush' to let you know he is from Alaska." Emil attended many fraternity social activities, including the 1914 picnic. The following year the picnic was held at Whidby Island in Puget Sound. Members and guests were transported by boat to the island, and his date was Gudrun.[9]

Dance programs show that Emil met and knew other college women as well. He attended a Kappa Sigma informal dance in October 1915 and a dance of the Puget Sound Alumni of Kappa Sigma in March 1916. His dance program for the Rose Hop of the same month shows that he had the seventh dance with Gudrun Andersen. In April 1916 he had the first dance with Gudrun at the Delta Delta Delta formal dance. According to the dance card, they danced to the tune "Are Your From Dixie?" She invited him to the Tri-Delta informal in November 1916.

Emil liked socializing with his college classmates. In May 1915 he attended the Junior Prom of the Class of 1916. In October of the same year, he went to the Annual Oval Club informal and the Rooters Club Dance. In April 1916 he attended the Campus Day Dance. In May 1916 he participated in the 50th Annual Military Ball at the National Guard Armory, as well as the Junior Prom held at the Hippodrome. In October 1916 he went to both the Annual Oval Club informal at the Gymnasium and the Halloween Dance. In December 1916 it was the University Varsity Ball.[10] As a clubman and a people person, Hurja kept a busy social schedule.

Emil became an avid football fan during his days in Seattle. The University of Washington coach Gilmour Dobie had an excellent record. During his years as coach of the Purple and Gold, the football teams were undefeated and only twice were tied, producing nine winning seasons. A graduate of the University of Minnesota, where he was quarterback on the team, he started coaching at Washington in 1907.

University of Washington fans traveled by boat to California to attend the Washington vs. California at Berkeley game on November 6, 1915. As general manager of the trip, Emil, with 300 others, left November 2 on a ship owned by the Pacific Coast Steamship Company. Washington gave California a 72–0 beating before 25,000 fans. They returned by ship November 9. He chronicled the trip in a four-page article for the *Washingtonian*, calling it "The Quest for the Golden Bear."

For a later prize song contest, he submitted words to a song he composed in 1917 titled "The Death of the Golden Bear." He wrote:

> The Golden Bear is creeping
> So bitterly it's weeping
> While Washington is keeping
> Her record spotless as of old
> Now see the bear is hobbling
> Upon his last legs wobbling
> It soon must fall a victim to the purple and the gold
> *Chorus:*
> Sing of Washington, for she is fairer than the rest,
> Proud and fearless leader of the hosts of the Golden West;
> Wide she flings her flag upon the breeze of every crest;
> Tremble now, you Native Sons, for our faith is all in Washington.

2nd verse:
The bear at last is calling
A death shout as he's falling
Back home the pelt we're hauling
That's what we did in days of old
A gold skin is a rare skin
We've got that golden bear skin,
It's just another trophy for the purple and the gold.

When University of California played in Seattle, Emil edited and arranged a game program in the shape of a football. In November 1916 he traveled to Eugene, Oregon, to see Washington play Oregon. The Ninth Champion Football Team was honored at a banquet on December 9, 1916, where Emil was an "invited guest." Emil committed himself with a passion in all of his endeavors, and football was no exception. At a time when college football was experiencing a growth spurt in the West, Emil plunged in.[11] His ability to focus all of his energies and passions on the task at hand, whether it was football, journalism, or later, polling, was already evident in his years as a student.

Other social activities filled his calendar. He attended the sophomore picnic at Wildwood Park on May 15, 1915. Students went by ferry to Wildwood Park, Lake Washington. Activities included a three-legged race, and the ladies had a candle race, carrying lit candles from one point to another. The following year, the junior day program on May 16, 1916, included a day filled with events such as tree planting, class luncheon, mixed double canoe race, log rolling, men's singles, girl's double canoe race, goose chase, greased pole walk, free-for-all swim, raft fight, interclass relay, canoe war, men's double canoe race, high dive, tub race, life-saving exhibition, tug-of-war, and Fir Tree Society initiation.

According to the Seattle *Times* of May 17, 1916, a total of 12 juniors and seniors were honored at a banquet at the Butler Hotel by being initiated into the Fir Tree Society, an honorary senior organization. The 12, including Emil, were pledged as the concluding event at the Junior Day Water Festival on May 6. As part of the initiation they "were obligated to garb themselves as pirates and walk the plank from a large barge moored off the shore." Other than Emil, all initiates were athletes or students involved in athletics.

The Annual Banquet of the University *Daily* staff on May 15, 1915, was held at the Boulevard. The menu included ripe olives, cream of tomato with boulevard wafers, lamb chops Madeira, new potatoes in butter, new peas, hot rolls, salad epinal, strawberry puffs, and coffee. As part of the program, five people spoke in what was called "Takes." Emil offered a "Take" on Alaska entitled "The Call of the Wild," in which he discussed the challenges one met for survival in the "great white North." The following year, the same banquet was held at the Northold Inn and he was accompanied by Gudrun.[12]

Emil returned regularly and during summer vacations to Alaska, and continued to write for publication. In the summer of 1914, Hurja accompanied a Chicago newspaper reporter named Lowell Thomas, who later became a well known radio broadcaster, to Alaska, where both were commissioned to write articles. With his knowledge of the region's natural resources, Hurja was a traveling special correspondent of the Mining & Scientific Press of San Francisco. An undated article notes: "Mr. Hurja, now in the employ of the Mining & Scientific Press of San Francisco and the Business Chronicle of Seattle, as Alaskan correspondent, arrived Juneau yesterday for a two week's visit. He will cover Southwestern Alaska from here, then going overland from Anchorage to Fairbanks over the route of the new government railroad and ending up with a visit to the principal Yukon camps." Alaskans wanted to publicize their accomplishments. The July 11, 1916, *Post Intelligencer* notes that University of Washington students and alumni voted to extend to President Henry Suzzallo an invitation to visit Alaska after Emil read greetings from Suzzallo at a banquet. An August 1, 1916, letter to Emil from President Suzzallo indicated his interest in trying to visit Alaska since he had never been there.[13]

Alaska needed an institution of higher learning, and Alaska's long-term congressional delegate, James Wickersham, introduced a bill in Congress providing for a University of Alaska. In support, Hurja extolled the territory's contributions in the *Post Intelligencer:* "this widely-scattered land of pioneers has increased the sum total of the world's wealth since 1867 by over $550,000,000. Two hundred and fifty million dollars has been produced in gold; two hundred millions in fish; seventy millions in furs; twenty millions in copper. The rest has been in a variety of mineral, timber, and lesser products." He wrote that in 590,884 square miles of territory, there was only one white inhabitant for every 16 square miles.

Not all of Emil's prognostications on Alaska were correct. In a 1914 article in the Overland *Monthly* entitled "Alaska, The World's Meat Shop," Emil predicted that the market for reindeer would increase as cattle ranges decreased and that in time, it would be almost universally used as meat in the United States.[14] Emil was obviously a bit ahead of his time. In the twenty-first century, with the increasing fear of the spread of mad-cow disease, it seems likely that grass- and lichen-fed reindeer would have had a large market.

FORD PEACE SHIP

World War I was raging in Europe while Emil was a student. A pacifist, Henry Ford, the automobile magnate, decided to personally fund an expedition to Europe to start peace talks to bring an end to the war. On November 27, 1915, he sent 150 invitations to prominent individuals he hoped would support his cause: pacifists, socialists, and feminists. In addition, all of the governors of U.S. states and territories were invited to accompany the ship or send a representative. On November 29, 1915, he contacted the presidents of 15 leading universities, asking each to select two students to accompany the group as non-voting observers. President Henry Suzzallo of the University of Washington received a Ford telegram inviting him to select two student representatives by the same standards that chose Rhodes Scholars. One requirement of student members was the mastery of a foreign language. Hurja knew German, as well as Finnish and some Swedish. Emil Hurja and another student were recommended and appointed by Suzzallo. While the other student could not respond in the short time frame (November 30 to December 4), Emil was given a leave of absence from the university and packed hurriedly, borrowing a fraternity brother's suit. Before departing, he contacted and secured credentials from Alaskan Governor J. F. A. Strong naming him the governor's personal representative. He also obtained a letter of introduction from Strong to the king of Sweden identifying Hurja as Alaska's official ambassador. He planned to travel east by railroad for the first time since leaving home six years earlier in the comfort of a coach seat, unlike his westward journey, when he rode the rods and empty freight cars. Then came a wire from Louis Lochner, one of the organizers of the expedition: "Hurja invited if he can make the boat."[15]

Then came a rush across the continental United States on a fast train leading eastward to catch the peace ship, with Emil uncertain if he could make it in time to sail on the *Oscar II*. President Suzzallo warned Emil in a memo: "You are taking your chances that Ford will forward you on the next steamer should you miss the peace ship; if he does not whatever expenses you incur are on your own cost." Undeterred, the adventurous college junior plugged onward. Not surprised, one of his journalism teachers, Frank Kane, wrote: "His Finnish substantiality meant perseverance, industry. His Alaskan environment taught him to extend his reach and take a chance." When the train reached Missoula, Montana, a messenger boarded the train with a telegram from the Ford expedition forwarded by President Suzzallo that read: "Keep Hurja coming. A second boat will leave December 8," thus assuring Emil, and many of the student and press invitees, of passage. Emil recalled that when he got the message, it was the "happiest experience of my life." En route and while switching trains in Chicago, Hurja was interviewed by the Chicago *American*. The press was all abuzz about Henry Ford's mantra: "Get the boys out of the trenches by Christmas." A realist knowledgeable about European public affairs, Hurja told the reporters: "this effort is not likely to stop the war at a word, but it is likely to bring about a conference that certainly is a great possibility for good."[16]

Emil arrived in New York after the *Oscar II* had sailed from Hoboken, New Jersey, on December 4. But Ford contracted with a second ship, the *Frederick VIII* to carry 23 late arrivals, who sailed on December 7. On December 17 the *Frederick VIII* was stopped by the British sea blockade in the Orkneys and detained at Kirkwell, Scotland, while the search for contraband took place. The legality of such searches greatly stirred the international community, and the German sympathizers poked fun at the British mantra "Britannia rules the waves." As they saw it, "Britannia waives the rules." Released from the search, the *Frederick VIII* joined the *Oscar II* party four days later in Christiana (now called Oslo), Norway. When they arrived on December 21, Norway was in the early stages of one of the coldest and snowiest winters Scandinavia had experienced in a century. Like the weather, Emil found the Norwegian officials cool and aloof, unlike the Norse students, who expressed more warmth and interest toward the peace mission.

The Ford Peace Expedition—led by American Peace Party leaders; Louis Lochner, a noted pacifist; and Hungarian suffragette, pacifist,and lecturer, Madame Rosika Schwimmer—planned to make landfall in Norway and then gather together representatives of several neutral nations, including Sweden, Denmark, Holland, and possibly others and meet at the Hague. As their plan stated, they hoped to "give central expression to the desire for peace and draft a document for the settlement of the war" and thus prevent "future wars." The peace delegates stressed this effort "was not hastily planned" but based on "confidential information," carried in Madame Schwimmer's mysterious "black bag." Although Schwimmer was tight-lipped in her exchanges with an adversarial press, she had let slip that she had solid information that the "belligerent powers are ready for peace even though officially they cannot admit it," and thus anxious to have neutrals join in a collective action for peace. Schwimmer refused the many press requests to see the documents in her black bag, which soon became an object of much attention and ridicule by the reporters on the expedition. Nevertheless, Schwimmer continued to assure the Peace Expedition delegates that the belligerents were anxious for peace. She stated that the mission hoped to bring about a just and lasting peace without victors or vanquished—strikingly similar language to that President Wilson would use in his "peace without victory" and "14 points" speeches a few years later.[17]

Henry Ford, however, had taken ill and was possibly discouraged by the adverse press that referred to the expedition as the "Loon Ship" and "Ship of Fools" and to the representatives as "nuts already cracked." Moreover, Rosika Schwimmer had received bad press in Norway, with some calling her "bossy," while others hinted she was a German agent and still others suggested she had bamboozled Ford into believing she was more influential in Scandinavia than she turned out to be. Ford on his doctor's advice quietly left the mission and sailed back to the United States on December 21, leaving the group without its most well known member.

Hurja noted that after Ford left, the student representatives were cut out of the plenary discussion sessions and no longer were accorded the service of porters and were required to carry their own luggage. For Emil and his fellow students it was a small inconvenience that was more than made up for by the social camaraderie of meeting Scandinavian students and by their cordial treatment at the official receptions.[18]

Being editor of the University of Washington *Daily* and a widely published reporter-journalist, Emil made the rounds of the Norwegian press and reported extensively on the fourth estate there. Accustomed to the bright liveliness of the American metropolitan press, he found "The Norwegian papers looked as cold and spiritless and severe as the journalist himself." Having interviewed the editor of Norway's largest newspaper, *Tidens Tign,* the editor, a Ph.D, told Emil about the structure of the Norse press: Most papers had few or no reporters in their employ and no "regular beats." A reporter was a person who made the rounds from one paper to another selling small items of news. After several years of such freelancing, a person might be eligible for a staff job, provided the person's formal education was sufficient. "Norwegian newspaper offices lacked the noise and life of an American press office," Hurja observed: There were "no papers on the floor and the rattle of typewriters was absent for not a single news paper man in Norway is able to write on a typewriter. All of the work is done longhand on copy paper." Hurja also faulted the writing style of the Norse freelancers— not only was the writing done in longhand, but "the ordinary rules of newspaper writing are not followed in Norway; each man writes as he pleases, for no semblance of order in the construction of story is observed." He concluded his observations with the fact that although an American-educated Norwegian scribe had tried to introduce modern American style changes, the Norse press lords had turned him down and would have none of it.

"The provincialism of the Norwegian press," Hurja continued, was in "sharp contrast to the brightness" of the Swedish papers. The press of Stockholm "showed more American influence especially in headline writing, leads into the story," and the like. About half of the staff of Sweden's *Dagens Nyheter* were able to use typewriters. Furthermore, the *Nyheter* of Stockholm was among the first in Scandinavia to introduce "the American system of headlines and lead writing." By 1915, according to Hurja, most of the Swedish press had initiated "the American system of headlines and lead writing."

When the peace mission arrived in Denmark, Hurja observed that the Danish press, like the Norse, remained "traditional to European writing."

The Danish *Politiken,* which immigrant-writer Jacob Riis once wrote for, had modernized to using telephone hookups to European capitals, and then fed the sound into a dictaphone from which typed copy could be accessed. Local social news, it appears, rarely broke into print. Denmark and Norway had had strong cultural links derived from the long period of Danish hegemony over the Norse. Thus, as Hurja concluded, in Norway "society news, dances, parties go unheralded; government news is of the keenest interest."[19]

Although nominally a student observer, Hurja, as personal representative of Governor Strong of Alaska, enjoyed certain perquisites, including first-class lodging and better meals than his fellow students. He wrote a series of articles published in the University of Washington *Daily* about his trip to Norway, Sweden, Denmark, Germany, and Holland while World War I was underway. In an undated article in the Juneau *Dispatch* after his peace ship trip, Emil wrote: "The peace ship has been woefully misunderstood. Mr. Ford's idea was not to pull the boys out of the trenches by Christmas, but rather to establish a neutral conference in some neutral European capital. The purpose of this conference was to discuss the issues involved in the war and to suggest ways and means for terminating the struggle." Emil was rapidly developing a sophisticated understanding of the complex geopolitics of war and peace.

On December 22 the peace mission embarked on a 24-hour train ride from Christiania to Stockholm, as Emil wrote, on a "slow and tiresome trip" without sleeping berths and inadequately heated. In cold weather, the peace argonauts often huddled in blankets to keep warm. Yet everyone's spirits turned up as they arrived in "Yuletide Stockholm." Light snow was falling and Emil recorded: "We received a splendid reception in Stockholm" and spent Christmas week there and attended a traditional Swedish *Julotta* service. There peace groups and student associations went out of their way to make the stay a pleasant one for the peace mission. The mayor put out a special welcome and a grand banquet was held. On Christmas Eve, Emil noted that people bustled about laden with packages amid the sounds of sleigh bells echoing through the light snowfall. Young Hurja described the city as being "like San Francisco at half speed." Emil went into a department store and met an "American-bred Irishman" who served him ice cream in the American section of the store.

The student representatives were lavishly hosted by their counterparts in Sweden and by the town mayor, with splendid receptions, concerts, and other entertainment. "Sweden, by universal consent of all who took part in the Peace Expedition," observed one of the organizers, Louis P. Lochner, "was the high-spot in our pilgrimage. Nowhere were arrangements so thoroughly and perfectly made as in Stockholm. . . . Nowhere was there more understanding of our aims and objectives than among these modern descendants of the Vikings." The Swedish metropolitan press also issued "encomiums of praise" on the Americans, the Washington *Daily* editor Hurja noted, and even the Norwegian press, following the Swedish lead, began to give the peace expedition more favorable coverage.[20]

On December 30 they left for Denmark, but were warned in advance that the mission could not hold any public meetings, which were banned by the Danish government since the beginning of the war. Nonetheless, the peace delegates in Denmark somehow managed to hold antiwar meetings, because they were technically "private," and thus skirted the law on no "public," meetings which the police observed but did not stop. The student delegation was also toured through museums, art galleries, and castles including "Elsinore of Shakespeare's Hamlet." Despite an occasional grumble by the University of Washington representative, Emil and the American students were full of gratitude for the cordial receptions and welcomes they received from all Scandinavian students from Norway onward to Denmark. Emil noted that "they all speak English," and some better than Americans. Not only did the expedition communicate well with young people, but in Denmark it also won an unexpected grand reception at the nation's leading newspaper, *Politiken*. There the leading senior writer concluded that "the peace pilgrims had won all Danish hearts," a quote that was published widely throughout Scandinavia.[21]

Then came the trip through Germany, where the peace pilgrims feared they might be treated roughly by the belligerent power. The choice was passage by land through Germany or by sea through mine-filled straits to get to the Hague in Holland, where the Continuous Mediation team would set up shop with hopes of ending the Great War. The mission decided on land transport and was warned by American and Scandinavian officials that Germany would let them pass through only in "sealed" railroad cars with windows blacked out and only by night. Furthermore, cameras and recording devices would be banned, and searches and inspections could be expected at numerous points. The mission, to their surprise, found the Germans were somewhat lenient, requiring no blacked-out windows. Peering into a darkened Deutschland, Emil recorded in his diary that he saw a "land of uniforms, a countryside ablaze with checkerboards of factory lights" supplying the "world's greatest fighting machine." At every depot he saw dramatically worded signs: "Soldaten Versicht In Sprech. Spionen gefahr": Soldiers beware what you say. Spies are listening. Hurja found German sentries to be more polite than he had expected, and compared them favorably against the British blockaders at Kirkwall, whom he recalled as being arrogant to a point of "disgust" because of their contempt for the American neutrality. Back in the states Henry Ford greeted the kaiser's decision to grant the peace mission permission to cross wartime Germany as a victory for the peace movement.[22]

The peace excursion was clearly a learning experience for the novitiate student journalist, who saw his writing skills challenged and honed by dealing with different cultures, languages, and issues. Emil's German-language facility served him well on the German-Dutch leg of the trip, and he even put his Finnish to use in Sweden, where some of the students and a few of the delegates were bilingual in Finnish and Swedish. Although the Hague mission failed to bring the belligerents to the peace table or to end the war, it did have an educative effect: it turned young Emil into an internationalist who strongly supported Woodrow Wilson's League of Nations and later Franklin Roosevelt's United Nations.

On January 11, 1916, the student representatives, most of the delegates, and the reporters set sail from Holland to the United States. A small cadre remained behind to set up the Neutral Conference for Continuous Mediation, which continued for the duration of the war and was a harbinger of the later to be formed League of Nations. The departing student delegates sent "a most heartfelt vote of thanks to Mr. Ford" for "all of the courtesies and kindnesses" throughout the trip. In fact the students were wined and dined so lavishly that Hurja recalled "that just for the novelty of it some refused champagne with our meals." On return Emil visited in Washington, D.C., for several days, meeting with the Alaska congressional delegate, and also with Secretary of State Robert Lansing, presumably for some kind of debriefing. Later he made his way back to Seattle and returned to an "enraged fraternity brother" the borrowed dress suit that the peace delegate had so hastily tucked into his suit case in his hurried departure.[23]

Although Ford had provided the necessities, delegates did need some spending money for nonessentials, and Emil returned with a mere 20 cents in the pocket of his borrowed suit. The University of Washington *Daily* and his replacement editor also had some fun with Emil, headlining the return of the prodigal editor with such lines as "HURJA IS BACK FROM SQUIRREL HUNT IN EUROPE" and a sidebar story kidding Emil about the fact that he had to make up military science drills missed with "PEACE DELEGATE BACK, PICKS UP GUN." The student editors mimicked the national press, which tended to poke fun at the Ford peace mission.

The university, Seattle, and Fairbanks press had extensively covered Hurja's trip, publishing his dispatches, letters, and reports to them. The result was that Emil was deluged with speaking invitations in Seattle and eastern Washington state. He became a sought-after speaker by church groups; Scandinavian clubs; municipal leagues; journalists; Rotarians; and civic, fraternal, and student groups.

Emil's speech giving, writing, and commentary on the Ford peace mission had won him new audiences and attention by new readers whom his football articles and Alaska reportage had not touched. During the summer of 1916, Emil again toured Alaska seeking information to write articles on its natural resource industries. He also acted as personal representative for President Suzzallo in setting up University of Washington alumni groups in Fairbanks, Skagway, Anchorage, Juneau, and Valdez.[24]

During his service as a journalist with the Fairbanks *Times* in 1911 and 1912, and his continuing work as Seattle *Post Intelligencer* correspondent to 1917, Emil published numerous pieces on Alaska's people, culture, natural resources, and mining industry. Hurja's interest in history prompted him to develop a library of original letters, documents, pamphlets, maps, and books relating to the history of the territory, with materials on the Russian period, and also on early Finnish settlers, which included one of the first Russian governors of the region. He wrote a weekly column for the Seattle *Post Intelligencer* on Alaskan mining activities as a student at the University of Washington and also served as special correspondent for the Mining and Scientific Press of San Francisco.

It was his Alaska knowledge and writing that won for him his next job. Leaving the University of Washington in 1917, Emil was taken on by the nonvoting Alaska territorial delegate to the United States Congress, Charles Sulzer, as secretary, at an annual salary of $500. For many decades Alaska had had no legislature except the United States Congress and had no representation in that Congress. Alaska had been recognized as a territory in May 1906, and a delegate to Congress was authorized, with a seat in the House of Representatives. All of the prerogatives of a congressman were given except the right to vote. A bicameral legislature was authorized in 1912. Meeting biennially, it had restricted powers. All laws enacted had to be submitted to the Congress of the United States, and if disapproved, they became void. In 1913, Congress authorized an investigation by the Alaskan Railroad Commission, and the following year there was enacted a law to construct a railroad to connect an open port on the Pacific Ocean with a navigable river in the interior. In 1915 the route from Seward to Fairbanks was designated, but construction was not completed until 1923. Floods, bank erosion, cave-ins, and rock and snow slides made maintenance expensive.

Emil's experiences in Congress were varied and interesting. He acquainted many committee chairs and members of Congress with Alaska's needs, propagandized about its future and potential wealth, and lobbied for more aid for Alaskan road development, becoming one of the spark plugs of a movement called "eight days to the states," which campaigned for solid, all-weather roadways from the United States to Alaska. Hurja noted: "Alaska's great need at that time was a closer liaison with the multitude of government departments, and this work fell to me because of my member's illness." He discovered that 44 federal government agencies had a hand in administering the territory of Alaska, thereby clogging the wheels of progress.[25]

During Hurja's employ in Congress for Sulzer, April 1917 to January 1918, the war clouds gathered as Germany resumed unrestricted submarine warfare following the unveiling of the Zimmerman Note (in which Germany threatened an alliance with Mexico against the United States) and the United States subsequently armed its merchant fleet to repel attacks. Then on April 2, Wilson convened a special session of Congress and asked for a Declaration of War against Germany. On April 4 and 6 the lower and upper houses of Congress passed the war resolution.[26]

Although Emil and Representative Sulzer arrived too late to hear the president's declaration, Emil heard Wilson's later speech on war preparation. Young man Emil was there in the chamber to hear the president, as he described it to Colonel P. W. Davidson: "Yesterday was a great day here, for President Wilson then delivered his great address to Congress. . . . I walked into the chamber just a few minutes before the President came in and stood right alongside of the Sergeant of Arms himself. During the whole address I was but a dozen feet from the President. Had anyone noticed me I probably would have had to answer to some of the Secret Service men. As it was I palmed myself off for a Representative for the half hour. It was a great experience, for it was the first time I had heard the President."

With the war underway and his work with Sulzer nearing completion, Hurja, the student peace delegate, had a change of mind about the prospects for peace. Fired up with the patriotism that swept through his generation of young men, Emil was anxious to enlist in the U.S. Army Air Corp, seeking a commission. His boss Representative Sulzer wrote Colonel Davidson: "I dislike to part with his services, but he is ambitious to do his bit in military channels, and realizing the crisis the nation is now in, I cannot oppose him or any other young men in such desires." Because of the difficulty of getting a commission, Hurja was advised to apply to the U.S. Army Signal Corp's, "spruce emergency division" created to meet the demand for lumber for aeroplane manufacture. Hurja assured the colonel that he knew the region, the transportation problems, and the nature of the industry in the Northwest and that he could be of service. Although Emil initially asked for the Air Corp's Quartermaster group, there were no vacancies. Emil asked Colonel Davidson to help him get into the military, writing, "I am full of anxiety to get into the service, for it offers the best opportunities for my special 'talents.' . . . I am greatly in earnest in this matter" and would appreciate what you could do to get me into the service.[27]

Having some training in the Cadet Corp at the University of Washington, and having knowledge of logging and powers of persuasion, Emil was inducted into the military service in the U.S. Army Air Force Signal Corp, located in Oregon and Washington. At the outbreak of the war, in April 1917, the United States had only 55 serviceable planes in the Signal Corp.

The Secretary of War, Newton Baker, mesmerized by the new war technology—airplanes—persuaded President Wilson to push through Congress a $1 billion bill to build "the greatest airfleet ever devised." This was the first war that saw the extensive use of airplanes in combat. Production problems plagued the army, which needed millions of board feet of straight spruce timber to build the air frames. The wizardry of metallurgy to produce lightweight metals and "metal skins" had not yet arrived in aircraft manufacturing. Weight was of paramount importance in building these "heavier-than-air" craft, and thus the prime choice for air frames and supports was lightweight and resilient spruce timber. Airplanes in 1917 were wooden-framed fuselages over which was stretched linen cloth that was lacquered to give it a metallic look. Very little metal was used at this time, except for the engines and machine guns.

Although Hurja expected to use his knowledge of Alaskan lumbering and transportation to help expedite the cutting and shipping of spruce timber, his superior wanted his talents as a journalist. Emil's main duties became editorial; putting out a pro-war-effort and morale-boosting paper called the *Peavey* (named after a tool loggers used to float timber down rivers). Hurja served in the Signal Corp through May 22, 1919, when he was discharged at the rank of captain. Before his discharge Hurja had sought on several occasions transfer to France, where he hoped to get airborne with flying aces such as Eddie Rickenbacker.[28]

Ironically the woman Emil was courting, Gudrun Andersen, had taken to flight before he could. The Seattle *Post Intelligencer* headlined the story: "UNIVERSITY GIRL TAKES FLIGHT WITH FORKNER AND SOARS 1,000 FEET ABOVE LAKE WASHINGTON:" There, pictured with leather helmet and protective goggles in the open cockpit of a Curtiss flying boat, was the smiling Nordic beauty. Gudrun reported that there "is an extraordinary charm about sailing through the air." She reported that her "tiny bit of misgiving" on takeoff blossomed into a "keen enthusiasm." As they soared over Seattle and near Mount Rainier, Gudrun related that this "first flight has given me a taste of unsuspected pleasure. I'll go again the first chance, for flying is surely a contradiction of the old saying, 'There's nothing new under the sun.'" When they descended from the heavens "with a light splashing pat upon the water" and deplaned back on shore, Gurdrun noted that an "ever present small boy" on the beach blinked and greeted her with "Pretty good for just a girl."[29]

Upon graduation in 1917, Gudrun worked for Emil's former employer, the Seattle *Post Intelligencer,* as the first woman beat reporter in the paper's history. When the United States entered World War I, Gudrun was the society editor and also wrote a daily column called "Women and the War," which was devoted to women's activities in support of the war effort. To get a feel for writing about flying machines and what aviators might experience in the war was the reason she doffed her leather helmet and went soaring above Lake Washington, one of the first women on campus to fly.[30]

At the war's conclusion, Hurja became publicity director for war savings in the state of Washington, promoting war stamps and liberty bonds. The next year Emil attended the Democratic National Convention in San Francisco as a delegate. James Cox was nominated for president, and former undersecretary of the navy Franklin Delano Roosevelt joined the ticket as vice president. Emil supported FDR's nomination.

A month later, on June 23, he married his college sweetheart, Gudrun Andersen. Gudrun, a talented actress and writer in her own right, had been the "belle of the campus" at the University of Washington. The Nordic beauty had a theatrical flair that nicely complemented Emil (with his more solid attachment to the material world). After marrying, it was on to an oil boom town, Breckinridge, Texas, where Emil was editor and publisher of the *Daily American* from 1920 to 1923. Hurja borrowed money to take over the paper. Breckinridge was a wild and woolly frontier oil-boom town. Emil recalled that the night he and Gudrun arrived, there had been a shooting and three corpses were laid out on the billiard table in one of the town's pool halls.

The *Daily American* prospered for a time under Emil's editorship, but then a disastrous fire wiped out the newspaper plant and half of the town. Overburdened with losses, the local insurance company failed to pay off on the loss, which left the Hurjas broke. Gudrun had gone with her father to visit his homeland, Denmark, in the summer of 1921, and had already tired of the rough-and-tumble frontier life of an oil boom town. By the end of 1921, Emil was telling his friends that his wife "will not take another year in Texas" and was preparing to leave Breckinridge He got the paper publishing again in a leased building and proudly boasted, "we didn't miss an issue." Nevertheless the setback meant starting again, and Emil privately told a fellow investor that he was "getting out when the getting is good." He told another investor he would "honor" his debt, but he "left Breckinridge penniless." What he had earned was a good reputation, for, as the local postmaster recalled in January of 1922, Emil "is considered by all to be the best newspaper man that ever hit this part of the country. . . . He is a good fellow, loved by all who know him, straight as a dye and always 'up and coming.' His integrity is above reproach and is one who never forgets his friends."[31]

In 1923 the Hurjas left Texas for California, where for two years, until 1926, Emil owned and edited a string of weekly newspapers in Santa Barbara, Beverly Hills, and El Segundo. Then in 1927 his knowledge of the oil industry attracted him back to Breckinridge, Texas, where he worked for another year as an oil industry analyst and writer. About the same time, he tried some real estate ventures during the Florida land boom, but they proved disappointing. One of his friends consoled him: "sorry to hear that your Pot of Gold was not on the end of the Florida rainbow." Better luck next time.[32]

Yet Hurja's work as an oil analyst, editor, and writer for the *Daily American* had gained him something of a reputation for keen insights into the extractive industries. All of his life, he had been familiar with mining in Michigan (once having planned to attend the Michigan College of Mines), Montana, and Alaska, and with a kindred industry, oil drilling. His Breckinridge *American* gained a considerable reputation in mining and oil drilling circles. A New Yorker acquainted with his expertise invited him to move to Manhattan to work for Joseph Gengler, a specialist in mining securities and oil stocks on the New York Stock Exchange. Hurja sold his paper and remaining interest, and in 1927, Emil and Gudrun moved to a Manhattan apartment on Riverside Drive where he would analyze and chart the flow of oil and gold output and market prices. As an analyst on oil and mining stocks, he met financiers Bernard Baruch and Frank Walker. When the stock market crashed in 1929, Emil suffered financial difficulties but continued to work in the financial markets, continuing to push Texas oil stocks as best he could. On one of his Alaskan jaunts in the 1920s, Hurja had met the well known stock market broker Ben "sell 'em all" Smith, the daring bear-market operator during the 1929 stock market crash. Emil continued to work with him after the crash. The friendship proved helpful in widening Emil's circle of acquaintances in the financial world as well as in national politics. After the crash, he worked with Smith on gold stocks and continued his interest in politics.

With his flair for figures and interest in voting trends, Hurja in 1928 tried to interest Democratic National Committee chair John J. Raskob and presidential candidate Alfred E. Smith in experimenting with polls for guiding their political campaign but got nowhere. A year later he made the same offer to Charles Michelson, director of publicity for the Democratic National Committee," offering my service in any capacity you may desire," but received no response. Hurja rushed through life possessed with the same restless spirit that brought his immigrant parents to these shores, observed his nephew, Dr. James Ojala. Emil constantly sought new frontiers—geographic, entrepreneurial, experiential, and intellectual. Like Frederick Jackson Turner, the author of *The Significance of the Frontier in American History,* Emil, who had studied and mountain-hiked with the famous American intellectual, moved from one frontier to another: from Michigan's Upper Peninsula to Montana, to Washington state, to Alaska, to the Texas oil boom, and finally to the frontier of public opinion polling. As we shall see in the next chapter, Emil was a pioneer on the cutting edge of experimenting, field testing, and applying the new science of sampling and polling for the first time to presidential campaigns, those of Franklin D. Roosevelt.[33]

CHAPTER 3

1932 PRESIDENTIAL ELECTION

POLITICAL HISTORIANS AND SOCIAL SCIENCE SCHOLARS HAVE tended to date heavy reliance upon public opinion polls used in political campaigns and to guide governance first to the 1960 John F. Kennedy election and to Louis Harris, allegedly the first big-time pollster to direct a presidential campaign, and then to Lyndon Johnson and his pollster consultant, Oliver Quayle. President Johnson was notorious not only for campaigning by the polls but for governing as well. He often defended his politics before pesky reporters and journalists by pulling out a recent poll from his vest pocket showing public support for his controversial policies. John Kennedy, although somewhat less overt, fine-tuned and revised his 1960 presidential campaign to be compatible with what Lou Harris and the polls told him. Pollster and consultant Pat Caddell may have eclipsed them both by putting candidate and later president Jimmy Carter on poll-pilot before, during, and after the 1976 presidential campaign. Yet it would be in the 1990s when the nation would witness its most poll-driven president in history, Bill Clinton, who not only used polls to guide his campaigns and shape his governance, but even checked out phrases for speeches using Dick Morris's "mall polls."[1]

Careful and painstaking research into the several Emil Hurja manuscript collections shows that Louis Harris and the John F. Kennedy campaign can no longer claim to be the "first." Governor Franklin D. Roosevelt was "flying" by the polls in his first presidential campaign, and even more so in his first administration and second campaign and to a much greater extent than is generally known or acknowledged. Roosevelt was the first president to make systematic use of public opinion polling for campaigning. His political navigator was a former captain from the World War I air force—then called the Signal Corp. Emil Hurja served as poll pilot and political consultant at the Democratic national campaign headquarters in the first presidential campaign to be guided by the newly developing science of public opinion polling and the political consulting business that would later grow from it. Hurja would remain on board for the New Deal in the role for the 1934 congressional and 1936 presidential elections.

Modern-day sampling and survey techniques were not available to candidates or political parties in the 1920s. Before presidential polling developed, other methods were used to predict elections and guide campaigns. Politicians depended upon field reports from precinct captains and county chairmen and on their own instincts. Precinct canvassers asked as many potential voters as possible how they intended to vote with little or no attention paid to apportioning their respondents by class, race, religion, or ethnicity. A precinct captain was expected to know the electorate and to be able to divine the public's voting sentiments.

Newspaper reporters and editors also attempted to gauge preelection sentiment and predict election outcomes. They ran nonscientific "straw" polls, often as clip-out questionnaires published in their newspapers or magazines, or as ballots that accompanied subscription advertising. The results were published primarily as circulation boosters. Those polled were generally subscribers, or potential subscribers, and did not represent a valid, scientific cross-section of the voting public.

Emil Hurja's fascination for polling and politics grew from his classes and discussions at the University of Washington with several notables, including Frederick Jackson Turner, a guest lecturer, and Vernon L. Parrington, who taught literature and history and a mineral analyst who lectured in the mining school. Parrington's *The Main Currents of American Thought,* a landmark work in literature supporting liberal humanism, was published in 1928, but Emil had the good fortune to hear the pre-pub lectures in 1916. The talks strengthened student Emil's political reformist impulse. Emil's interest in political reform also owed something to his early hometown days on the Upper Peninsula's mining range, where young Emil witnessed how the mining companies fraudulently voted immigrant miners en masse and solidly locked the GOP into power in those districts. Hurja also heard Turner's seminal lectures on the importance of the frontier in spreading democracy in the United States, and on how the populism of Western and Midwestern farmers, miners, workers, and frontiersmen put them ahead of the East in democratizing the political system on a series of important issues, ranging from granting women the vote to the popular election of U.S. senators.[2] Not surprisingly the rhetoric of New Deal reform would resonate favorably with Emil.

Hurja's education at the University of Washington, along with his work as an extractive industry journalist in Alaska and Texas and as a mining stock analyst, helped prepare him to enter the new science of public opinion polling. Autodidact Emil read Turner's 1912 book on sectionalism that called for new methods in historical studies that incorporated data drawn from literature, politics, economics, and sociology. Above all Turner importuned that "the method of the statistician . . . is absolutely essential." Hurja took Turner's work to heart and soon began to identify his own political research with statistical methods to such a degree that many 1930s news reporters called him the "New Deal statistician." (The word "pollster" had not yet been coined.) Emil's knowledge of sampling theory, which underlay scientific public opinion polling, was learned from lectures by mining expert Donald Campbell, who gave campus talks on sampling procedures for ore assaying and mineral analysis.[3] Evidence of this influence abounds, for Hurja used mining and mineral assaying metaphors, and not mathematical ones, when describing what he was doing to the D.C. press. As Emil explained to newsmen:

> You apply the same test to public opinion that you do to ore. In mining you take several samples from the face of the ore, pulverize them, and find out what the average pay per ton will be. In politics you take sections of voters, check new trends against past performances, establish percentage shift among different voting strata, supplement this information from competent observers in the field, and you can accurately predict an election result.[4]

What Hurja described with his mining metaphors were statistical techniques known today by names such as "random sampling," "quotas," "weighting," and "representative cross sections of the unit being measured," along with "historical behavior of the unit to measure stability and change." None of these concepts previously had been applied successfully in predicting presidential elections on a national scale. Although at this time sampling theory was known to pure statisticians and had been applied to commodities such as iron ore and produce, no one had applied the theory to national voting behavior.[5] Furthermore, evidence and experience suggested that statistical techniques applied to homogenous materials such as corn crops or gold ore veins might not pertain to a heterogeneous national population of Americans drawn from a hundred ethnic groups with a variety of racial, religious, regional, class, and occupational differences. The problem of finding a representative cross-section out of such a melting pot had seemed statistically insurmountable. Emil was up to the challenge. Hurja's entry into the new science of public opinion polling was another chapter in the life of frontiersman facing yet another frontier—only this time it was an intellectual one.

Hurja, then a mining stock analyst for a Wall Street brokerage firm, tried in 1928 to persuade the Democratic National Committee, which was managing Alfred E. Smith's presidential campaign, to use his methods for forecasting electoral support for the Democratic nominee and for guiding his campaign. However, Hurja was unable to win over the committee; its chairman, John J. Raskob, dismissed him as a crank with a crackpot idea. Raskob and the committee in 1928 relied upon field reports of precinct captains and county chairmen and their own instincts to direct the campaign. The Democrats lost the presidential election.[6]

Hurja prepared to try again in 1932. First Hurja, capitalizing upon his old Alaska connections, got himself slated as an Alaskan delegate to the Democratic National Convention in Chicago. He again offered his services to the Democratic National Committee. Hurja made his case for guiding campaigns by polling by pointing out how the DNC under Raskob in 1928 had wasted scarce campaign funds on states that were hopelessly Republican, despite what local precinct captains said. Scarce funds and valuable campaign resources, Hurja argued, should be expended where the political payoff was probable; in undecided states and in those leaning or weakly Democratic. Spending time and money on solid GOP areas such as New England, or on traditionally Democratic states in the Solid South, was a needless dissipation of resources. Hurja understood, of course, that the South's defection to Hoover in 1928 was caused mostly by Al Smith's Catholicism and his super-wetness on prohibition, but Hurja classified that as aberrant behavior. Public and private opinion polls could be used to correct such faulty strategies, Hurja told the DNC.[7]

The existing polls of the 1920s and early 1930s were called "straw" polls in that they were not drawn from random samples of the nation's population nor from representative samples of states, counties, or cities in which they were conducted. Even so, the *Literary Digest,* which ran "unrepresentative" mail polls of subscribers and potential subscribers culled from telephone and automobile registration lists, had amassed an impressive record in the past decade of predicting in advance the winning presidential candidate. In 1924 the *Digest* predicted correctly the vote of all states in the electoral college save two, and in 1928 placed correctly all the states in the electoral college except four, lending, as the pioneer scholar of polling Claude E. Robinson noted, "an air of unfounded infallibility" to the *Digest* polls. The number polled was large, sometimes running into the millions of returned postcards or mail ballots, which led to a widely shared belief (erroneous as it later turned out) by the public as well as many pollsters that the larger the poll, the greater the accuracy in predicting results.[8]

SETTING UP CAMPAIGN CENTRAL

Emil Hurja proposed in the summer of 1932 to harness this public pulse taking, using the Hearst press and the *Literary Digest* because of their national scope, along with precinct and state canvasses undertaken by party workers, and to put this information to use in running the presidential campaign. As Hurja told the DNC that year in his "Memorandum and Out-line," he wanted to establish a "definite method of statistical control and analysis of political sentiment during the coming campaign." He asked that "a division or section be created in the party organization to handle and col-lect this information and tabulate it on a uniform basis for the benefit of the national organization, and for the various state and regional organizations that will function during the campaign." Hurja advised that through his "close personal contact" with the "pollers" much of the poll data and raw re-turns of the *Literary Digest* and Hearst polls could sometimes be obtained before their publication and analyzed in advance for the party's good. Hurja asked that the "Minute Men of the Democratic Party" be organized as a na-tional group and be assigned the task of gathering raw data on voter senti-ment, as well as completed polls. The information, including both numerical and anecdotal data, would be sent to a central bureau within the DNC where it "could be correlated and analyzed for the benefit of the or-ganization leaders" by Hurja.[9]

Hurja then outlined how he, the statistical analyst, would establish benchmarks from the 1928 and 1930 congressional election results, as well as the polls, and follow them progressively through the presidential cam-paign of 1932 from August to November. This he promised the party would give them a moving "picture of sentiment" as it evolved over the campaign, which he called the "trend analysis method." He would chart this data on a weekly and even daily basis, as the various tests of political sentiment from the 48 states and dozens of counties and cities flowed in, and would assem-ble it into a master chart. All raw data would be computed in percentages to make comparability and tracking possible. The "Advantages" to be gained for the presidential campaign, Hurja advised, were that it would be possible "at any time to test the effect of a particular speech of the Candidate or the Opposition with a test poll conducted on the street through our own work-ers." Why? Hurja answered his own question: "Test polls should prove of tremendous value if only to save needless expenditure of campaign funds in districts where not needed." He "pointed out that during the 1928 cam-paign, the closeness of the *Literary Digest* poll in Rhode Island and Massa-chusetts caused a strong finale of Democratic Campaign Orators to be sent to those states with the result that, although the *Digest* poll indicated a Re-publican victory, Smith carried Massachusetts by 127,192 and Rhode Island by 1,451 votes." On the other side of the ledger, Emil told the party bigwigs that by ignoring the polls and various tests of political sentiment and failing to analyze them, the DNC wasted all kinds of effort and money in Pennsyl-vania, which in 1928, in Emil's view, was hopelessly Republican and beyond capture by a campaign blitzkrieg. Hurja, through DNC treasurer Frank C. Walker and publicity director Charles Michelson, got a hearing with the

DNC, which signed him on as a political consultant to Chairman James A. Farley.[10] Emil's "Memorandum and Outline" became the blueprint for the 1932 campaign.

Hurja's insight into how the statistically flawed straw polls could be corrected served the Roosevelt campaign well. Emil understood why the heralded *Literary Digest* polls could be right as well as wrong. Part of the *Digest's* success in the previous decade in calling in advance the presidential victories derived from the non-class nature of the vote and the fact that the groups whom the *Digest* targeted, middle and upper income voters, were respondents who approximated very closely the vote of lower-income groups, as well as other segments of the voting population. Thus skewed and unrepresentative samples got it right, partly by luck. Hurja read the 1932 *Digest* and Hearst polls by comparing them to their margin of error in 1928, which he used to "correct" them. He also reran some of the state, county, city, and congressional district poll returns and reweighted them in accordance with the percent they represented in the local or national population of the unit being measured.[11] He generally calculated voter turnout levels from previous turnouts, although he was helped by one of the *Digest* poll questions, which asked the respondent for whom, if anyone, he/she had voted in previous election. This was helpful in identifying new voters, or to use Emil's language, "doping out the first time voters."[12] The "weighting" and "correcting" unrepresentative polls, for an outdoorsman and hunter like Hurja, was the equivalent of trying to shoot straight from a crooked gun barrel. It could be done by compensating for the bend in the barrel, along with conducting windage checks when firing shots.

Hurja also developed what he labeled "trend analysis," which he used to track change over the course of a campaign and to check the effectiveness of Roosevelt's speeches or newly announced program promises. In 1932, Emil was in the experimental stage. By the 1934 congressional and 1936 presidential campaigns, he had developed a systematic method. An agricultural economist named Louis Bean would later publicize trend analysis and the reweighting of unrepresentative polls in his article publications and book chapters with such eye-catching titles that sought to rehabilitate the old chestnut "As Goes Maine So Goes the Nation," which became discredited after the early September Maine elections failed to predict the national elections results in November.[13] Wags were thereafter ridiculing the idea with the saying "As goes Maine so goes Vermont." Nonetheless Hurja and later Bean knew that the early September Maine vote, when compared to previous elections, could be factored into trend analysis.

Hurja used trend analysis to help manage three DNC campaigns in the first New Deal, from 1932 through 1936. After a long hiatus, trend analysis would be developed into a fine art in the post-1960 presidential campaigns with the use of overnight tracking polls. In the Roosevelt campaigns, Hurja knew that as long as the polling organization was reasonably consistent in its methodology (which the Hearst and *Digest* organizations were) he could be confident that the numbers would reveal trends that could be factored into running a political campaign.[14]

When it came time in 1932 for Emil to sell the DNC on his idea that poll numbers could be used to direct campaigns, serendipity intervened. Independent of Farley and the DNC a well-to-do business Democrat and president of Macy's in New York, Jesse L. Straus, had polled convention delegates in advance of their conclave to nominate a presidential candidate. The Straus canvass of presidential preferences, which was widely covered by the press, reported that a majority of preconvention delegates favored New York governor Franklin D. Roosevelt.[15]

Many news commentators and some scholars were persuaded after Roosevelt was nominated that the Straus polls had been the single most important stratagem in persuading some favored-son delegates and supporters of rival candidates (who numbered nearly a dozen) to tip the scales in favor of Franklin Roosevelt. Two political scholars who observed the preconvention and convention maneuvering wrote of the Straus surveys: "The value of these surveys to the Roosevelt candidacy cannot be overestimated. . . . They . . . went a long way in making his nomination inevitable. . . . Truly, no piece of strategy in the pre-convention period was more successful than these surveys. Furthermore, their use must be reckoned the most unique maneuver of the campaign."[16]

There is no doubt that the delegate preference polls created momentum for the governor; made him the most talked- and written-about candidate, next to Smith; and likely moved some delegates toward the New York governor, enabling him to secure a simple majority by convention time. Yet it is not entirely persuasive that the Straus polls did it all by themselves: the Democratic Rules Committee in Chicago hung tight to its two-thirds rule for nomination, and many of the lead contenders, including Alfred E. Smith and J. Nance Garner, thought they could emerge as compromise candidates and possibly win the nomination from a "deadlocked" convention. The prospect of a deadlock was serious enough so that Roosevelt tried to change the Rules Committee requirement from a two-thirds vote needed for nomination to a simple majority, but after charges of trying to change the rules in mid-game and being charged with "bad sportsmanship" the Roosevelt forces backed off and began bargaining for the remaining delegate votes they needed. Newspaper publisher William Randolph Hearst turned out to be the "kingmaker" or "Warwick" of the Chicago convention when he arranged to swing the California and Texas delegates to Governor Roosevelt in exchange for a deal to name Texan J. Nance Garner as vice president. Thus FDR finally won the nomination on the fourth ballot.[17]

The Straus poll served to strengthen in Democratic National Committee director James Farley's mind the political influence of polls. Farley, who never fully understood how polls worked, saw their principal influence as creating hoopla, "ballyhoo," and the "bandwagon" effect.[18] Other New Dealers did not understand how the polls worked either, and FDR's close confidante and long-time aide Louis M. Howe called statistician Hurja "Weege," a phonetic rendering of Ouija, a popular board game of the 1920s, which presumably had mystical predictive values.[19] Even so, Farley was increasingly inclined, as the 1932 campaign progressed, to seek out poll briefings by Hurja for campaign guidance and sought Emil's advice for his predictive press releases. By late September and through October to election day Hurja was writing Farley's press releases, predicting a coming Democratic victory and offering specifics as to the state vote, the electoral vote, and the regional direction of voting.[20]

Hurja told the editor of the Juneau *Daily Empire,* a former employer from his college days, that senators such as Pat Harrison sought his advice on "how the trend was in the farm belt." . . . I wrote Farley's last statement, and today I wrote another, which is enclosed. He likes them, as does Charley Michelson, and Louis Howe." A week and a half later Emil developed these themes further, noting to the Juneau editor, "Virtually all of the statements Farley makes that involve predictions, I have prepared." Elaborating further, he stated: "Farley likes them, and calls on me daily. But that is only one face of the work; the other is the real value of statistics to campaign managers—the women's department calls up every day for 'dope.' I have had a call to send material daily to Edward M. House among others."[21] As Emil pointed out, political managers were adjusting their campaigns in accordance with poll findings.

The Democratic standard bearer also consulted with "Weege" before starting on his October cross-country barnstorming campaign: "On Monday I was called to Albany to consult with Gov. Roosevelt before he started on his trip," Emil noted. "He [Roosevelt] said he had read my state reports with interest (my analysis of the past vote and present indications in each state, based on my polls), and asked me a lot of questions. I suggested poking a little fun at Hoover as a good means of combating the last-minute efforts. He said he was going to put in a little of it on this trip." Hurja closed his letter to his Juneau editor saying, "in July when I wrote you—a landslide of major proportions. No one would believe me then . . . but now many of them are beginning to see the light."[22]

HURJA POLL ANALYSIS 1932

The summer and fall of 1932 was Hurja's trial run for using polls to pilot a political campaign. Tracking the campaign from August through November

1932, Emil was busy disaggregating the polls of state and congressional districts. Drawing upon the Hearst newspaper polls and data from the *Literary Digest,* the latter which was gathered from all 48 states and many congressional districts, Emil was busy crunching numbers. The 1928 poll numbers and election returns, along with the 1930 congressional returns, formed his benchmark for tracking changes and trends. Emil forewarned his DNC colleagues that the *Literary Digest* polls could not be read at face value: with their middle- and upper-income respondents gleaned from telephone and auto registration lists, they had a Republican bias and "understated the Democratic strength in the case of every one of the 48 states." The last *Digest* poll of 1928 had under-predicted the Al Smith vote, stating the Democrat would pull only 36 percent of the popular vote, whereas the final numbers showed that 41 percent of the public voted for the nation's first plausible Catholic presidential candidate. But biases did not render polls unusable. Emil in 1932 knew that one could correct for biases by over- and under-weighting certain segments of the poll electorate and correcting the returns to the proportion of the population that the voter segment represented. Even more to the point, Hurja argued, one could read the numbers as "trends and not necessarily absolute percentages" of the projected and anticipated vote. The Hearst polls, Hurja noted, had some of the "same biases" but were nonetheless useful in spotting trends and detecting troublespots and campaign mistakes, and showing the "drift of the voters since 1928."[23]

In his "Supplementary Memorandum on Interpretation of Hearst Poll," Hurja on September 7, 1932, again cautioned Farley and the DNC that the published numbers of the Hearst polls could not be accepted at face value, but had to be reanalyzed to correct their built-in biases. The Hearst surveys were "obtained by sending a reply postcard to every tenth name in telephone books, strictly on the basis of the voting strength of the county." An "investigation at the statistical department of the American Telephone and Telegraph Company," Emil continued, "discloses" that "roughly speaking" approximately "three-quarters of the telephones came from the upper one-half of the economic strata of the country; the remaining one-fourth comes from the lower one-half of the economic strata." Another point "revealed" by the investigation at A.T. and T., Emil told the Democrats, is that the "very rural portion of the population of the country is not in the main represented by listing in telephone directories. The rural subscribers are usually tied to a mutual telephone company, which frequently does not issue directories or lists of any kind. This kind of telephone user, then, is not included in the Hearts poll." The "probable error . . . might run over five percent," Emil concluded, but happily is "in favor of Roosevelt."

The Hearst survey of "southern states is likely to show an ever greater percentage error," Emil reasoned; because of a "lack of special issues which aroused the south in 1928" (such as Prohibition and Al Smith's Catholicism), the turnout would be down and the Solid South would return to the Democratic fold. Emil was correct in his prediction that the Solid South would return to the Democratic fold on Election Day, and he was partly right in forecasting a lower turnout than in 1928: this occurred in four southern and border states in 1932.[24]

Hurja delved deeply into state- and city-level polls to understand their biases and see if anything usable could be salvaged from poorly designed "straws." In his "Review of Colorado Statistics" and "Trend of the Polls" he placed Colorado as a "doubtful" state for the Democrats. In his analysis he factored in the 1930 congressional and senate elections, and came up with a "Composite of All Elections" that put a favorable light on Roosevelt's chances in the mountain state. Although the Hearst and *Literary Digest* polls since August had shown a steady erosion of the projected Democratic presidential vote, which stood at 49 percent for Roosevelt as of September 10, Hurja took into account the GOP bias of both polls and suggested that with such corrections Roosevelt could be shown carrying Colorado by a small margin. Hurja also took comfort in his prediction when the Denver *Post* conducted a survey at the automobile license bureau that showed the renewal applicants giving Roosevelt a sizable lead from that segment of the electorate. Finally, as Hurja reported to Farley, the newspaper editors in the Denver region showed a 4-to-2 bias in favor of Roosevelt. Roosevelt would carry Colorado on election Tuesday, as predicted.[25]

GENDER GAP

One of Hurja's biggest finds in early polling history occurred on September 10, when he detected a growing gender gap in the polls: he headlined his memo to Farley and the DNC: "FARM BELT SHOWS HOOVER GAINS AMONG WOMEN." He then dug further into the Hearst polls, which showed such results and corrected their bias. He discovered that the Hearst poll, based on the 1928 turnout rates, had sent two-thirds of its ballots to men and one-third to women, which, by the standards of the day and the empirical evidence available, was a reasonable methodology. Yet when Hurja dug further into the numbers, he discovered that "women returned ballots in excess of their numbers in the population." He then corrected the overpolling and told Roosevelt's political handlers: "By making allowances for the excess of women's representation in the polls, the probable Democratic percentages for election itself would be materially higher from these states." Nevertheless, Hurja warned: "substantial losses have been suffered in the women's vote throughout the farm belt, and consideration should be given to stop losses." In probing for the cause of the gender losses, Hurja, in his

"South Dakota Special Report" on September 21, deduced that the decline in the women's support for Roosevelt was "apparently due to the reaction of women generally in the farm belt to the prohibition question" on which Roosevelt had thumped for repeal in his Sea Girt speech. Roosevelt's "wetness" sat poorly with Midwestern farm wives.[26]

The east coast also showed some September losses among women voters, although some of the losses were in some cases offset by gains by male voters. Hurja's report told the DNC: "Gains in Pennsylvania Among New Voters and Losses Among Women Voters." The polls of September 15 showed 61 percent of men favoring Roosevelt but only 47 percent of women doing so. The male vote, as Hurja tracked it, showed a consistent and steady increase from a low of 47 percent on August 20 to 61 percent on September 15, while women voters had "shown a corresponding decline." In this instance the male-female differentials in turnout were not sufficient to carry the state, and Pennsylvania went for the GOP's Hoover in 1932.[27]

In examining the trends in New York and New Jersey, Hurja found that although the New York governor was still leading in his home state by a 52 percent showing, the scandal case of Tammany Hall Democratic Mayor Jimmy Walker was taking its toll in dulling enthusiasm for Roosevelt. In neighboring New Jersey, Hurja was still waiting for some follow-up polls to measure the success or failure of Roosevelt's Sea Girt speech, delivered at a "monster rally" orchestrated by corrupt Jersey City boss Frank "I am the Law" Hague.[28] In the speech Roosevelt came out strongly for the repeal of Prohibition. The candidate's pro-liquor position and the association of Roosevelt's campaign with big-city bossism, Hurja feared, would lose votes in middle America. As he noted to the governor and the DNC director, "it is evident that the effect of the combination of the Sea Girt speech and the Walker case is becoming noticeable in the ballot being currently received in the count."[29]

Although Roosevelt's pro-drink and anti-Tammany positions should have offset each other, as Hurja read public sentiment, it was clear that Roosevelt's anti-Tammany stand was hurting more than pro-drink was helping. Irish Americans and machine Democrats, especially in New York and New Jersey, were annoyed when Governor Roosevelt took the presidential nomination from their hero, the "Happy Warrior" Al Smith, and now doubly annoyed when the governor went after their corrupt but debonair and ever-popular "let-the-good-times-roll" Tammany favorite, Mayor Jimmy Walker. As the Roosevelts' close advisor, Louis M. Howe's secretary Lela Stiles saw it in 1932: "The whole country, it seemed to us, was sitting out there watching what FDR would do. If he didn't remove Walker from office, the country would say 'Tammany controlled.' If he did remove him, Tammany would go against him. And we had to have New York to win."[30] Providentially, and with no forewarning, the tainted Tammany mayor resigned, sparing Governor Roosevelt the agony of a hard decision.

In Missouri the gender loss was less damaging to Roosevelt because of a strong male pro-Roosevelt sentiment being expressed in the polls. Hurja, on September 12, labeled it "safely Democratic this year," and he was proven right in November. In the Midwest, however, Emil expressed real concern about an even larger gender gap: the polls for Indiana and Illinois showed 64 percent of male voters favoring Roosevelt, but a meager 22 percent of female voters choosing the New York governor, as of September 9. He told Farley, "this should call for some drastic action." The Hearst poll in Massachusetts also showed a similar "alarming" drop off in the women's vote, with only 20 percent favoring the Democratic candidate. Yet when Hurja corrected the biases in the poll, he told Farley such reweighting raised Roosevelt to about 49 percent, which, combined with the majority male total, made the Bay State likely to vote Democratic in 1932. And indeed it did, for despite Herbert Hoover's sweep of northern New England, Massachusetts voted for Roosevelt .[31]

Hurja then followed up with advice to the DNC about where to put extra effort with campaign oratory, additional campaign funding, speakers, broadcasts, and newspaper advertising, and how to address the special needs of the soft spots in building the Democratic vote coalition. On September 10, Hurja analyzed and reanalyzed three Hearst polls for Wisconsin (8/26, 9/1, and 9/9) and detected an "unexpected drift" away from Roosevelt and called for a "measure to check it." A day earlier he told Farley, "the decline in Indiana and Ohio is particularly severe" and called for "drastic action," which generally translated into more campaign funds for more orators, more public advertising, and more political rallies.[32] Deciding where Democratic Party resources should be used to win elections was Hurja's contribution of the practical application of polling to campaigns.

Elsewhere in the nation he offered additional advice on where time, effort, and money should be put into the campaign and where it was not needed: in the governor's home state of New York, Hurja warned that Roosevelt was polling lower among women than men and that the "trend has been downward since the beginning of September." In Michigan, on the other hand, the trend by October 11 was showing an uptick, and Hurja advised that extra effort be put there, where the "work will count for the most." On the border states Hurja summarized his analysis with one-liners that read: "Maryland—Better with women than men; no need for special effort. Tennessee—Better with women than men; no need for special work. West Virginia—Running better with women than with men; percentage appears entirely safe." In the farm belt Hurja advised: "Iowa—State is Safe, but farm women likely to be against Roosevelt in generous measure. Kansas—Recent improvement with women; losses with Men. Both need some work. North Dakota—Women running about 50%. No need for special work here . . . Believe women won't turn out in anywhere nearly the same proportion as in other states of the farm belt. Wisconsin—Recent slump with women, but men are running at exceptionally high rate. Believe that women's vote here will be like that of North Dakota, small in proportion to that of men." On the mountain states Hurja advised: "Colorado—Some work can be done here. Women running 43.9%, men 57.6%. Utah—Women running higher than men; no need for work. Other mountain and coast states are O.K."[33] Overall the gender gap was a problem for Roosevelt in his first election. But as New Deal labor secretary Frances Perkins noted, Roosevelt "learned" and "in 1932 he discovered anew the power and influence of the women's vote."[34] With their newly established Womens Division, headed by Mary "Molly" Dewson, the Democrats began a generation-long remediation that would reverse the numbers by the latter part of the twentieth century. By 1999 the Roper Center's *Public Perspective* reported that an analysis combing all Gallup surveys of the previous six years shows that "women in 1999 are about 10 percentage points more likely than men to identify with the Democratic party."[35]

Other issues also disturbed Democratic bigwigs. Roosevelt and the party leaders were concerned about the falling-out between the two main contenders for the Democratic nomination, Roosevelt and Al Smith, who had been the 1928 presidential candidate. With the Depression underway the Democrats smelled victory in the air. After the stock market crash of 1929, two perceptive political scientists who had interviewed party leaders and attended both nominating conventions noted that "no stock depreciated more in value than that of the G.O.P."[36] The Democrats swept the 1930 gubernatorial and congressional elections, and took control of the House of Representatives, and reduced Republican control in the Senate to one vote. Al Smith, who had carried the party's banner in the previous election, was thought by his friends and supporters to be the deserving nominee for 1932, now that victory was in sight. But alas, Governor Roosevelt beat out the Empire State's former governor, and bitterness and bad feelings ensued. Party leaders feared that a split between these two prominent Democrats might destroy hope for victory just as the William H. Taft–Theodore Roosevelt schism had done to the Republicans in 1912. The DNC feared that Catholic Smith followers were defecting to Hoover, and Hurja conducted an analysis of the 1928 and 1932 Hearst and *Digest* polls to determine the defection rate. Hurja reported on October 12 that there was a sizable Catholic Democratic defection to Hoover, which ranged from 6 to 8 percent in the midwestern states to as high as 15 percent on the eastern seaboard and New England states, and which Hurja in his report tabbed "Percentage of state population that is Roman Catholic." Percent defection and percent Catholic showed a high positive correlation. Political consultant (although the word was not in currency then) Hurja advised the Roosevelt campaign that special efforts should be made to schedule a "Smith speaking tour, or a more formal and vigorous endorsement" of candidate Roosevelt by the convention loser. To that end Hurja recommended: "Special handbills, or flyers; special posters, special art work showing Governor Roosevelt and Governor Smith together . . . as well as . . . special radio appeals in the more important states and cities" to publicly heal the wound and call back the defectors into the Democratic vote column. Some effort was made in that direction, and a Smith endorsement of Roosevelt in September was widely publicized.[37]

To measure how the Roosevelt campaign was progressing Hurja developed a large U.S. map with each of the states color coded to indicate how the polls and other information showed the state leaning in the presidential campaign. Blue-colored states were positively for Roosevelt, and light blue were not so definite but were leaning toward Roosevelt. Red was for states that were positively for Hoover, and light red for those leaning toward Hoover. Markings on his map also showed where Democratic radio broadcasts were not effective and where circulation by strong Republican newspapers was believed to have influenced Republican leanings. Hurja also catalogued letters from citizens that gave clues to sentiments and issues that influenced voters, but he mostly relied on opinion polls—private, public, straw—and his own surveys.[38]

The Hurja method in 1932 involved examining every scrap of information about potential voter preferences, even including private house-to-house polls made by bookmakers and gamblers, who placed odds on them for purposes of betting. The massive storehouse of information that Hurja assembled was then digested and synthesized into a two-page analysis of how the Democratic campaign was progressing—where it was slumping and where voter sentiments were shifting. He also indicated where the party should shift its battalions of orators and mimeograph machines, radio talks, and campaign advertising. Light-blue states, those leaning toward Roosevelt, got most of the attention. Thus Hurja, during the 1932 presidential campaign, performed as the brain machine and backroom intelligence directing Roosevelt's try for the presidency.

Finally, as the campaign was swinging into the last three weeks, Hurja did a "Poll Story Special" for Farley to release to the press that took note of the urban vote coalition abuilding for Roosevelt. (Sam Lubell would later bring this urban coalition to the attention of scholars and the public.) The Democratic candidate "has such a commanding lead" as shown by the polls, Hurja wrote, that "he will carry nearly all of the one thousand largest cities of the country. . . . Only forty-one of the one thousand largest cities in the country can be considered doubtful at this time. Of the 93 cities having 100,000 population or more, and representing about 30% of the total population of the country, the *Literary Digest* and other polls show Governor Roosevelt building a preponderant lead in all but eighteen, six of which are in Massachusetts. In the five largest cities of the country—all save one, Philadelphia—Governor Roosevelt is shown ahead by the *Literary Digest* statistics." And Hurja concluded by pointing to a separate poll, then being conducted, that showed Roosevelt surging into the lead even in Philadelphia. However, the surge would not prove enough for the Democrats to carry Pennsylvania on Election Day.[39]

By late October, Hurja was writing all of the memos and press releases for the DNC and, in one such memo he explained: "This tabulation shows that the clean sweep we've been talking about is not an idle dream—that it is possible if the swing continues." Hurja ground out a mounting stack of press releases for Farley, with reports such as "We have tabbed 387 different polls taken by newspapers, magazines, volunteers on radio, trains, ships, airplanes for 1,921,000 votes and show Roosevelt winning an overwhelming vote . . . we have checked and rechecked . . . eliminated bias by weighting" for states and even counties. "A single straw ballot doesn't mean a thing but a million straws in the air tell which way the wind is blowing . . . a whirlwind for Roosevelt." Hurja had earlier written his financier friend Bernard Baruch, telling him, "Roosevelt has it in the bag. I doubt if anything can keep him from getting the election." On October 14, Hurja provided Farley with "Suggested Release to All Daily Papers," which read, "Roosevelt is as good as elected president," conceding that only Maine and Vermont were "doubtful."[40]

On Friday, November 4, the last weekend before the election, Hurja handed Farley a press release stating the Republican party "is going to sink to the lowest state that it has experienced in two party contests since the Civil War," and that Roosevelt could win by a 10 million popular majority. "Next Tuesday," continued Hurja," we shall see a revolution at the ballot box." Farley released the statement under his signature on election weekend. The results on Election Tuesday confirmed the Hurja prediction. Farley and the DNC based their predictions on Hurja's charts, graphs, and polls, and were amazingly accurate in calling the outcome in November. The results showed that Hurja had predicted eight mountain states for Roosevelt by a plurality of 300,000 votes, and the actual plurality was 295,000 votes, with an average error of only 564 per state. Hurja predicted a 185,000 margin for the Dakotas, and the actual vote was a 190,000 plurality. He also called the South correctly by predicting a 2 million plurality (actual result: a 2.3 million plurality) and the border states with a 1 million plurality (actual result: 1.2 million plurality). In state after state and region after region, Hurja forecast a Democratic plurality of 7.5 million votes; the actual result was 7.2 million votes. Hurja was wrong only in Delaware, Pennsylvania, and Connecticut, which he called for Roosevelt by narrow margins.[41]

Roosevelt won a smashing victory. His vote plurality over Herbert Hoover in the electoral college was by a landslide proportion of 472 to 59, which was the largest margin of victory in the electoral college since the Civil War. Governor Roosevelt carried 42 states to six for incumbent Hoover, who hung on barely in northern New England. The general turnout was up about 12 percent, although the women's vote, which was an estimated 42 percent, was down slightly from the 1928 record of 43 percent of the popular vote.[42] The results show that consultant Hurja's advice was generally on target. Although the scholarly literature generally dates campaigning by the polls to John F. Kennedy and Louis Harris in 1960, and governing by the polls to Lyndon Johnson and Oliver Quayle, we can see from a careful study of Hurja papers and other political collections at the Roosevelt Library that the right date is not 1960, but 1932. The United States had gone through its first presidential election guided by the polls when Governor Franklin Roosevelt defeated incumbent President Herbert Hoover in 1932. Political scientist Robert Eisinger, who has researched the polling data at the Roosevelt Library, concluded recently that Emil Hurja's polls for FDR and Hadley Cantril's during World War II "signaled the birth of presidential polling and . . . transformed the presidency and American politics."[43]

EPILOGUE

Because the *Literary Digest* poll was so wrong in its 1936 prediction of a Republican victory, and because it was based on an unrepresentative sample derived from telephone owners and automobile registrants, poll experts and scholars have tended to dismiss all *Digest* polls as "pre-scientific" (which they were) and useless, and therefore hardly worth studying or writing about. But as research into Emil Hurja's methods of imaginatively and ingeniously correcting biases, reweighting voting groups, and using trend analysis to direct a presidential campaign shows, it was and is possible to use a flawed compass to direct a political campaign. "Trend analysis," which Hurja introduced into American presidential politics was the key to it all. After correcting for biases and unrepresentative sampling, and reweighting results and rerunning and reanalyzing statistics and raw data from the *Literary Digest* and Hearst polls, Hurja was able to point the DNC to where the Roosevelt campaign was slumping, gaining, and holding even; where the gender gap was hurting the governor; and where "something should be done," "nothing need be done," or "drastic action" should be taken. For the first time in history a presidential campaign had been conducted under the guidance of the newly developing science of public opinion polling. As *Fortune* magazine observed, the Democratic National Committee had "adapted its campaign expenditures to Mr. Hurja's figures. Down to 1932 political parties had largely used the scatter-gun method. A campaign chairman . . . would spill his funds equitably and inefficiently over an entire map. Armed with Hurja's prognostications Mr. Farley avoided such errors."[44]

A study of the Emil Hurja papers shows that it was not John F. Kennedy and Lyndon Johnson who were the first to campaign and govern by the polls but that FDR was "flying by the polls" in his first campaign to a much greater extent than is generally known or acknowledged. Hurja was there as poll pilot and functioned in that role through the 1934 and 1936 election campaigns, and also on policy matters after 1934. After Hurja left the administration in 1937, there seem to have been no poll-driven political consultants in the White House until the eve of World War II, when FDR resumed his reliance on polls on issues of neutrality legislation, aid to Britain, and other defense-preparation measures. During FDR's third administration, in World War II, it is clear that Hadley Cantril and others ran secret polls related to the popularity of the president's policies. To take one striking example, Roosevelt had secret polls conducted on the American Catholic response to the bombing of the holy city of Rome. When he discovered that American Catholics were not overly opposed provided the Vatican was not targeted, the president gave the go-ahead order and Rome was bombed. Roosevelt's consciousness of Catholic voter sentiments was not something born in the exigencies of war, for clearly Hurja was examining Catholic voter data in critical New England and the eastern states, and Al Smith defections on religious grounds.[45]

It has been only recently that a few scholars have recognized Roosevelt's reliance on polls from 1940 onward. But research into the Hurja files shows that it happened much earlier and that we can date the beginning of electioneering by the polls to Roosevelt's 1932 presidential campaign. Jesse L. Straus blazed the way with the preconvention delegate preference polls in 1932, and Hurja paved the road for polling by demonstrating its utility for campaigning, and to some extent even for governing.[46]

CHAPTER 4

POLLING AND PATRONAGE FOR ROOSEVELT AND THE NEW DEAL

HAVING HELPED WIN THE PRESIDENTIAL ELECTION, Hurja during the years 1933 to 1934 also made himself exceedingly useful in other areas of the Roosevelt presidency. He had become, for example, a principal in the direction of patronage policy for the administration. Hurja first worked for the Reconstruction Finance Corporation, replacing Hoover appointees with New Deal loyalists. He then switched to the Department of Interior to handle political appointments under Secretary Harold Ickes, a Republican anti-machine reformer from Chicago who was adamantly opposed to the spoils system. As the New Deal's "point man" in the potentially patronage-rich Interior Department, Hurja had to maneuver very carefully to get appointments by the "curmudgeonly" Ickes. Ickes had his fill of ward heelers and no-show jobs from the free-and-easy machine politics of 1920s Chicago. Thus Hurja was careful to screen out the blatantly "unqualified," although occasionally a no-show political hack slipped through—not surprising, given the thousands of new jobs created by FDR's "alphabetical agencies." Easing the political appointment process, Roosevelt supported congressional measures to "exempt" many of the newly minted agency jobs from civil service. Hurja slowly brought skeptical Ickes along to accept political appointments by starting off with a 30-day "provisional" appointment system, a kind of probationary period with the understanding that if the new appointees proved unsatisfactory, they could be dismissed. Ickes was pleasantly surprised that Hurja could find so many qualified New Deal FRBC loyalists who proved satisfactory on the job. For Roosevelt Before Chicago (FRBC)

was a reference to Democrats who supported FDR before the 1932 nominating convention. Very few of Hurja's "provisionals" were discharged, and
gradually Secretary Ickes became "less suspicious and slowly yielded to the
system," noted a spoils expert in 1934 in *Current History*.[1]

New Deal patronage in a widely circulated article published in *American
Magazine* (August 1933) in which Farley wrote: "Patronage is a reward for
those who have worked for party victory. It is also of assistance for building
the party machine for the next election." Farley would later regret his im-
politic revelations, because "Farleyism," as many writers observed, was becoming synonymous with "corruption." Farley lamented that the public
thought he had invented "patronage" as a "diabolical scheme" to wreck the
federal civil service.[2] After undergoing a hailstorm of criticism, Farley gave
up patronage operations and handed over much of the day-to-day management and detail to Hurja to sort out.

One can easily understand why. Postmaster General Farley, as the traditional patronage director, was swamped in the first months of 1933 with loy-
alist Democrats clamoring for jobs. The Democrats, having been out of the
White House for three administrations, were lean and hungry and eager to
replace the Republican-packed federal agencies, as well as to move into the
thousands of new jobs created by Roosevelt's alphabetical agencies and emergency relief programs. Farley groaned as "droves of office seekers" descended
on his office; as he recalled, "it seemed as though they were arriving by the
trainloads." Aggravated by the worst year of the Great Depression, Farley
was "swamped by job hunters": he complained that they "thronged his outer
office," stopped him in the street, "came to my table at restaurants," and
"snowed me under" with a "mountain of letters and telegrams." Job suppli-
cants literally jammed venues where Farley was rumored to be and even
bothered him at the hotel where he stayed. One desperate job seeker followed him into his bathroom, and Farley feared the man might try to get
into the bathtub with him. The postmaster grumbled that he had to slip
back and forth to his office "like a man dodging a sheriff's writ."[3]

Members of Congress felt some of the same pressures. A Kentucky De-
mocrat telegraphed Senator Albin Barkley: "Don't come home. It isn't safe."
An Indiana senator hid out in a remote corner of an adjacent state, and anxious job seekers were informed that he was "in seclusion in Michigan."
Straightaway hundreds of letters turned up in the local post offices directed
to "Senator Frederick Van Nuys, Seclusion, Michigan." As political writer
Ray Tucker observed: "patronage problems make cowards of statesmen."[4]
Little wonder that Postmaster Farley was anxious to given up much of the
routine management of patronage and leave it to Hurja to sort out.

Hurja dramatically changed and revolutionized patronage for the New
Deal. A systems man with an engineer's drive for problem solving and effi-

ciency, Hurja worked out what he called a "model system of political clearance" that ended the "hit-and-miss" practice. Hurja established a tightly controlled screening-and-selection process to separate the worthy from the unworthy applicants.[5] Every federal job seeker was required to provide in triplicate endorsements from local Democratic leaders that included the name of applicant, the kind of job desired, and the name of a sponsor. Hurja then consulted loose-leaf binders of information about every state and congressional district, the Democratic vote in each district, previous years' election results, the results of private and public opinion polls, how voters in the district reacted to Roosevelt's policies, the political biography of the congressman asking for the favor, and most importantly, a carefully kept table on how every congressman voted on bills sent by the president to Congress. If the congressman had voted against the president, his friends were not likely to get jobs. Hurja used color-coded stationery to carry his recommendations forward: if the job seeker carried a buff-colored letter, it meant that Hurja was merely recommending the person for a job; if the applicant carried a white letter, it meant that he/she was to be given a job if one were available. The highest form of recommendation was written on blue stationery. It opened every federal agency door and practically guaranteed the supplicant a federal job. The ultimate test of loyalty was whether delegates had supported Roosevelt's nomination before the 1932 convention—those FRBC loyalists Hurja judged the most worthy of employment. This extensive record keeping and the analytical tables enabled Hurja to transform spoilsmanship into a quasi-scientific exercise in personnel management, which greatly strengthened the executive arm of government.[6]

Hurja also kept an up-to-date card index that showed the 60 to 70 districts where Democrats faced their closest fights in congressional elections. Those districts were receiving more patronage than those that were hopelessly lost to the opposition or those that were lead-pipe cinch Democrat. Charts were also kept by Hurja on the distribution of jobs, so as to keep some balance among the states. He also calculated a system of quotas to reward political loyalty as well s recruit new followers. Out of every 1,000 jobs, New York was entitled to 101 and Arizona to 4, and so on. Yet another chart recorded the flow of federal money to state salaries. "By watching these charts no State ever gets too far out of line or has for long a complaint that it is not receiving its share," noted one observer. Patronage was not only used to reward friends and build for future political strength, but it also gave FDR more control over Congress. Hurja kept a record of all of the Democratic members of Congress, recording their "aye and no" votes. During the first congressional session of the Roosevelt presidency, the administration handed out "as few jobs as possible until the session was over." As Brain Truster Raymond Moley recalled: "Patronage would be used, if not as a club, then as a steel-pointed pic." As political writer Harold Brayman put it: "those who stood by the New Deal have had their rewards increased while the backsliders have been punished."[7]

When public criticism erupted over Hurja's rewarding the friends of Roosevelt and punishing his enemies, Hurja defended himself. He struck back, arguing, "Patronage is guarding the government against disloyalty. If you place your friends in office, the government benefits. They work out of loyalty and don't do just a routine job." Furthermore," Hurja added, "we have never asked any bureau to take anyone who is not qualified."[8] Paradoxically, although Emil had been a lifelong merit employee, as his record shows, he had become a scholarly devotee of President Andrew Jackson, the patron saint of American spoilsmanship. At the time Emil was intellectually persuaded that there was a link between effective national leadership and the discretionary power to hire and fire "at will." Twelve portraits of Andy Jackson adorned his office.

HOW EFFECTIVE WAS THE HURJA-FARLEY SYSTEM IN PAYING POLITICAL DIVIDENDS TO ROOSEVELT AND HIS PARTY?

Gavin Wright, in an econometric analysis of New Deal spending and patronage, examined the proposition that federal spending "can be explained in large part" as an effort to win electoral votes. On purely rational grounds, Wright wrote that during one of the nation's worst depressions one might hypothesize that the poorest areas of the nation and lowest-income districts would reap most from the New Deal federal spending. But in matter of fact the "inequities" in New Deal spending Wright observed "seem perverse in that they favor states with high income. In particular, the West seems to have received far more than its per-capita share of benefits, while the South—far behind in income—received little." Why? Because "the South was safely in the Democratic fold" while the West was "uncertain." On specific New Deal programs Wright asked, Was the Works Progress Administration (WPA) used as a political tool for elections, or did it function to offset low employment and poverty? It is here, concludes Wright, that Roosevelt critics find their strongest evidence, for "WPA employment reached peaks in the fall of election years," but statistically the "distribution of jobs" was also "strongly related to relief and unemployment" needs. Overall, was the political strategy effective? Do vote returns correlate positively with high spending? To the extent that that question is answerable statistically, Wright concludes that his study "contains modest evidence that the effect of the spending patterns of the New Deal did indeed have an effect on the vote."[9]

What was the larger meaning of Hurja's redesign of the patronage system? One immediate impact was that decision making on jobs gravitated toward the executive branch and away from local party control. By reengineering patronage Hurja helped the Roosevelt administration undermine the traditional party patronage system, whereby patronage jobs were decided locally. Hurja's statistical and management techniques helped decide who would receive patronage jobs and guaranteed loyalty to Roosevelt and the executive branch. Hurja's new methods of patronage control were part of Roosevelt's attempt to strengthen the executive branch by making it less dependent on local Democratic Party bosses. This "signaled a historic change in the evolution of American politics," observed two political scientists.[10] It was also the beginning of the growth of executive power at the price of the other branches of government.

POLLING FOR ROOSEVELT AND THE NEW DEAL

After Hurja had served about a year and a half handing out jobs as patronage dispenser and assistant secretary of interior, he was transferred back to the Democratic National Committee as deputy director in April 1934. The move occurred for two important reasons: partly to defuse the fire of criticism being rained upon Postmaster General James A. Farley, who also functioned as chairman of the DNC, and also to move Hurja into a position to direct, as political consultant, the 1934 congressional elections. Farley in his appointment letter named Hurja executive director, in effect making him acting chairman.[11] Farley hoped to ease some of the criticism that he, as postmaster and DNC chairman, was corrupting the civil service with his heavy-handed awarding of jobs for political reasons. Postmaster Farley had come under a barrage of public denunciation for awarding no-bid contracts for airmail service to carriers believed to be friends of the administration. Reeling under criticism, he canceled the contracts. In February, Farley switched all of the mail service to the Army Air Corps, but that turned out, as Farley lamented, to be "disaster after disaster." The country experienced a bad winter, with weather that contributed to causing several airplane crashes. As Farley recalled: "Ten brave young fliers lost their lives, as the country was swept by storms and gales" and "the wrath of an aroused public descended upon my head. . . . I was called a murderer." Twisting in the hurricane of criticism, Farley looked to the White House for help, but no help came: "a kind word would have been a great help when the lashes were falling," recalled a chastened and resentful Farley. Handing over major responsibility for the more political of his two offices, the DNC, to Emil Hurja seemed like a wise thing to do. The hope was that it would diminish the "lashes" falling on the postmaster general.[12]

1934 MIDTERM CONGRESSIONAL ELECTION

With the 1934 midterm congressional elections in the offing Hurja began sounding out public opinion; polling, consulting, and helping to direct DNC resources where they could do the most good for Democratic candidates. The case of West Virginia is illustrative. As Hurja advised, "Taking ten counties in a certain Congressional district—in three of these there is no chance of victory; in three others there is no chance of defeat. Of the remaining four, two are small and two are large. Concentrate on the two largest and the district will be won." Hurja's advice was followed; Jim Farley later boasted that the Democrats would carry the district, and they did win the congressional seat in question for the Democratic camp.[13] In other states Hurja sent bulletins to Democratic congressional candidates showing "Federal appropriations segregated by department for your state. You can use this any way you like—in speeches, radio talks or newspaper interviews." Hurja was also able to remind Maine voters that Roosevelt promised federal money for a hydroelectric project at Passamaquoddy Bay. There appeared to be a political payoff: the Democrats uncharacteristically won the early statewide September elections in the traditionally Republican state of Maine.[14]

President Roosevelt, through Hurja and the DNC, more vigorously inserted the White House into congressional elections than hitherto had been the case. Hurja mapped out for the president's closest personal friend and aide, Louis M. Howe, a strategy of how Roosevelt and the White House could take a controlling interest in how key congressmen ran their campaigns. Hurja first ordered the mapping of all local, state, and national election returns in each congressional district since 1932. This data, once prepared, Hurja said, could be placed in the hands of "political counselors . . . to be given charge of certain areas and certain districts—their duty being . . . to contact congressmen in their district" and "go over problems with them, etc." Hurja declared: "This sort of service to congressmen will be different from anything hitherto attempted in Washington, and will be the best kind of 'big stick' when it comes to legislation." This, Hurja continued, is likely to "obtain a high degree of cooperation" from the victorious representatives.[15] Clearly, here was an idea and a stratagem for advancing Roosevelt's executive power over the legislative branch, and the beginnings of what Arthur M. Schlesinger, Jr. calls the "Imperial Presidency." Four years later, in 1938, Roosevelt attempted his purge of maverick House Democrats. Once in a fight with Congress, Roosevelt said he would like to unleash 16 lions on the legislative branch of government, but someone objected that the lions might make a mistake. FDR answered: "Not if they stayed there long enough."[16]

Characteristically, the off-year, midterm congressional elections were won by the party not in the White House. Accordingly many political pundits and newspaper editors predicted a Republican victory in 1934. The optimists in the Democratic camp predicted at the most a gain of four Senate seats. Hurja confidently predicted ten, and the Democrats actually won nine. Most experts asserted the Republicans would probably pick up 35 new seats in the House of Representatives, whereas Hurja predicted they would suffer losses and that the Democrats would pick up new seats, which they did. Hurja predicted the outcome state by state and by congressional district, naming the winners in advance of the election. He erred only with the results in Minnesota and Vermont.[17]

Using public-opinion soundings and polls to guide the campaign had paid dividends. Hurja over the previous two years had been honing his techniques and making them much more applicable to the routine of day-to-day campaigning. The question was where to invest political resources such as advertising, campaign rallies, and announcements of new public works projects. Hurja had the answer, and political resources were directed where Emil's poll analysis showed the Democrats needed to strengthen their candidates. The Democratic congressional victory in 1934 was historic in that it was the first time since 1902 that the president's party had won a midterm election by gaining seats in both houses. It would also turn out to be the biggest midterm victory for the party in the White House in the twentieth century, surpassing Theodore Roosevelt's smaller 1902 win and Bill Clinton's much smaller 1998 gains in the House of Representatives. Franklin D. Roosevelt was amazed by both the results and the predictions that came from Hurja, the DNC, and Farley. The president told Farley that it was the "most remarkable thing" he had ever experienced or heard of during his entire political career.[18]

The 1934 congressional election cinched Hurja's reputation as a seer and prophet, and as a political advisor without peer. By then the national press corps in Washington was buzzing, demanding to know how the Democratic National Committee chair Jim Farley could predict elections so accurately. Farley had kept Hurja out of the limelight and hidden away in back rooms, far from the press. In 1935, however, after putting off the press and raising the level of excitement, Farley with fanfare unveiled his secret weapon: Emil Hurja, the "crystal gazer from Crystal Falls" who labored away with his slide rule, polls, and election maps, writing forecast results for the national chairman. The revelation propelled Hurja forward in such a dramatic way that he rocketed from obscurity to a key position in national politics almost overnight.[19]

In addition to directing the congressional campaign, Hurja sampled public reaction to Roosevelt's policy initiatives and speeches, and even plumbed public opinion on who the president's most formidable rivals were likely to be in the opposing parties. Hurja sent WPA workers in key states and cities questionnaires to track public sentiment as it appeared in newspapers, and also to conduct street-level polls as a measures of anti- and pro–New Deal views.[20]

There is much evidence for 1935 and 1936 that FDR made increasing use of the public- opinion polls and other measures of public sentiment assembled by Hurja and the DNC. FDR had become an avid consumer of surveys, and a poll in the Hurja collection bears Roosevelt's approving signature.[21] Some writers have attributed the president's uncanny feel for public opinion to his personal perspicacity, his "sixth sense," and extolled him for being on the cutting edge of public will and ahead of the shapers of public sentiment, such as newspaper editors. Speech writer Stanley High, who joined Roosevelt late in his first term, asserted: "The President seldom goes wrong in his forecast of popular reaction. He is sensitive to public opinion as some people are sensitive to weather. . . . He can break down public opinion section by section. . . . I have heard awestruck Congressmen, with ears flattened from having so long been kept close to the ground, admit after conversation with the President that he knew more than they did about the state of mind of their constituents." High asserted that FDR relied on "hunches and intuition." He "is amazingly expressive of the spirit and temper of the times," concluded High. When senators and representatives were called to the president's office, "they were seldom asked what the state of the public mind in their particular area was. They were told what the state of the public mind in those areas was." High observed: "Word got around Capitol Hill that the President knows more about our constituents than we do."[22]

Yet it was more than personal perspicacity, "hunches and intuition" that sharpened Roosevelt's feel for the public pulse. It was Hurja's systematic study of public opinion, and not merely FDR's reading random letters that were written to him, that gave him what many public observers attributed to a great intuitive political instinct. Hurja assembled the thousands of letters and other communications that flowed into the DNC into stacks labeled pro, con, and neutral, and statistically noted the stacks by numbers and percentages for the president. Even more helpful in psyching out the public will, Hurja interpreted the public polls; reweighted the unrepresentative ones, such as the *Literary Digest's,* and also ran his own "secret " polls measuring public response to the New Deal and to the president. Hurja often had access to pre-publication Gallup, *Literary Digest,* and other polls, which were passed on to Roosevelt and gave the president his "edge" in being ahead of the press and Congress in understanding and expressing the public will.[23]

Hurja also sent out mail questionnaires to party chiefs in every county where the Agricultural Adjustment Act and the Public Works Administration operated, seeking to find out which agencies were "favorably regarded" and which caused dissatisfaction with the public. Some of the "make-work projects," including the PWA, were generating a lot of editorial and cartoon criticism that depicted these projects as "shovel-leaning" and involved with useless make work. Hurja also ran a survey of impacted congressional districts, asking which three New Deal agencies were "most popular in your district" and which received the "greatest number of complaints." He also explained to the elected representatives how this knowledge, along with his polls, could be useful in reelection campaigns.[24]

During these years he also exchanged information with George Gallup on issues of reliability and sample size. Hurja told Gallup in their discussions that running samples between 100 to 600, his own tests showed that small numbers revealed the same answers as the larger-sized samples. Yet Gallup, experimenting with weighting his quota samples, ran numbers in 1936 that exceeded 300,000 per sampling. As an avid historical researcher into the Jacksonian period, Hurja found evidence of the "first" straw poll, reported in July 1824 in the Harrisburg *Pennsylvanian* newspaper, showing Andrew Jackson then in the lead for the presidency. Emil sent Gallup the information which George published in his 1940 book, *The Pulse of Democracy.*[25]

The poll results in 1935, during the natal days of scientific polling, sometimes seemed contradictory: Eugene Meyer, editor of the Washington *Post,* which ran the newly launched American Institute of Public Opinion, quizzed its director in a radio talk:

> Meyer: "I'd like to ask you about some of the results of your surveys. For example, one nation wide straw vote says that America is against the New Deal, that only 45% of the voters favor the New Deal policies. Yet 'America Speaks' said that 53% of America is for Roosevelt."
>
> Gallup: "Both statements are correct. . . . Many people at this time do not approve of New Deal policies but vote for President Roosevelt regardless. Partly, this is because [for] many Democrats . . . the blame for unpopular policies falls on the president's advisors, rather than upon Roosevelt himself. You undoubtedly have heard people say that they think the President is trying to do the right thing but is being misled by the Brain Trust."[26]

This kind of paradox of like and dislike would pop up again in 1998–99 in reverse form during the impeachment scandal, when the polls showed the public disapproved of Bill Clinton's personal behavior and moral character, but approved of the president's policies. Emil Hurja understood this kind of public ambivalence about FDR and some of his New Deal policies, especially the unpopular ones, which the public blamed on the "brain trusters." Hurja tabulated newspaper columns across the nation on FDR's leading Brain Truster, Rexford Tugwell, and turned over the results to Roosevelt.

After the court had invalidated some of Roosevelt's pet measures, such as the National Industrial Recovery Act and the Guffey-Snyder Coal Stabilization Act, as unconstitutional, the president unleashed a series of demagogic attacks on big business, "entrenched wealth," and greedy capitalists. Hurja's own polls and his interpretations of the Gallup's data showed Roosevelt's approval ratings had been dropping steadily (at 1 percent a month), from a high of 69 percent approval in February 1934 to a low of 50 percent in September 1935. Low poll ratings appear to have caused the president to relent in his attacks on business and the court and to give business a "breathing spell." Thereafter, Roosevelt's popularity with the voters slowly began to recover through the last months of 1935 and into 1936, and improved month by month until campaign time, when the incumbent was leading by a comfortable majority. We cannot say for certain that it was Hurja's advice that moderated the president's behavior, but what we can say is that Roosevelt was the first president to make systematic use of public-opinion polls such as Hurja's to measure reaction to his policies and speeches. Because of poll analyses, the president appeared to make a mid-course correction, overruling his own instincts and altering the disastrous course he had been following in early 1935. Hurja's numbers seemed to have convinced Roosevelt to stop the assault on American institutions that was causing his low levels of public support. One writer noted that Hurja was a practical "antidote to the impractical brain trusters and reformers" who surrounded Roosevelt, and to their "impractical legislative" schemes.[27] Yet the "breathing spell" for business was short lived, for the thunder on the left and Hurja's new poll may have propelled the president leftward.[28]

Democrats in 1935 were also concerned about the radical protest organizations on the political left of the New Deal, which they believed might pose a threat to Roosevelt's reelection campaign in 1936. Francis Townsend's Old Age Pension clubs, Father Charles E. Coughlin's National Union for Social Justice, and Senator Huey Long's Share Our Wealth clubs claimed millions of members, and Long was rapidly emerging as the left's challenger to FDR. Hurja then ran a "secret" poll, sent to all voting units in proportion to their 1932 vote, asking whether the public favored Roosevelt or Long. "The President, Emil Hurja and I went over the poll which Hurja had prepared," Farley recalled. "The President was greatly interested in the poll."[29]

The poll, which Hurja shared with FDR, Farley, and Louis Howe over dinner, was staggering: Long's Share Our Wealth program was attracting great strength in the industrial and farm areas of the North, and Long, as a third-party presidential candidate, was attracting support from 3 to 4 million potential voters. Long was "high in our thoughts," Farley recalled, for Hurja's poll showed that Long controlled 100,000 votes in New York state and was "recruiting Democrats rather than Republicans." New York was still an important state in the Democrats' minds, for it had swung elections in the past, and furthermore it was Roosevelt's home state. Hurja and Farley also pointed out to FDR that he had "lost ground since 1932," and that his approval ratings since 1934 had slipped.[30] Finally, Farley observed that the president was "jumpy" in the spring of 1935 because Hurja's "secret poll found him weaker than at any time since inauguration."[31]

In addition to Roosevelt's other travails, the Supreme Court "was overhauling the New Deal" with a number of key decisions that invalidated the Railroad Retirement Act and the Coal Conservation Act, and with the big blow that declared the National Industrial Recovery Act to be an unconstitutional usurpation of power by the bureaucracy. The president, as Farley recalled, was "bitterly disappointed and angry" and "wrongly convinced" that the public supported the NRA. He was sure that his declining popularity was caused in part by these court decisions.[32] Along with many White House aides, the president misinterpreted the drop in his popularity through most of 1935 and part of 1936 as being caused by the Supreme Court's invalidation of the New Deal's "dashing experiments," the NRA and the Agricultural Adjustment Act. The president had misjudged the public acceptance of his pet projects. Hurja cautioned the president that his assessments were wrong and that the public was deeply offended by some of his centralized-government regulatory programs. Hurja had found this out through a secret public-opinion questionnaire that sought "An Expression of Public Reaction To The Decision Rendered by the Supreme Court," and whether the respondents "Approve, Disapprove or were Non-committal."[33]

As Hurja's and other polls showed, the president's approval ratings began to drop long before the court decisions, and they only began to rise after the court had killed off the president's pet projects. As Hurja told reporter Alva Johnson, Roosevelt's rise in popularity came only after the Supreme Court had invalidated what the president wrongly thought were "his greatest achievements," the NRA and AAA, the "very things that were sinking him in 1935."[34] The same year, as summer moved into fall, there was more disappointing news for the Democrats, who lost control of the New York State Assembly and failed to win the city elections in Philadelphia.[35]

In the beginning of the presidential election year, 1936, the news for Roosevelt was not good. That seems retrospectively ironic. Professor William Leuchtenburg noted that "So decisive were the election results that it seems in retrospect, that everyone must have recognized that the campaign would end in a landslide victory. But at the beginning of 1936, the outcome seemed very much in doubt." A January poll by the American Institute of Public Opinion found that if Roosevelt held five states listed as borderline Democrat, he would win, but by the small majority of 25 electoral votes. Also alarming to the Democrats were the findings of the *Literary Digest* poll, which had come within 1 percent of predicting FDR's popular majority in 1932. In the fall of 1935, the *Digest* asked in a straw poll what people thought of the New Deal. It drew a 63 percent disapproval rating. In addition Democratic statistician Hurja virtually wrote off New York and Illinois and saw only an outside chance in Ohio, Indiana, and Minnesota.[36] When Harold Ickes saw Hurja's "confidential polls," the interior secretary was shocked and recorded in his secret diary that the "results were alarming." They tracked the fall in FDR's support since 1932.[37] In addition the Democratic record of the past three quarters of a century included short one-term presidencies with the Republicans returned to the White House.

By 1935, Emil Hurja had become a national celebrity in his own right. The capital's press corps had begun to byline political forecasts with the phrase, "as Hurja says." Never before had a public-opinion pollster worked for an American presidential candidate or forecast elections so accurately as had the "crystal gazer from Crystal Falls." The nation's leading magazines, including *Colliers, Newsweek,* the *Saturday Evening Post,* and the *American Magazine,* wrote feature articles on the person they called "the Democratic guess man," the "soothsayer," the "magic forecaster," and the "wizard of Washington." In March 1936 came the ultimate accolade: Hurja was pictured on the cover of *Time* magazine, an honor usually reserved for the likes of Franklin Roosevelt, Joseph Stalin, Winston Churchill, or sports heroes. Hurja was the first public-opinion pollster to make the cover of *Time.* He was the toast of the town, believed in 1936 to have the powers of a delphic oracle.[38]

The year 1936 saw Hurja again laboring away in his back-room office at the Democratic national headquarters. His work environment looked more like an engineer's construction shack than a political director's office. In it were newspaper files, clippings, history books, records of previous political campaigns, almanacs, legislative reports, slide rules, adding and calculating machines, books of logarithms, colored crayons, and indexes that showed what type of voter lived in what locality and what economic situations existed in every square inch of the nation. Hurja told his assistants: "Politics is a matter of geography plus economics. There isn't any magic in this; it's work." Hurja had U.S. maps showing editorial opinions on Roosevelt; charts showing the subjects most discussed in the newspapers each week; an electoral map of the nation; and every opinion poll he could muster, including his own. In addition, he had the full popular vote county disaggregated to the smallest units for which measurement was possible.[39]

Hurja's methodology was eclectic and experimental, as was the presidential polling profession at this time. He clearly used what is called "quota" methods of creating mini-universes of voters—farmers, factory workers, Catholics, women, etc., and he also reweighted unrepresentative samples, as did George Gallup.[40] But the main thrust of Hurja's polling was trend analysis. By focusing on the population that voted in previous elections, he diminished or minimized the problem of polling nonvoters, which was and still remains a bugbear in the polling business. By polling and studying other polls that asked how the respondents voted in the last election, he was also able to pick out the new voters, most of whom, in Hurja's analysis in 1936, were going Democratic. A second powerful guide for Hurja was the "Urban and Rural" vote, which he charted with great care and precision, and which by 1936 he was persuaded was the best single short-cut to fathoming national voter opinion. Hurja's mapping of the vote demonstrated that big cities were becoming increasingly Democratic during the New Deal years, and that rural and small-town America was becoming more Republican. This was a dramatic shift from the 1920s, when Republican presidential candidates had carried the big-city vote.[41]

The "geography" of the vote was also very important to Hurja in his analysis. As he said, understanding the voters was a matter of calculating "geography plus economics." He realized, for example, that many of the straw polls were never national in the sense of covering all 48 states. To address this problem Hurja used a proto-version of "area sampling" and employed local Democratic Party members, Works Progress administrators, and state officials to sample public opinion. This was not true "pinpoint" or "random-area" sampling, in which every voting-age person in the nation has an equal chance of being polled. It was area sampling to ensure that all of the 48 states (with electoral votes) were covered by the use of rural-urban and economic quotas. The Hurja mix of "quota" sampling and "area" sampling was the state of the applied-art and would be used by mainline pollsters through the 1948 presidential election.

Like all pollsters and political consultants, then and now, he was looking for efficient and less-costly shortcuts to understanding national election trends, and he sometimes sought or used "banner" counties, local units that had been on the winning side in previous elections. With banner counties or mini-universes of this kind he compared the most recent poll findings to the previous voting record of the unit and thus became a pioneer in the application of "trend analysis," which many reporters in the mid-thirties were calling the "Hurja method."[42]

Among the new campaign ideas introduced by Hurja was sending out "boiler plate" (ready-to-print news articles and speeches favorable to Roosevelt and the New Deal) to the press. As Hurja saw it, the small-town newspapers had "little time or typesetting money" and were glad to use ready-to-print boiler plate as page filler.[43]

To start off the presidential campaign, Hurja ran a poll in early February 1936 to size up Roosevelt's potential Republican opponents. The national poll, of 1,000 ballots, was sent to a national sample sorted by region and urban and rural respondents. It tested which opponent—Alfred Landon, Senator William Borah, Franklin Knox, or Herbert Hoover—would prove the strongest; Landon turned out to be the one. Many of Hurja's polls were conducted under the name National Inquirer, so as not to identify the White House or the DNC as the source.[44]

Hurja also directed the running of state polls from the DNC headquarters, and the Michigan poll serves as a good example of how state-level choices were shaped by the national administration and the DNC. Michigan was a critical state, with two popular Republican senators, Republicans James Couzens and Arthur Vandenberg, both of whom were often mentioned as presidential timber. In the Wolverine state the poll was directed by the business manager of the State Highway Commission, G. D. Kennedy, who explained: "The work was conducted under the approved scientific methods used by Emil Hurja of the Democratic National Committee." Kennedy explained to Philippine high commissioner Frank Murphy that some 9,639 ballots had been "mailed to the registered owners of automobiles in proportion to the population of various counties of the state . . . [they were] selected at random, being every 50th, every 100th, every 150th, every 200th registered owner, depending upon the ratio of automobiles owned within a particular county." The problem that auto lists are unrepresentative of the voting population was well known to Hurja, who regularly weighted *Literary Digest* polls because of the upper-income bias of such national lists. Yet in the automobile manufacturing capitol of the nation it was different. Kennedy argued, and Hurja agreed, that "Particularly in the state of Michigan the automobile is about as typical of the citizen of the state as any known medium of registration. For example, the telephone subscribers would not reach into the lower brackets of the population as well as do automobiles. It is quite significant that in Michigan even a great many welfare clients are owners of automobiles, and it is concluded after careful study, that this furnished the best cross-section of any available list." In addition the questionnaire ballot asked the respondent to declare how he/she voted in 1932, as well as their 1936 preference. "This method," Kennedy noted, "eliminates what might seem to be an apparent cause of error, the fact that more Republican votes are returned than Democratic." By identifying Republican voters by their 1932 vote behavior and comparing that to the actual number of GOP votes in Michigan that year, the pollsters were able to weight the 1936 preferences to correct the Republicans bias. The results of the Hurja-DNC-directed poll, along with other samplings, showed that if Franklin Roosevelt hoped to carry Michigan and "if the Democratic cause is to win in 1936, Frank Murphy must be the candidate" for governor.[45] At the president's request the popular Murphy gave up the high commissionership of the Philippines and returned to Michigan to make a successful run for the governorship, which helped Roosevelt carry the state. In Michigan, as well as in some other states, the choice of statewide candidates was often decided on what was best for the White House and the national administration, and shaped by the DNC and Hurja's polling organization.

Hurja's "secret poll" on presidential aspirant Huey Long showed that third-party threats were also a matter of concern. The death by assassination of Huey Long in September 1935 did not end the third-party challenge to the Democratic ticket. The Coughlin, Townsend, and Share Our Wealth movements then coalesced into a single party, called the Union Party, with North Dakota congressman William Lemke as its presidential candidate. Again the Democrats worried, because as the Gallup and Hurja polls showed, the Union Party drew most of its support from former FDR supporters. The Lemke party did not expect to win outright, but as the Coughlinites calculated it, Lemke need only carry 6 percent of the popular vote to throw the election into the House of Representatives, where their political leverage for pet programs would increase. Many political pundits considered it a plausible scenario, for the Share Our Wealth clubs claimed 6 million supporters, the National Union for Social Justice claimed a nominal 9 million followers, and several million supported the Townsend Old Age Pension clubs. The problem that Lemke and the Union Party would eventually meet was disunity among these fragmented parts.[46]

In the new year came more bad news: the defection of national Democratic leader Alfred E. Smith, the party's standard bearer in 1928, who delivered his open invitation for Democrats to defect with his "I'll take a walk" speech on January 25, 1936, before the American Liberty League. There was major panic among White House operatives and the DNC. Hurja telegraphed all of the county and local Democratic chairmen in the nation, asking them to quickly wire back to him a "20-word digest of each editorial [in their area] giving salient points, the name of the newspaper carrying the editorial and the attitude which the editorial expressed. . . . That is whether the attitude expressed is favorable, unfavorable or neutral to the administration," after the Smith bombshell. Where Smith would lead disgruntled Democrats was a matter of pressing concern.[47]

Turning to the newspapers, Hurja worked out a systematic plan to keep tabs on the national press for Roosevelt. Sizing up the problem of monitoring political opinion of the nation's dailies and weeklies, he estimated the cost to be $428,000 per year to track and document political views of 12,964 dailies and weeklies. Recognizing that "it would be very difficult, if not impossible, to analyze a large volume of papers accurately, speedily and at a reasonable cost," the Hurja operation proposed instead that the press views of the Roosevelt administration be derived from the 175 newspapers that "furnish news to all papers in the country." Citing Walter Lippman's study of public opinion, the DNC report declared that these 175 papers "constitute the press for the general news. They are key papers which collect the news dealing with great events, and even the people who do not read any of one of the one hundred and seventy-five depend ultimately upon them for news." The benefits would be twofold: the sample would cost only a "fraction of the estimate given and would insure speedy delivery of press opinion to the president." A standardized format, enabling easy and fast comparison, would then be sent to Democratic chairmen and precinct workers, who would carefully note each story by page number, size of type, placement on the page, size of the headline, and the paper's political affiliation.[48] Hurja also monitored radio station "attitudes" toward Roosevelt and the New Deal.[49]

In addition to monitoring the media and editorial opinion, Hurja systematically tracked all of the state polls and vote returns since the last election and organized the states by percent Democratic. He advised that "borderline" states should get most of the attention, pointing out that a "number of important States are borderline and will become Democratic on exercise of intelligent campaigning. Money, time and effort should not be wasted, but applied in those States close to the fifty percent Line and carrying the largest possible Electoral Vote at the least expense." Hurja continued: "Attention must also be paid to present Democratic States also close to the fifty percent line, for they can be maintained with minimum effort and their loss to Republicans would make more serious the necessity of winning presently Republican States at greater cost."[50]

Hurja strewed maps on the floor and studied them all day, sometimes superimposing tissue-paper colored maps on top of the base map to demonstrate how sentiment was shifting in the nation. He then played with calculating machines, took pencil and pad in hand, and came up with information on where to concentrate Democratic speakers and propaganda in certain counties to carry particular districts. With notepad in hand, Hurja would tell the Democratic high command, "We have this state for sure—waste no effort on it. We are certainly to lose that state. Ignore it." And then, "Now here is a doubtful state that may be lost or won." With Hurja's advice, Postmaster General Farley, who directed the flow of funds for the Democrats, would signal the announcement of new WPA projects and relief programs or designate speakers and campaign materials for those states that Hurja's notebook indicated were doubtful.[51]

Hurja's own polls under the cover name of National Inquirer sampled opinion in midwestern cities before and after Roosevelt's "Western tour." Hurja told Roosevelt that the president's favorable ratings had picked up after the whistle stops in the hustings. The ballots that "hit two days after your visit" showed an average increase of "13.9% taking the same number of the same type of samples in each city, before and after your visit." The polls conducted on October 1 and October 21, Hurja noted, "surpassed my expectations. I had not supposed that a visit would bring such material improvement in the voting expectations of the cities visited." A few days later, Hurja delivered the good news to the president on his visit to Roosevelt's home in Hyde Park. The president was pleased with the findings of his "magic forecaster."[52]

Hurja had noted nearly a month earlier to FDR the powerful pickup in urban support for the Democrats, and how the urban trend lines were running in favor of the party. Hurja told his friend Aiken that "to dope out election trends is not to hit the nail on the head" but to detect the direction and speed of change. The trend is your friend, argued Hurja: "Trends are great things. Don't fight a trend, accelerate it . . . if it is in your favor help it along." Hurja continued: "I don't want to go into the morals of these things—I'm interested in mechanics," and he also explained "how to utilize the trend—which I like to describe as opinion in motion."[53]

Hurja has "broadened the study of trends until it is something distinctive in American politics," journalist Ray Tucker observed in March 1936. "He now applies it to the mood and mind of the electorate. With questionnaires and frequent samplings of public opinion, he checks up reaction to administration policies, to presidential speeches and conferences, to attitudes of congressional blocs on both sides of the aisle, to Republican lines of attack. . . . When he detects a waning of sympathy for the party or man in the White House, he investigates the whys and wherefores. All these ups and downs he records in his files or paints on his map."[54]

Hurja also pioneered another aspect of political campaign management, which Lawrence Jacobs and Robert Shapiro call "priming." Jacobs and Shapiro, in their noteworthy studies of polling in the John F. Kennedy, Lyndon Johnson, and Richard Nixon campaigns, persuasively argue that their presidential polls were employed to "prime" the electorate by polling only on the issues that the candidates wished to discuss and could manage successfully. By publicizing such polls they set the public agenda by focusing attention on a selected and limited number of topics, on which the candidates would be viewed favorably. Hurja appeared to be engaging in an early protoversion of "priming." Alva Johnson, who had been following Hurja's campaign management, wrote in June 1936 that one of Hurja's key management techniques was to "steer conversation or what people were talking about " in reference to Roosevelt and the New Deal.[55]

Hurja and his principal number cruncher, R.H. Tatlow, kept tabs on the variety of new polls on the scene in 1936. Both were puzzled by Harvard Professor W.L. Crum's adjustments of the *Literary Digest* polls, especially because Crum understood scientific polling. Crum made several adjustments to the *Digest* polls based on his assumption that 10 percent of the 1932 electorate had died and that the new votes that would make up 10 percent of the final returns were falling away from the Democrats. According to Crum's adjustments, the Republican presidential candidate Alfred Landon would defeat FDR by an electoral college vote of 318 to 213.[56] Hurja disagreed and sought to understand what he saw as Crum's flawed numbers. Hurja, in addition to running his own polls, reweighted the *Digest* polls by socioeconomic and demographic quotas, and the results confirmed his and other findings that gave FDR a winning majority of the electoral votes.[57]

By election year 1936, Hurja was no longer the sole "scientific method" pollster on the scene. The grandfather of free-standing public-opinion polls, Dr. George Gallup, had founded his American Institute of Public Opinion and begun publishing his polls in 67 newspapers in October 1935. Gallup was then an unknown quantity and an unproven force, and he was regarded by some politicians and newspaper editors with skepticism and even outright disbelief. Also on the scene were Elmo Roper and P. T. Cherington of the *Fortune* magazine poll: they were joined in 1936 by Archibald Crossley, who worked for the Hearst newspapers. These three, plus Emil Hurja for the DNC, were the leading candidates for the polling "sweepstakes" of 1936. All four were considered "scientific" in that they sought representative samples through "quotas" and "cross-sections" (and in Hurja's case urban-rural categories) and used weighting and shied away from the raw-mail ballot technique of the *Literary Digest,* whose polls were primarily considered to be circulation boosters. Scientific polling in predicting elections was in its infancy in 1936. As Gallup, Hurja, and others recognized, the presidential race of 1936 would be the real test, measuring the efficacy of preelection polling.[58]

As early as March, Hurja was predicting confidently that not a single Republican candidate could carry even his home state against President Roosevelt, and as it turned out, FDR was reelected by a landslide that year. Even though Hurja had correctly forecast President Roosevelt's victory, he had underestimated the size of the landslide, calling 376 electoral votes for Roosevelt. The president, in his preelection forecast, picked 360 as his winning number in the electoral college.[59] Hurja's boss, Jim Farley, hit the number right on the head with his prediction of a Roosevelt win with 523 votes to 8 for his hapless opponent. Farley took particular delight in needling the "wizard of Washington" for his conservative forecast, asserting later that some of Hurja's figures were "worthless." Because of Hurja's national publicity, Farley had grown envious of the genie from Crystal Falls and worked to diminish his public standing by claiming for himself much of the credit for the press release forecasts and Roosevelt's victory. Actually, Farley's "reputation as a prophet, of which he is very proud," one writer concluded in 1939, "is the result of the theory and system of vote analysis developed by Emil Hurja."[60]

All three of the commercial pollsters correctly called in advance the winner of the 1936 presidential election, although their "accuracy" varied, as did the size of their preelection balloting. The *Fortune* poll under Elmo Roper and P. T. Cherington, although it was the smallest, eliciting the views of only 4,500 respondents, was the most accurate and came within 1 percent of Roosevelt's actual popular vote. The *Fortune* poll was "national" in that it did not seek to predict state, congressional district, or electoral college votes, as did the others such as Gallup's and Hurja's. Gallup, by contrast, sent out 300,000 preelection ballots, whereas the nonscientific *Literary Digest* flooded automobile and telephone owners with 10 million ballots. Hurja had tried to persuade Gallup in private talks that a smaller sampling size, of even 600 per state, properly weighted, could produce the same results as mega-sized polls. Hurja's confidence in smaller-sized samples is carried forth by today's modern pollsters and consultants, who often run 1,500 respondents for a national survey. Pure "random" sampling, or "pinpoint" sampling, as it was then called, was not attempted by any of the polls (all used quotas and "weighted" their samples). This led two sharp-eyed experts to observe that "weighted polls were on public trial for the first time" in 1936.[61] Poll practitioner Archibald Crossley noted that this was the "first time" "voter quotas" had been tried publicly and that "voter quotas had to be learned by experience."[62]

The election results confirmed the use of the then state-of-the-art, scientific statistical principles over the popular straw polls of the *Literary Digest* type. The *Digest,* which had wrongly predicted victory for the Republican presidential candidate, Alfred Landon, became a laughing stock and the object of endless ridicule, contributing to its demise. The *Digest* was "not hooted out of business" because of its error-stricken 1936 forecast, Jean Converse argues, but rather because it was in serious economic trouble, with its circulation halved and its advertising revenue dropping because of new competition by new publications, such as *Time.* The Landon prediction was simply the coup de grace, the last straw that felled the king of the straw polls.

The *Digest* debacle underlined dramatically that scientifically based representative samples, despite their small size, were far superior to the unrepresentative mega-polls. The automobile and telephone ownership lists used by the *Digest* were skewed toward the upper-income registers and thus far off the mark. The unrepresentativeness of the *Digest's* polling lists was made worse because 1936 saw the most class-based presidential vote since 1896.[63] Of the publicly visible pollsters, *Fortune* magazine took the grand prize, coming within 1 percent of predicting FDR's popular vote victory.[64]

Two leading students of public opinion, Daniel Katz and Hadley Cantril, noted that "under Emil Hurja the Democratic National Committee has developed an elaborate machine, adapted to party needs, for measuring the public pulse."[65] In his post-election analysis Hurja weighted the differences between the popular vote and the electoral vote, which had some meaning for future campaigns. In a close election, he declared, it is well to bear in mind that victory in some sections pays bigger dividends in electoral votes than in other sections, and electoral votes are the ones that count. "The Solid South pays two for one," he asserted, for "its popular vote produces twice the weight in electoral votes." Whereas 11 percent of Roosevelt's popular vote came from the ten states of the South, these states produced 22 percent of his electoral vote. The eastern seaboard, on the other hand, produced 27 percent of Roosevelt's popular vote but only 22 percent of the electoral vote. Roosevelt had to win two-and-one half times as many popular votes in the East to equal the South's electoral vote.[66]

Hurja's post-election analysis also underscored the urban nature of FDR's 1936 landslide and confirmed Emil's formulation that rural areas were Republican and big cities Democratic, and that city size was also a good predictor: the larger the city, the higher the probability it would vote Democratic. In that year Roosevelt gained voting strength in 143 of the nation's 157 urban counties (those with cities in the 50,000-plus population class). The 14 in which Roosevelt's strength eroded compared to 1932 were in the South, the border states, and New York. Roosevelt's gains in the majority of urban counties "was emphatic." "You will find," Hurja said, "a definite cleavage of opinion based on the size of the city. . . . In other words, the character of the Roosevelt victory in 1936 was entirely different from his earlier victory in 1932. His major strength in one was rural and in the other, urban."[67] Hurja's analysis of the realignment in the urban vote came several years before Samuel Lubell's better known and pathbreaking "Revolt of the City" in his widely read *The Future of American Politics* (1951).[68]

The larger historic meaning of Hurja's work for FDR as a pollster and a political consultant was the beginning of the process of using private polls to enlarge, enhance, and expand the executive power of the nation's chief executive. Roosevelt sought to strengthen the presidency in order to achieve a large measure of independence from the Democratic Party, the media, Congress, and other special interest groups. FDR's "secret weapon" until 1935, when Farley spilled the beans, was Emil Hurja. Emil's secret polls and numerous other measures of public opinion gave Roosevelt a political prescience that stunned congressmen and the media, and freed the president from dependence upon county and state chairmen, local representatives, and a press that used to think of itself as more perceptive of the public will than most politicians. Roosevelt reversed that process, and it was only in the spring and summer of 1935 that the press learned the source of FDR's perspicacity and political clairvoyance. The use of private polling "served as a historic turning point in American politics," observed two perceptive political scientists.[69] The growth of the executive branch under FDR signaled a profound change in the American political system, a process started by the polls conducted by

Emil Hurja. Many of Hurja's polls, including the 1935 survey measuring how much damage Huey Long would do to FDR's reelection campaign, were kept secret because FDR did not want to be labeled a "manipulative ruler" pandering to the public's shifting sentiments. Instead he wanted to be seen as a deeply principled executive exercising "true leadership."

LEGISLATIVE LOBBYIST

Hurja worked in other capacities in serving the New Deal, including lobbying and persuading congressmen to support Roosevelt's measures. In August 1935, the Public Utility Holding Company Act passed, giving the Federal Power Commission authority to regulate the interstate transmission of electrical power and the Federal Trade Commission authority over gas pipelines. It also called for electric and gas holding companies to confine their operations to a single and concentrated system and area, and forbade "pyramiding," or efforts to monopolize power sales. To that end the bill set up a five-year "death sentence" clause, which meant that at the end of such a period a holding company that could not demonstrate its localized, useful, and efficient operation could be dissolved. Public utility holding companies vigorously opposed the "death sentence" clause, and Illinois senator William H. Dieterich advanced an amendment to kill the "death sentence" provision. The Democrats were six votes short of stopping Dieterich's motion to abolish the "death sentence." The White House then sent its political operative Thomas Corcoran and Emil Hurja to work the Senate and kill the Dieterich amendment.

Hurja reasoned, and Corcoran agreed, that if they could show some defection from the Dieterich amendment early in the roll-call vote of the Senate, the suspicion might arise that the administration had bought off somebody, and other defections would follow. It followed that some of the weaker supporters of the Dieterich amendment might fear they were joining a losing cause by attacking the "death sentence" and would reap the consequences of White House retribution. The challenge that Hurja and Corcoran faced was to turn around the first Senate voter, who was Senator Alva B. Adams of Colorado. Hurja, described by one of his contemporaries as a man of great personal charm and an uncanny ability to get cooperation from the most obstinate sources" talked with Senator Adams to find out what he wanted from the White House in return for deserting the Dieterich amendment. Adams wanted a mini-office from the Securities and Exchange Commission, located in Denver. Hurja consulted with Corcoran, and Tommy told Emil that FDR would put the office in Denver if Senator Adams abstained from supporting Dieterich. That did the trick. Adams voted for the president. Thereafter followed murmuring in the Senate chamber, and enough of the questionable votes shifted to save the "death sentence" by one vote. Hurja's tactical skills were not only useful for campaigning and enlarging the powers of the president, but for legislating, as the rescue of the "death sentence" clause shows.[70]

THE CAPITAL SOCIAL SWIRL

The Hurjas had been and were among the movers and shakers in social and sociopolitical circles in Washington, D.C. Emil was a member of the Burning Tree Club, where, according to one columnist, the "New Deal and the Old Guard, the Lame Ducks and the Young Ducks learning to quack" met, golfed, and traded stories. He also belonged to the Congressional Country Club and the Nineteen Twenty-Five F. Street Club. Because of his journalism background, he joined the National Press Club, and he continued his fraternity affiliation with the alumni chapter of Kappa Sigma Fraternity in Washington, D.C. An avid collector of historical memorabilia, he was a member of the National Society of Autograph Collectors, and he had located and facilitated the movement of several historical collections to the Library of Congress and other repositories. As member of the Temple Noyes Lodge No. 32 of the Masons, Hurja had been honored with a master mason degree in June 1936. His boss, the president, had been scheduled to attend but had canceled because of a political trip to Texas.[71]

Emil's wife Gudrun Hurja was a highly visible socialite: she was a member of the American Newspaper Women's Club, president of the D.C. Art Association, and a well known Washington hostess whose activities were covered extensively in the society pages of the newspapers. The Hurjas received more social invitations than they could manage. Mrs. Hurja was an accomplished pianist and played informally for the amusement of her many friends at social gatherings. She presided over "sing for your supper" dinner parties, in which guests gathered around the piano as Goody played and led with her soft soprano voice. Capital luminaries such as Justice Felix Frankfurter, General Omar Bradley, and Justice Robert Jackson and many of the capital's diplomatic corps partook in this pioneer sentimentality that recalled Gudrun's Yukon days. In December 1935, Gudrun attended a "bal-masque" at the White House hosted by the first lady, Eleanor Roosevelt. Goody came dressed as an Eskimo in mukluks and a white fur parka, and carried a hunting harpoon. The Hurjas were pleased to present symbolic forms of their loyalty to the Yukon, frontier America, and Alaska. Mrs. Hurja was described by the press as a "Talented Capital Hostess who Entertains Frequently" and as the "Darling of the Klondike [Who] Spurs Washington Arts." She was also an active patroness in planning the President's Birthday Ball.[72]

After the close of the Democratic Convention, Gudrun took a short respite from her social labors. In the summer of 1936, when Emil was busy with Jim Farley running Roosevelt's reelection campaign, Gudrun and her father, Anders Andresen, set sail on the Polish liner *Batory* for her father's homeland, Denmark. They spent several weeks motoring through the picturesque Danish countryside and returned to Washington in mid-August. No sooner had she returned than she was back in the social and political swirl, hosting a fashionable luncheon at the Mayflower Hotel for German baroness Juliana von Bottinger and others.

After the election and the exhausting 14-hour campaign days were over, the Hurjas in late 1936 set sail on the *Queen Mary* for a relaxing trip abroad. They visited London, Paris, Berlin, and Stockholm. Then they flew to Helsinki and spent time in the home of Emil's forbears, whom he had not visited previously. In Helsinki, with the celebration of the anniversary of Finland's independence underway, they attended a ball at the palace given by Finland's president Pehr Evind Svinhufvud and Mme. Svinhufvud. They returned to Washington in time to spend Christmas in their Georgetown home. According to the Washington *Post* they were among the first "New Dealers" to move to Georgetown.[73]

In February 1937 the Hurjas entertained at a tea at their Georgetown residence, a party attended by many prominent people in diplomatic and official circles. The names of the guests would read like a "Who's Who." Although men usually did not attend teas, this party was an exception. The rooms were jammed with guests, including the German ambassador Hans Luther, along with the ministers from Norway and Greece, the Italian ambassador's wife Matilda de Suvich, Mme. Troyanovsky from the Soviet Embassy, and other foreign dignitaries. Also in attendance were several senators' wives; a bevy of U.S. congressmen, including Chicago's Fred Britten; and Rear Admiral and Mrs. Mark Bristol. A patroness of the arts, Gudrun invited the Greek minister Demetrios Sicilianos, who spoke to the attendees about his newly acquired El Greco painting.[74]

The party and home were described in the Washington *Post:* "Their yellow brick residence at 1909 Thirtieth Street is entered through a charming courtyard at one side. The dining room is on the first floor, the drawing room on the second. The latter is reached by a narrow staircase, the ceiling of which is so low that many a tall and dignified diplomat yesterday had to stoop to keep from bumping. . . . On the walls at the head of the stairway hang old prints and documents belonging to Mr. Hurja's collection of Andrew Jackson relics, his favorite hobby. One picture, a political broadside used in his Administration, had rather a familiar look and guests recognized it as one used by the Hurjas as a Christmas card last season. They found it in a little shop in Stockholm, of all places." The *Post* continued: "In the dining room is a large Chinese screen of green and gold in subdued hues which the Hurjas brought back with them from the Orient when they attended the Inauguration of President Quezon of the Philippine Commonwealth. A low lacquered table, another souvenir of the trip, is in the drawing room upstairs. . . . There were almost as many men as women at yesterday's tea, a situation rare enough in Washington to come under the heading of news."[75]

In June 1937 the Hurjas flew to London for the king's coronation. They watched the royal procession moving slowly and majestically toward Westminster Abbey and attended the coronation ball. They viewed the entire entertainment from a box next to one occupied by the Duke of Gloucester and his family. They met visitors from around the globe. Gudrun was entranced by the ceremony, saying, "It was all so wonderful, I'm sorry it is over." In July, they traveled to California, and then on to a trip to the Smoky Mountains in Tennessee. On these nationwide junkets they were often met and entertained by senators or other New Deal leading lights while talking political business and enjoying fishing or hiking.[76]

Leaving the New Deal would diminish the Hurjas' political and diplomatic social roles. Gudrun, who had entertained and cohosted with the First Lady, saw her social swirl shrink. Other factors also impacted negatively on the social life of the district. The shock of the 1937 Roosevelt recession, the president's controversial and ill-fated "Supreme Court packing" bill of the same year, and Roosevelt's ill-advised effort to purge the Democratic Party of conservatives created new conflict and foes of the administration that seeped into the social life of the capital. Thus Emil Hurja's departure from the New Deal would be only a small part of the disintegration of the sociopolitical life of Washington.

CHAPTER 5

POST–NEW DEAL HURJA

FLUSHED WITH VICTORY FROM AN UNPRECEDENTED LANDSLIDE of historic proportions, second-term Roosevelt was emboldened to strike at his political enemies with new vigor and venom. Angered by the invalidation of much New Deal legislation by what a White House aide sneeringly called a "horse and buggy" Supreme Court, the president launched his fight against the justices. His proposed Judicial Reform bill would have enabled the president to appoint six new Supreme Court justices for every member past age 70 who refused to retire. Eighty-year-old Justice Louis D. Brandeis, a liberal pro–New Dealer, was shocked and believed that Roosevelt had made a serious mistake. Democratic national chairman James Farley, although he publicly cooperated with the president in rounding up congressional votes for the measure, was known to privately oppose what became known as the "Court packing" bill. Democratic floor leaders in Congress who had received little or no advanced notice were even more annoyed by the president's bombshell. Democratic majority leader in the Senate Joe Robinson was opposed, as was a passel of New Deal and liberal senators, including Burton K. Wheeler, Joseph C. Mahoney, David Walsh and George Norris. Wheeler, in a radio talk, warned Americans that Roosevelt was trying to create a "political court" controlled by the president that might at some future time "cut down those guarantees of liberty written by the blood of your forefathers." Vice President J. Nance Garner, when he heard of the bill, reportedly held his nose, pointed his thumbs down, and left Washington on a five-week vacation, unwilling to fight for the measure in the Senate. Even the president's wife, Eleanor, thought that FDR had stumbled badly with his attack on the court and feared that he had lost his common political sense, now that his close friend and confidante Louis M. Howe was dead.[1] A second loss was Emil Hurja, who at this time was quietly packing his bags and preparing to leave the administration and no longer offering FDR poll advice and interpretations.

Roosevelt's popularity dropped precipitously: only weeks after the Judicial Reform bill was presented, George Gallup's polls showed 53 percent of Americans opposing the president's "court packing." The president's critics, and even a few of his friends, raged in the press that Roosevelt was trying to establish a "dictatorship," an easy analog since Europe was marching to the tune of newly born and evolving fascist and communist dictatorships. By July 1937, the Judicial Reform bill was dead on arrival, as were several of the other measures that Roosevelt pushed in the 1937 legislative session. Historian David Kennedy observed that FDR had "woefully underestimated the strength of popular devotion to the Court's traditional role."[2]

The historical context in which Roosevelt pushed his court packing did not make it attractive to the American public or even Progressives Era reformers. This was an age in which the excesses and brutalism of fascist and communist dictatorships were all over the newspapers and newsreels. As Otis Graham has shown, the "writings of the progressives are strewn with worried references to Mussolini and Hitler and Stalin, to the emergence of malignant totalitarian regimes." The powerful state and the all-powerful leader were of keen concern to them, and they feared that "those who proposed to grant further power to government in the cause of social reform were headed in the wrong direction." One prominent progressive writer, Oswald Garrison Villard, cited what he saw in Nazi Germany as his reason for opposing FDR's judicial reorganization bill. He wrote: "I share with Dorothy Thompson's feelings that this proposal opens the way to a dictatorship." Another liberal writer, Amos Pinchot, warned Roosevelt in a letter that what was happening in Europe showed "clear enough, that, if a leader pursues the path of bureaucratic regimentation of industry and agriculture, he must go forward into dictatorship, whether he wants to or not."[3]

Undeterred by critics on the political left and furious that his own Democratic Party, which controlled Congress, had turned against him on the court packing, FDR vowed vengeance and planned to politically cleanse the Democratic Congress of its dissenters. To that end Roosevelt launched his "purge" of 1938, campaigning to defeat Democratic congressional candidates whom he called "Copperheads" and incumbents who failed to toe the executive office line. Roosevelt went after some of the big names in the Senate, including Walter George, Millard Tydings, and "Cotton" Ed Smith, and campaigned against them in their state primaries. Some 69 percent of the public polled by Gallup in July said the Roosevelt "purge" was "wrong." As Brain Truster Raymond Moley noted, the Roosevelt purge "created shrieks of public protest against presidential intervention in the primaries." Writer Nathan Miller detected that the "purge" had a chilling parallel to the Soviet purges and executions of the same period, and that "the purge created the sinister specter of concentration camps, forced labor and firing squads." In the end Roosevelt's purge failed miserably. As Moley put it, "only one victim marked for excision had fallen." The Republicans won the mid-term elections, capturing 81 new seats in the House and 8 in the Senate, and had a net gain of 13 governorships. Two leading New Deal liberals, Governors Frank Murphy of Michigan and Philip La Follette of Wisconsin, were defeated. In addition the failed "court packing" and "purge" had created a new coalition of moderate and conservative Democrats who joined with Republicans to frustrate New Deal initiatives. Professor Kennedy's study showed that FDR would "never again" control Congress as he had from 1933 to 1936, and that although New Deal laws were preserved, no new ambitious programs would be passed.[4]

It was in the stormy and turbulent political climate of "court packing" in 1937 that Emil Hurja decided to leave the Roosevelt administration and pursue his career in the private sector. Hurja was disappointed by what he considered the president's political mistakes and uneasy about the attack on the independence of the judiciary. He was also uncomfortable with the collectivist direction of the second New Deal and the president's increasing and politically unwise contempt for the other branches of government. FDR's attack on business intensified in his campaign, and in his wrap-up speech in Madison Square Garden in 1936 he called businessmen the "forces of selfishness and lust for power," and warned them that in his coming second administration "those forces have met their master." FDR's "punch line" disturbed Hurja, who, as he was leaving Madison Square Garden, told his fellow New Dealer Tommy Corcoran: "that punch is going to hurt the President more than it is going to help him. . . . I wish he hadn't felt he had to say that." In addition Hurja's relationship with Farley had cooled considerably when Jim took umbrage over the flush of favorable publicity for Hurja and the fact that newsmen more often sought out Hurja than Farley for "dope" on polls and campaigning. Finally Hurja felt that his labors had not been rewarded appropriately, for he had been promised a diplomatic job as minister to Finland, the land of his forebears. After the 1936 election, Emil and his wife Gudrun had traveled to Finland, where they had an audience with the Finnish president and took part in the anniversary celebration of Finnish independence. Despite all of his efforts the diplomatic job was not forthcoming. He then sought the territorial governorship of Alaska, an appointive position. Neither came through, and Hurja left the administration in March 1937. Many newspapers conjectured that FDR had lost his "political compass."[5]

Although it is difficult to know whether FDR's lack of guidance from Howe and Hurja caused him to stumble politically through 1937 and 1938, nonetheless the evidence is suggestive. Roosevelt had experienced a great hubris (what Greeks call the victory disease) and was puffed up from his 1936 landslide. That, coupled with the lack of sure-footed political guidance from close friend Louis Howe and Hurja's numbers, was a critical factor in explaining Roosevelt's missteps in 1937 and 1938. Without pollster Hurja and long-time aide Louie Howe, who died in 1936, Roosevelt experienced the worst two years of his presidency. Roosevelt's fumbling and stumbling through the beginning of his second term, with the ill-fated "court packing" and equally disastrous and failed 1938 "purge" of conservative Democrats, has raised questions. As presidential leadership scholar Erwin Hargrove put it: "Why did Roosevelt, who was the very model of prudence, make such dramatic mistakes, one after the other, thereby weakening his presidency? . . . Why did he misfire so badly in his second term?" Hargrove offers an explanation: that FDR may have confused his 1936 electoral victory "with a mandate to do whatever he wished" and thus "prudence gave way to hubris." That certainly may have been one of the operative factors, but the evidence in the Hurja papers and other political sources suggest another important element. No longer the sure-footed political mule who could pick his way daintily around the legislative crevasses and political "black holes," Roosevelt behaved in a way that was out of character with his first term. The principal reason is the president had lost his political counselor and political "compass" in Louis Howe and Emil Hurja. Roosevelt's misreading of the changing political and cultural climate of both the Congress and the nation seems in marked contrast to the approach of the political high-wire artist who had traversed the first term with the ability of a "great Wallenda." Without his advisors to tell him how his behavior showed eerie resemblances to the abuse of executive authority, FDR had temporarily gone tone deaf politically. The types of attitude surveys begun by Hurja in 1935 were broken off in 1937 when Hurja left the administration.[6]

ENLARGING PRESIDENTIAL POWER

The use of secret and public polls, the control of patronage, and the enormous growth of presidential power under Roosevelt prompted questions that were revisited during President Richard Nixon's tenure and the Watergate scandal. The Nixon abuse of presidential power prompted Arthur M. Schlesinger, Jr. to examine the augmenting of executive authority and write a widely noted study, *The Imperial Presidency*. Schlesinger, a Roosevelt biographer, goes easy on FDR and saddles the blame on Harry Truman, Lyndon B. Johnson, and Richard M. Nixon. Schlesinger scathingly writes: "Truman, Johnson and Nixon almost came to see the sharing of power with Congress in foreign policy as a derogation of the Presidency." Schlesinger's "critical tests of the imperial presidency are threefold: the war-making power; the secrecy system; and the employment against the American people of emergency authority acquired for use against foreign enemies." Although Schlesinger does not concede this, it is clear that Roosevelt qualifies for at last two of the three criteria: "the secrecy system" and "the employment against the American people of emergency authority acquired for use against" a domestic crisis. If one extends the story into FDR's third term, it is clear, as several scholars have shown, that the president's stretching of the "war-making power" also fits this four-term president. As Robert Eisinger and Jeremy Brown's, Richard Steele's and even Cantril's work shows, FDR made good use of "war-making" powers to conceal his "secret" polls and efforts to manipulate public opinion.[7]

The "dean" of the New Deal scholars, William E. Leuchtenburg, asked the critical question: "Does the imperial presidency have its roots in the 1930s, and is FDR the godfather of Watergate?" The dean then cites an address on Watergate by California senator Alan Cranston, a liberal Democrat, who declared: "Those who tried to warn us back at the beginnings of the New Deal of the dangers of one-man rule that lay ahead on the path we were taking toward strong, centralized government may not have been so wrong." Leuchtenburg observed that "In the First Hundred Days of 1933, Roosevelt initiated an enormous expansion of the federal government, with proliferating alphabet agencies lodged under the executive wing. Vast powers were delegated to presidential appointees, with little or no Congressional oversight," and he argues that during the prelude to WWII, "in foreign affairs, Roosevelt bent the law in order to speed aid to the Allies." The dean concludes: "The notion that the origins of the Watergate scandal lie in the age of Roosevelt has a certain plausibility."[8]

The power of the presidency had been enormously scaled up by FDR and made possible, in part, by the work of Emil Hurja and James A. Farley, through the clever use of polling and centralizing patronage control in the presidency. Whether Roosevelt would have used cruder, less sophisticated, and more arbitrary methods (unleashing lions on Congress) to enlarge his powers were Hurja and Farley not there is a matter of conjecture. We can't redo the experiment before 1936. But what we can do is to ask what happened after Hurja left the administration and Farley privately and publicly opposed FDR's efforts to use his newly enlarged executive authority. What is clear is that other methods got Roosevelt into much more trouble with the electorate and Congress than he faced before 1936. Hurja left the administration when FDR embarked on his "court packing" plan in February 1937. In 1938 he was even more disappointed when the president launched his fumbling effort to "purge" the Democratic Party of its dissenters. The "purge," which resembled in some ways the Soviet purges of the time, angered Farley, who opposed the president on the issue, as did many Democrats. As David M. Kennedy wrote, the "New Deal's political momentum was exhausted by mid-1937." Never again would Roosevelt control Congress as he had in his first term. Although the threat to the court saved the New Deal laws on the books, very few New Deal laws were passed thereafter. As New Dealer Henry Wallace observed: "The whole New Deal went up in smoke as a result of the Supreme Court fight."[9]

Somewhat soured by politics, the New Deal's ex-pollster had first intended to take an executive position with a New York life insurance company, but then he told his friend Saul Haas, "I have changed my mind . . . for reasons that US Life . . . has undertaken to initiate its foreign business in Shanghai, with a result that they are due for an unholy licking from all accounts." The Sino-Japanese War did not augur well for business. Instead Hurja opened up a public relations consulting firm in the National Press Building in Washington, D.C. and hoped to contract with five or six clients. With Emil off the DNC payroll, the Hurjas planned in late 1937 to move out of their Georgetown home to less expensive digs. Meanwhile Emil was working on another book, a study of a Jacksonian era politician, Robert J. Walker, which he hoped to finish before his client load developed. With his keen interest in preserving historical documents Hurja also midwifed the purchase of Confederate vice president Alexander Stephen's papers for the Library of Congress, through a generous gift from his friend Bernard Baruch.[10]

Hurja had already authored two books. His *History of Presidential Inaugurations* was published in 1933, just after FDR had taken his oath of office. A second book, *Westward Ho Fare Paid* (1936), was the result of a 1935 world tour that he and his wife Gudrun took after accompanying a congressional delegation to Manila to attend the inauguration of the new commonwealth government of the Philippines. This event was prescribed by the Tydings-McDuffie Act (1934), which provided for a constitution, the election of a president, and a large degree of self government that would eventually lead to independence. In his book Emil recorded some dangers to the new commonwealth: already in December 1935, Japan showed ominous signs of "expansion," and Hurja noted that the public justification was that Nippon needed territory for its congested population and markets for its expanding industrial factory sector, an Asian echo of "Lebensraum." Hurja warned that Japan was eye-ing China, Russia, and possibly even the Philippines in her expansionist zest for empire. Shanghai and Hong Kong, by contrast, he found "colorful" and peaceful, but in Egypt, Hurja again noted the ominous signs of war, with Italian war vessels moving through the Suez Canal to support Italian troops in Ethiopia. The congressional party and Hurja, after attending the Philippine inauguration, returned to the United States in January 1936.[11]

LEAVING THE NEW DEAL

After leaving the Roosevelt administration in March, Hurja in the late spring and summer of 1937 took on his first public relations job for the Walgreen Drug Company, one of the sponsors of the Anglo-American Goodwill Coronation Flight, which commemorated the coronation of English king George VI. On May 9, 1937, aviators Dick Merrill and Jack Lambie took off from New York City with a twin-engine Electra Lockheed (similar to Amelia Earhart's plane) and landed near London, where they had first-day stamp covers canceled and picked up coronation pictures for the return flight. They flew some 7,000 miles, establishing a new Atlantic crossing record of 45 hours, 53 minutes of flying time. Hurja in his National Press Building office, assisted by his brother Arthur, handled much of the press work for Walgreen and arranged for a touchdown of the two aviators at Chicago's Municipal Airport, where a happy crowd greeted them, anxious to buy first-day stamp covers and see pictures of King George's accession. The flight was also notable for its early use of a new radio compass that enabled the fliers to reckon their position from commercial radio broadcasts and the use of an experimental "Gyro pilot," which, Hurja explained in his press release, "actually flies the airplane without human hands at the controls." His second consulting contract was for the Norwegian government in 1937, when he handled the planning, routing, and publicity for the Crown Prince of Norway on his trip through the United States. For his efforts Hurja was awarded the Order of St. Olav by King Haakon.[12]

But no sooner had the crown prince finished his tour than Hurja was back lining up polling jobs for the next year's elections and talking with his friend George Gallup about delegate and political attitude surveys. Once a psephologist, always a psephologist. Hurja and his brother Art, working out of their Washington and Chicago offices, organized, conducted, and directed a series of 1938 polls for candidates and political organizations in various states. In Kansas they polled for statewide candidates under the name of the Kansas Reference Bureau: they ran a mail ballot directed to a sample of heads of households. In California they conducted their work under the name of the California Reference Bureau, polling for gubernatorial and senatorial primaries, and were also under contract to set up an organization to oppose a referendum on a redistributionist measure, which Hurja called "a screwy $30 a week phony money idea." In other states they worked for single candidates or sometimes the statewide Democratic or Republican organization. In Ohio, under the name National Inquirer, they polled the gubernatorial, senatorial, and congressional campaigns. There they employed a mix of mail ballots and personal interviewing. In the personal interviews, which were employed to elicit opinions of low-income groups who were the least likely to respond to mail ballots, the Hurjas used training instructions for interviewers from Opinion Research, Inc., a Gallup interviewing subsidiary. The 1938 midterm election, unlike 1934, followed the normal pattern of the party in the White House losing seats in Congress. This was the first national election in which the Roosevelt presidency found itself on the losing side. The Democratic majority in both houses remained, but was reduced in size. Arthur and Emil had polled for a number of winning candidates.[13]

Hurja had been involved in using polling for campaign strategizing for two of the most notable midterm congressional elections in the twentieth century. In the 1934 election, which he had guided for the party in the White House, the Democrats had won more new seats in both houses than in any midterm election in the twentieth century. Now, in the 1938 election, when he worked for a number of candidates from the GOP, the party not in the White House, the Republicans had won more seats in both houses than in any other midterm election carried by the GOP, even including the Republican sweep in 1994.

DELAWARE TERCENTENARY

Not only was Emil Hurja busy working with clients in 1937–38, but, he also took on a pro-bono labor of love—developing a Tercentenary Celebration for the 300th anniversary of the founding of New Sweden in the Delaware Valley in 1638. The Swedish government and Swedish American organizations were well along with their planning for the June 1938 celebration and had received promises of cooperation from the three participating states, Delaware, Pennsylvania, and New Jersey. Congress had also passed a joint resolution signed by the president inviting Sweden and Swedish Americans to the Delaware Tercentenary. Finland, although in 1638 a part of the kingdom of Sweden, had been left out of the planning, which by spring 1938 was well advanced and had taken on a "Sweden-only" character. Research by scholars had shown that half or more of the colonists of New Sweden were Finnish speakers of Finnish descent: John Morton, one of the principal signers of the American Declaration of Independence, was of Finnish stock, and the colony's governor, Johan Printz, was a Swede-Finn who had led Finnish shock troops during the Thirty Years War and recruited some of New Sweden's settlers from the district near his manor in Vaasa, Finland. Many of the other Finnish speakers had come from the Swedish province of Varmland.[14]

Finnish Americans felt left out and formed a committee led by Professors John Wuorinen of Columbia University and John B. Olli of City College, Minnesota ex-congressman Oscar Larson, and others. Because Hurja had worked for FDR and had good contacts with congressmen, the committee

(Left)
Figure 1. Young man Emil Hurja at age eight peddling the Crystal Falls *Diamond Drill* and other papers such as the Finnish language *Paivalehti*. Emil also worked in his father's grocery store and ran a one-man print shop in the back room. On his off-time, workaholic Emil was an avid reader of political history and seemed destined to become a journalist, publisher, and pollster. Photo courtesy of the Iron County Museum Archives, Caspian, Michigan.

(Below)   Figure 2.   Emil Hurja, on the left, is seen out big game hunting in Alaska with two companions in 1912. Sharpshooter Hurja learned to shoot straight even from a crooked gun barrel. Emil applied that metaphor later when he described how he could use unscientific and unrepresentative polls such as the *Literary Digest* and correct them by "re-weighting" to make political sense of them. Photo courtesy of the Finnish-American Heritage Center.

Figure 3. Lieutenant Emil Hurja in 1918 of the U.S. Army Signal Corps and his college sweetheart G[u]drun Anderson, whom he later married. Gudrun, one of the first female reporters, remained in Seatt[le] writing a column, "Women and the War," for the *Post Intelligencer,* while Emil served as an officer as we[ll] as editor for the Army's Spruce Division. Photo courtesy of the Finnish-American Heritage Center.

Figure 4.   Emil Hurja, seated on the left, wrote all of Democratic National Chairman James Farley's press releases for the 1932, 1934, and 1936 presidential and congressional campaigns. Seen above is Emil handing Farley a press release based on Emil's "secret polls" and re-weighting of other polls showing Franklin Roosevelt in the lead in 1932. Photo courtesy of the FDR Library.

Figure 5.   Emil Hurja, the first public opinion pollster to harness "scientific" sampling procedures and polling is shown here mapping out the potential Democratic vote for the 1934 mid-term Congressional elections. His polling and advice on campaigning helped the presidential party in the White House win the first off-year election since 1902. Photo courtesy of the FDR Library.

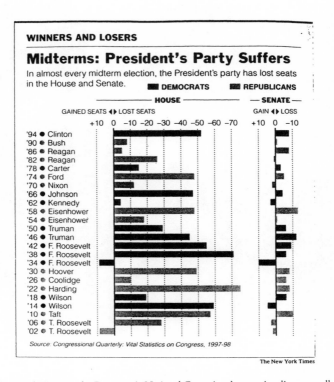

WINNERS AND LOSERS

Midterms: President's Party Suffers

In almost every midterm election, the President's party has lost seats in the House and Senate.　■ DEMOCRATS　■ REPUBLICANS

————— HOUSE ————— ——— SENATE ———

GAINED SEATS ◀▶ LOST SEATS　　　　　　　　GAIN ◀▶ LOSS

+10　0　–10 –20 –30 –40 –50 –60 –70　　+10　0　–10

'94 ● Clinton
'90 ◉ Bush
'86 ◉ Reagan
'82 ◉ Reagan
'78 ● Carter
'74 ◉ Ford
'70 ◉ Nixon
'66 ● Johnson
'62 ● Kennedy
'58 ◉ Eisenhower
'54 ◉ Eisenhower
'50 ● Truman
'46 ● Truman
'42 ● F. Roosevelt
'38 ● F. Roosevelt
'34 ● F. Roosevelt
'30 ◉ Hoover
'26 ◉ Coolidge
'22 ◉ Harding
'18 ● Wilson
'14 ● Wilson
'10 ◉ Taft
'06 ◉ T. Roosevelt
'02 ◉ T. Roosevelt

Source: Congressional Quarterly: Vital Statistics on Congress, 1997-98

The New York Times

Figure 6.　Emil Hurja, as the Democratic National Committee's executive director, polled "secretly" and planned the winning strategy for the Congressional mid-term election of 1934, which reversed the pattern of the president's party losing seats. Roosevelt told Farley it was the "most remarkable thing" he had ever seen in his entire political career.　Image courtesy of the FDR Library.

(Right)　Figure 7. Emil Hurja in 1935 ran a secret poll that showed that populist Senator Huey Long as a presidential candidate would seriously damage President Roosevelt's re-election prospects. Hurja also monitored newspaper editorials and stories on Long and two White House aides, brain truster, Rex Tugell, and Donald Richberg. Image courtesy of the FDR Library.

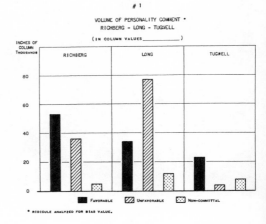

1

VOLUME OF PERSONALITY COMMENT *
RICHBERG - LONG - TUGWELL

(IN COLUMN VALUES_____)

INCHES OF
COLUMN
THOUSANDS

RICHBERG　　　　LONG　　　　TUGWELL

■ FAVORABLE　▨ UNFAVORABLE　▦ NON-COMMITTAL

* RIDICULE ANALYZED FOR BIAS VALUE.

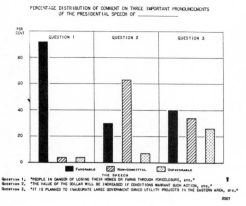

PERCENTAGE DISTRIBUTION OF COMMENT ON THREE IMPORTANT PRONOUNCEMENTS
OF THE PRESIDENTIAL SPEECH OF _____

QUESTION 1. "PEOPLE IN DANGER OF LOSING THEIR HOMES OR FARMS THROUGH FORECLOSURE, ETC."
QUESTION 2. "THE VALUE OF THE DOLLAR WILL BE INCREASED IF CONDITIONS WARRANT SUCH ACTION, ETC."
QUESTION 3. "IT IS PLANNED TO INAUGURATE LARGE GOVERNMENT OWNED UTILITY PROJECTS IN THE EASTERN AREA, ETC."

2067

(Left)   Figure 8.   Emil Hurja used his polls not only to measure the popularity of Roosevelt's New Deal programs such as the Agricultural Adjustment Act, the National Industrial Recovery Act, and the Farm Mortgage legislation but also to measure public reaction to new proposals being aired in the president's speeches. Image courtesy of the FDR Library.

Figure 9.   Emil Hurja in 1936 applying his poll results to a U.S. map and plotting strategies for Roosevelt's re-election campaign. Hurja, whose "secret" polling for FDR had been made public in 1935 by DNC Chair Farley, was known by the capital press corps as "the magic forecaster," and the "Wizard of Washington." Photo courtesy of the FDR Library.

Figure 10.   In 1935 Emil Hurja, second from right, was a member of the U.S. special mission that went to the Philippines for the inauguration of the Commonwealth government. Seen second from the left is General Douglas MacArthur and third from the left is Manuel Quezon, the first president of the Commonwealth. Photo courtesy of the Iron County Museum Archives, Caspian, Michigan.

Figure 11.   The first lady, Eleanor Roosevelt, on the left, draws a prize-winning number at a raffle held at a Democratic Women's party arranged by Gudrun Hurja, center of photo. During the New Deal years, Gudrun was one of the best known capital hostesses. Photo courtesy of the FDR Library.

(Right) Figure 12. When Hurja took over *Pathfinder* in 1939, the magazine was on the verge of bankruptcy. Hurja nursed it back to life by expanding its political coverage with perceptive articles on worldwide military buildups and the U.S. Navy's rapid expansion which won his magazine readers in some of the world's trouble spots such as Guam, Wake Island, Midway, and the Hawaiian Islands. Image courtesy of the Historical Archives, Finlandia University.

(Left) Figure 13. Emil Hurja's 1940 presidential poll was confined to *Pathfinder* readers and labeled as a "family poll" which as the above ballot shows mis-predicted the election for Republican Wendell Willkie. Image courtesy of the Historical Archives, Finlandia University.

For Release Wednesday, Oct. 23

FDR Would Trail Behind Willkie If There Were No War in Europe, Latest Gallup Survey Reveals

Effect of War On President's Strength Measured

If there were no war in Europe today, which candidate would you vote for?

WILLKIE .. 53%
ROOSEVELT .. 47

(Left) Figure 14.   George Gallup's American Institute of Public Opinion pre-election polling and Emil Hurja's post-election polling confirmed *Pathfinder* editor Hurja's suspicion that it was the looming war that enabled President Roosevelt to break the two-term tradition and win the election of 1940. Image courtesy of the Historical Archives, Finlandia University.

THE DETROIT NEWS, SUNDAY, OCTOBER 19, 1952

Roosevelt's Ballot Expert Predicts Landslide for

14 — Part I   The Dallas Morning News   Monday, November 3, 1952

Ike to Win Texas by 200,000, Carry Dallas, Hurja Asserts

12A   St. Louis Globe-Democrat.   Sunday, Nov.

Ike Sure of 32 States, Political Analyst Say

(Right) Figure 15.   Emil Hurja recaptured his polling reputation by predicting a Dwight Eisenhower landslide in 1952. Hurja's bold pre-election polls stood out even more because as Professor Harold Gosnell observed: "Frightened by their errors in 1948, the pollsters were cautious in predicting the outcome of the election of 1952." Hurja was not and boldly forecast a Republican victory with Ike carrying 55 percent of the popular vote to Democrat Adlai Stevenson's 44 percent. The Washington staff writers of the Pittsburgh *Post Gazette* summed it up writing the "most accurate of all the pollsters in this election was Emil Hurja . . . who predicted 411 electoral votes for Eisenhower." Image courtesy of the Historical Archives, Finlandia University.

invited him aboard what became the American Finnish Delaware Tercentenary Central Committee.

The problems and challenges facing the Delaware Tercentenary Committee in April 1937 fell under several headings, and at the time seemed nearly insurmountable. They were

1. to get an official resolution from the U.S. Congress and President Roosevelt inviting Finland and Finnish Americans;
2. to get the name of Finland and the Finns added to the U.S. official commemorative postage stamp, which was to read 1638–1938 "the landing of the Swedes";
3. to get the three states of the Delaware Valley—Delaware, Pennsylvania, and New Jersey—to cooperate in inviting Finland and Finnish Americans;
4. to find a site for an appropriate sculpture or memorial and to persuade a city to cooperate by giving park land and space, in time for a memorial celebration;
5. to make the Finnish aspect of the Delaware tercentenary distinctive so that it would stand on its own and not be swallowed up by the well-organized and long-planned Swedish celebration of the Delaware tercentenary;
6. to publish and publicize a modern history of Finnish Delaware by a recognized American scholar;
7. and to commission an official memorial.

THE TERCENTENARY COMMITTEE

The last problem was the easiest to solve, since the Finnish government was anxious to participate and commissioned famous sculptor Vaino Aaltonen to carve a suitable memorial. Yet before that could be done there had to be an official invitation by the U.S. government, the president, and the tercentenary states, inviting the government of Finland and Finnish Americans to attend. The reason is that unlike today's privately held celebrations, this event in 1938 was an official celebration sanctioned by the U.S. government and the president. As a result of congressional action, an official Tercentenary Commission had been formed in 1936, with five members appointed by the House of Representatives, five by the U.S. Senate, and five by the president, with a small appropriation of funds to meet expenses. The states of Delaware, Pennsylvania, and New Jersey had formed state Delaware Commissions, and finally the government of Sweden and Swedish Americans had been called by a formal joint resolution passed by Congress that invited Sweden, Swedish

Americans, "and other individuals" to participate in the 300th anniversary of permanent settlement in the Delaware Valley. The congressional resolution had been guided through by Swedish American representatives and Swedish American lodges and fraternal groups that had been planning the anniversary since 1931.[15]

A scholarly two-volume study by Amandus Johnson, published in 1911, and a more recent one in 1931 by Christopher Ward had laid the intellectual basis for New Sweden's tercentenary. To boot, the Swedish government had accepted the invitation, promising to send the crown prince and princess and an official Swedish delegation. Famous sculptor Carl Milles had also been commissioned to execute an appropriate Swedish memorial, to be dedicated in Wilmington at a site called "the Rocks," where the first Swedish and Finnish settlers had landed.[16]

That was the situation in April 1937. At that time Finland and Finnish Americans had not been invited. The first job of the Finnish Delaware Committee was to establish an intellectually respectable claim to being part of the Delaware settlement. To that end committee member Dr. John Wuorinen of Columbia University was commissioned to write a modern history of the Finnish role in Delaware, and Columbia University Press was scheduled to publish the book in a rather large run of 5,000 copies. (Large for an academic book and especially during the Depression years of the 1930s.) The Wuorinen book, *The Finns on the Delaware* (1938), was published on time, and the many popular articles and press releases derived from it would help to lend academic respectability and prestige to the Finnish side of the story. Wuorinen drew extensively upon Solomon Ilmonen's diligent research, which showed the clear and undeniable presence of large numbers of Finns (accounting for possibly half or more of the residents of New Sweden). Additional research was done by Hurja and others to find the site of the original colony named "Finland." It turned out to be Chester, Pennsylvania, which was chosen as the site of the Finnish celebration and the Aaltonen sculpted memorial. These findings were widely publicized in 1938 with the help of Hurja's public relations firm. The Finnish American and American newspaper response was more than the organizers expected. Finnish American Delaware stories, including a radio play, were widely disseminated in the press and on radio. The Wuorinen book helped to reestablish the claim of Finns to having been among the first permanent settlers of the Delaware Valley.[17]

In April 1937, at the time Wuorinen's book was being written, the problem of getting an official invitation from the U.S. government was still unresolved. To that end the committee directed its most politically influential member, Emil Hurja. Hurja's work experience from 1932 to 1936 as a political advisor, pollster, patronage dispenser, and lobbyist for Roosevelt proved invaluable. Having represented the White House in negotiations with Congress, Hurja knew how that body operated, and he knew many of the members on a personal basis. He had, for example, been the go-between for many of the congressmen who had wanted patronage jobs and favors from the U.S. Postal Service or the U.S. Interior Department, where Hurja had handled patronage and job matters on numerous federal projects. Thus when Hurja brought the Finnish issue to individual senators and representatives, he was talking in many cases to old friends.

Even so the job was formidable, for Swedish Americans were one year ahead of the Finns and wanted the Delaware Tercentenary exclusively for themselves. Hurja in the spring of 1937 requested that both houses of Congress amend the 1936 Joint Resolution that had invited only Sweden and include in it language that would invite the government of Finland and Finnish Americans as well. The joint resolution inviting Finland easily passed the upper house in May 1937, where Hurja's contacts were very good. In the House of Representatives, the "include Finland" resolution faltered and languished in committee meetings.[18] There a Swedish-born congressman from Massachusetts, Pehr (Peter) Holmes, had been instructed to stop the include-Finland resolution at all costs. Congressmen Holmes objected on two grounds: First, he argued that the Finns were Johnny-come-latelys, since Swedish Americans had been planning the celebration since 1931 and had gotten an exclusive formal invitation in 1936 to participate. Second, Holmes told Congress:

> I do not think it is quite fair to the Government of Sweden at this stage to include a resolution inviting Finland as a coequal of the government which was originally invited to participate in this celebration. Three hundred years ago Finland was a province of Sweden and the two countries were under one flag, the Swedish flag . . . the land was purchased in the name of Sweden.[19]

Holmes also repeated several times that the original and first request had come from Delaware, which had asked Congress invite Sweden, and not Finland. He also alluded to what he called the "diplomatic situation" and implied that Sweden might be offended if it had to share with Finland coequal status in the Delaware Tercentenary.

Holmes' argument for retaining the Sweden-only joint resolution had been rebutted several times by congressmen supporting Finland who had argued that Finland deserved to be included because she paid her debts to the United States. That, as it turned out, would be the straw that broke the back of the Sweden-only joint resolution. Hurja had worked hard among congressional leaders, reminding them that only Finland had met her debt obligations from World War I, paying the debt and interest on time.

In the discussion, Congressman Robert Allen of Pennsylvania said Finland should be invited, adding, "it is not going to detract from the glory of Sweden in any respect. It is merely extending a little recognition to Finland." Allen also alluded to the "kindly feeling" Americans had toward Finland for paying her debts. His statement was followed by applause. Answering Allen was Representative Holmes, who said he also admired Finland for her "honesty" and "meeting her obligations to the United States," but that Finland should be honored separately at some time in the future and not at the 1938 Delaware celebration. This prompted Representative Frank Hook from Michigan's Upper Peninsula, an area of heavy Finnish settlement, to give a stem-winding speech. Praising Finland and Finnish American virtues of hard work, thrift, and honesty, Hook finished his speech with the words: "It is the only nation that has paid its debt to the United States, and in recognition of that fact alone, they should be given a right to participate in this celebration."[20]

Hook's closing line brought down the House with widespread and thunderous applause. Hurja had helped Hook write this speech, which would later be included in the copper box that was sealed into the Aaltonen memorial at Chester. Representative J. Parnell Thomas of New Jersey, one of the three states involved, also spoke vigorously on behalf of Finland, saying the governor of his state supported inviting Finland and concluding," I think the people of Finland should be invited to every celebration held in the United States." Applause interrupted his remarks.

Thomas continued:

> If there is one country in the world that we should invite to a celebration or that we should have a special celebration for, it is Finland. They are an incentive to the whole world, they are an example to the whole world, and they have certainly shown us that if there is one country in this world friendly to the United States, it is Finland, by having paid its obligations to us on the day they were due, and I hope this resolution passes.

The Speaker of the House of Representatives noted that two states, Pennsylvania and New Jersey, had concurred in changing the resolution to include Finland, and in the Speaker's words, "it would be embarrassing if we did not do this." The speaker called upon Representative Holmes to withdraw his objections and for unanimous support for the measure. He concluded, saying, "I know it will give great satisfaction to them and to the people at large who so greatly admire the Finnish Government for keeping their obligations with the American people."[21]

The Speaker's remarks about Finland's paying its debts met with applause, and the measure passed the House. On August 21, 1937, Finland

and Finnish Americans were officially invited to attend the Delaware Tercentenary. Hurja's wide friendship and knowledge of Congress had helped
the joint resolution through. As Eero K. Djerf of the Delaware Central
Committee observed: "you can see the important position . . . Emil Hurja
plays with respect to the Congressional Resolutions. . . . His assistance has
helped us to surmount unpredictable difficulties."[22]

The other and perhaps equally important factor was the decision of the
Finnish government to continue paying the interest on its World War I debt
obligations to the United States when all other nations had defaulted. This
was of signal importance, for the average American who knew anything
about Finland during the 1930s knew two things: Finland paid its debts,
and Finland was the land of Olympic gold medalist Paavo Nurmi. The debt
repaid Finland many times in good will in the United States and the timely
payments helped win an official invitation to the Delaware Tercentenary. In
a footnote to the joint resolution to include Finland, Hurja told Finland's
foreign minister Rudolph Holsti in a memorandum that Swedish opposition
had not come from the government of Sweden but from "the misguided jeal-
ousy of American Swedes, resentful that Finland had the temerity" to ask for
its "place in the sun." The Swedish government had voiced very few objections, and in fact had extended an invitation to the Finnish delegation to accompany Swedish emissaries on the Swedish motorship Kungsholm. The
Finns accepted.[23]

THE DELAWARE STAMP QUESTION

The second important challenge on the federal front was to somehow
squeeze Finland into sharing with Sweden the glory on the official commemorative Delaware stamp. The stamp issue would prove a high hurdle to
cross over. By the late winter of 1938, the design for the stamp had already
been accepted by the postmaster general and President Roosevelt (who took
a personal interest in stamps and was an avid collector). Roosevelt had also
approved the design and caption, which read 300th anniversary of "the landing of the Swedes" and had a sketch of Swedish soldiers disembarking. The
die for the stamp, we are told, was already half made. Thus to change the
stamp at that late date in 1938 looked almost hopeless.

Yet Emil Hurja, with the support of the Delaware Committee, struck out
in two directions to get Finland on the Tercentenary stamp. He first contacted distinguished Finnish-born architect and designer Eliel Saarinen, then
at the Cranbrook School of Art near Detroit, asking him to design the
Delaware stamp. Hurja's thought was that it would be difficult for the Post
Office to turn down the design of such a distinguished artist. But Saarinen
declined. Next Hurja went back to pulling political strings, as he did in the

joint resolution matter, and pleaded with his friend and old boss, Postmaster James Farley. Hurja also personally contacted the president on the matter, knowing of FDR's keen interest in commemorative stamps.[24]

The documents at the Presidential Library in Hyde Park, New York, indicate that Franklin Roosevelt not only took an interest in the matter, but personally approved this last-minute change of design, which necessitated throwing out the old design and the half-made die. This was no small matter to a government trying to economize during the Depression years. The memo from an aide to the president read: "Hurja believes Finns should be included" on the stamp. Hurja had suggested that the new version should read: "Landing of the Swedes and Finns." FDR noted below the request: "Yes, landing of the Swedes and Finns," and that is how the tercentenary stamp was printed. Hurja also won from the Post Office the right to use a special canceling die for the Chester, Pennsylvania, post office during the celebration. This privilege, according to Hurja, was seldom extended to ethnic organizations but generally reserved in the 1930s for charitable groups, such as the Red Cross.[25]

A PLACE IN THE DELAWARE SUN

The third challenge before the American Finnish Delaware Committee was to prevent the Finnish aspect from being swallowed up by what threatened to be a Swedish monopoly of the tercentenary. The existing plan allowed Swedish ethnic content to dominate most of the three-day celebration, beginning with the arrival of the Swedish ship *Kungsholm* and the official Swedish party, and the royal representatives. They would be greeted at the original landfall, "the Rocks," in Wilmington, and it was there that the world-famous Swedish sculptor Carl Milles would erect his Swedish memorial. The official Finnish delegation, led by Foreign Minister Rudolph Holsti, five members of Parliament, and a representative of the church, Reverend Sigfrid Sirenius, would arrive with the Swedish party on the Swedish ship. President Roosevelt would greet the party at Wilmington, and there the Finns would have a minor role with Holsti presenting President Roosevelt, the Swedish royals, and the Finnish prime minister with commemorative gold medals struck from Lapland gold. The ceremonies at the various historic sites, including the John Morton homestead, the Old Swedish Church, Governor Johan Printz Park, etc., would be largely Swedish productions, but with Finns like Holsti invited to make cameo appearances.[26]

The tercentenary took place as scheduled on a rainy June 27, in Wilmington, Delaware. President Roosevelt accepted the Swedish monument at Fort Christina Park. In his address he thanked the "generosity of the people of Sweden" and praised the "fine qualities of good citizenship" of Swedish

Americans, reminding the audience that Sweden was the first neutral European power to "negotiate a treaty of amity and trade with our young and
struggling nation" in the eighteenth century. Roosevelt also added, "I am
proud that Swedish blood runs in my veins," for one of his ancestors, Mar-
tinus Hoffman, was an early Swedish settler of New Amsterdam. He added
a touch of humor with some verse about the overweight Swedish governor,
Johan Printz, who is said to have tipped the scales at more than 300 pounds:

> No Governor of Delaware
> Before or Since
> Has weighed as much
> As Johan Printz. (laughter)

The president concluded his speech by extending to Finland and her immigrants an "equally hearty welcome," saying they had "also contributed
greatly to our American civilization." Recognizing that Finland was the only
World War I borrower nation paying her debts, the president added: "Finland, small in size but mighty in honor, occupies an especially warm place
in the American heart."[27] The president had responded gracefully to sugges-
tions made by his former pollster, Emil Hurja.

The Finnish committee decided to make the dedication of the Aaltonen
immigrant monument at Chester the centerpiece of its part in the tercentenary. Eero Djerf of the committee promised that it would be more than simply formal ceremonies and windy speeches but would have ethnic and folk
content that would appeal to the average Finnish American attending. Accordingly the day of June 29 was stretched into a kind of Finnish festival,
with marching bands such as Humina, the Chicago Sibelius Chorus, the
Runeberg Chorus from New York, folk dancers, and other entertainment
that had widespread popular appeal. The Swedish crown prince was respect-
fully present at the Aaltonen monument unveiling, and the Suomi Synod
president, the Reverend John Wargelin, gave the invocation. Foreign Minister Rudolph Holsti presented the monument to the United States, and U.S.
Solicitor General Robert Jackson, as a personal representative of the president, graciously accepted and gave a short speech written by Hurja, high-
lighting Finnish achievements. Governor George Earle accepted on behalf of
the State of Pennsylvania and the mayor of Chester, William Ward, accepted
for his city. As it turned out the committee had an easy time persuading the
mayor of Chester to cooperate, since his niece, Jean Harvey, an attractive
young lady, was a descendant of the early Finnish settlers. The mayor's niece
unveiled the Aaltonen sculpture in Chester's Crozer Park.[28]

The U.S. Navy band played the American and Finnish national anthems
conducted by guest Turku Symphony conductor Tauno Hannikainen, who

came specifically for that purpose. The rest of the day was taken up with band concerts, folk dancing, and speeches by various Finnish American dignitaries, including historian Elis Sulkanen. The Delaware committee and Hurja had succeeded in establishing a distinctly Finnish day at the tercentenary. The monument depicting the early settlement was an exquisite piece of work that brought appreciative "oohs" and "aahs" from the audience and the more than 2,000 Finnish Americans who attended. All seemed to enjoy the ceremony enormously.

The tercentenary appeared to be an enormous success, for the celebration brought together for the first time religious, political, fraternal, and language groups, including Church Finns, "Red Finns" or socialists, cooperators, fraternal lodges, and temperance associations. Swedish-speaking Finns were also included in many aspects of the programs. "For the first time in Finnish-American history, Swedish speaking and Finnish speaking Americans have been brought together successfully in a common cause," wrote Djerf. A survey by the committee of 25 major Finnish American newspapers and periodicals indicated generally favorable press for the event.[29] The survey pioneer Emil Hurja had played a key role in making the tercentenary a success; he pushed through the U.S. Congress the "include Finland" resolution and got FDR to alter the official stamp to include the Finns. Emil had also helped to produce a radio program that dramatized the landing, and with his public relations firm circulated it widely to broadcast stations.

In the larger national perspective the Delaware undertaking was also a success. Having reviewed the history of the U.S. founding fathers, the Finnish committee was able to point out the presence of John Morton (Marttinen), a man of Finnish ancestry who cast the decisive vote of the 13 colonies for the Declaration of Independence in 1776. Finnish Americans could share vicariously in the founding of the new nation, as could Swedes, with another founding father, John Hanson, the first president under the Articles of Confederation.[30]

From an international perspective the 1938 Delaware tercentenary was also important. As war clouds gathered over Europe and totalitarian regimes in Germany and Communist Russia threatened the peace, all made it doubly important for Finland and Sweden to associate their democratic political systems with the Western democracies and to advertise that fact. The Delaware tercentenary provided the ideal opportunity to link Finland and Sweden to the foundation stones of one of the West's largest democracies, the United States, and to acquaint Americans with their Nordic political kin in Europe.

CHAPTER 6

1939—PUBLISHING, POLLING, CONSULTING

AFTER TWO YEARS IN THE PUBLIC RELATIONS BUSINESS, Hurja returned to what had been his first occupation, news reporting, but this time it was not with a newspaper as in Alaska or Texas, but as publisher-editor of a Washington, D.C., news magazine, *Pathfinder*. Advertised as one of the nation's largest weekly news magazines, *Pathfinder*, with a circulation of more than one million, was outselling *Time, Newsweek,* and *US. News and World Report*. When Hurja acquired *Pathfinder*, the publication employed about 100 people, with a payroll exceeding one half million dollars, and had its own printing plant and editorial offices.

He purchased the news weekly in July 1939 from Sevellon Brown, editor-publisher of the Providence *Evening Bulletin. Pathfinder* was deeply in debt, with multiple mortgages, including second and even third mortgages, on some of its physical plants. Its stockholders and note holders had not been paid for several years. On July 17, when Hurja took over, the magazine was, as Emil said, "on the verge of bankruptcy for the staff had not been paid and the current notes were over due by five days." Rival *Newsweek* correctly sized up Emil's new venture, describing it as a "wobbly publication . . . virtually in a state of suspension due to financial difficulties." The magazine is "cheaply produced on newsprint," and most of its circulation was in small towns. In the first months Hurja worked desperately to buy out short-term notes, putting in $30,000 of his own money, which later grew to $80,000, to keep the enterprise afloat. It was a struggle, as Emil described to one of the note holders, to "make a silk purse out of a sow's ear." Hurja did not draw a salary for the first two years.[1]

As editor, publisher, and financial manager his first challenge was to straighten out the circulation mess. Ironically, it would appear on the surface of matters that *Pathfinder's* enormous circulation (for its time) of

1,250,000 would have been a real plus, but it was not. As the seller Brown admitted to Hurja, some 400,000 of the subscribers were a year or more in arrears, which meant that the magazine had all of the costs of printing and circulation for nearly one-third of the subscribers, who paid nothing. How could such a thing happen? The previous owner of the newsweekly had used what Hurja called the "crew method" of boosting circulation, which meant that the subscription agency kept most of the subscriber payments they collected. In addition sub-agents sometimes linked one magazine with one or two others to boost sales and in effect gave away *Pathfinder* at no cost and no return. As Hurja discovered, the subscribers generated by the "crew method" rarely re-subscribed directly to *Pathfinder,* and thus the magazine carried a heavy debt load in servicing some 400,000 nonpaying and nonrenewing subscribers. The only way to keep the circulation up above the other news magazines was to employ the "crew method" continuously.[2]

Why would a publication engage in such unprofitable activity? Mostly because the price of advertising was based on the volume of subscribers, and theoretically 1,250,000 should have commanded a high price and greatly increased advertising revenue. Yet in practice this did not happen for several reasons: First, because many of the subscribers were in arrears and in effect got free magazines, there was no way to assure potential advertisers that the magazine was read or the advertising noticed. Second, as *Newsweek* pointed out, *Pathfinder* was "cheaply produced on newsprint" and not glossy magazine paper as were its smaller-circulation rivals such as *Time* and *Newsweek* which could thus charge more for advertising. Third, more than two-thirds of *Pathfinder*'s circulation came from rural areas and small towns, while only one-third came from big-city markets. *Time, Newsweek,* and *US News* circulated in the large, upscale urban and metropolitan markets, and even though their numbers were smaller than *Pathfinder*'s, they charged more for advertising, creaming off many of the choice accounts and generating larger advertising revenue.[3]

Hurja's first challenge was to cut out the unprofitable circulation, since it did not add to *Pathfinder*'s advertising revenue and only created a publishing deficit. Next, since the slicker-appearing news magazines dominated metropolitan sales, Hurja decided to target a special niche market, rural areas and small-town America, state and national legislators, public officeholders, and public employees in general, by exploiting his keen knowledge of how national and state politics operated. Although Hurja felt comfortable with rural and small-town America and national politics and policy-making, his other reason for making *Pathfinder* what he called "Middle America's" news magazine was that he could sell advertisers on a specialty market, which in 1940 included 52 percent of the nation's population. The other news magazines already had the urban market, but none of them was as small town and rural focused as *Pathfinder.* His target was farmers and residents of hamlets, villages, small towns, and cities with populations under 100,000. Hurja knew the market reasonably well from his polling days with the New Deal, and he hoped to bring a level of political analysis and feature stories to this public that other news magazines did not. By 1940, Hurja had discarded the previous owner's "crew method" and slimmed circulation to what the news business described as 700,000 "guarantees." As he refined the market more, the circulation was trimmed to a 500,000 advertisers "guarantee." "Guarantees" were actual paid subscriptions, which advertisers were assured were more likely to read the magazine and its advertising copy than were recipients of "giveaways" or "bonus" magazines generated by the "crew" method to boost circulation He was also taking measures to improve the paper quality.[4]

Hurja also began upgrading the quality of advertising carried in the magazine in hopes of appealing to large national corporate advertisers of automobiles, appliances, and industrial products. He focused on cleansing the advertising pages of ads that promoted "Baby for You," "Women Delayed, Sexual Rejuvenation" remedies, alcohol and tobacco abstinence potions, or patent medicines for prostate and epilepsy. "Nuhair," "violent ray lamps," "diarythmic machines" and "anything smacking of aches and pains and ills in headlines and copy which gives the appearance of patent medicine" or is "distasteful" is "unacceptable," ruled editor Hurja. He told the sales staff he wanted to "elevate" the type of advertising run in *Pathfinder* and that we "will never get the better big advertisers while we continue running trash." He instructed the ad staff to examine carefully the *Saturday Evening Post, Time, Colliers,* and *Country Gentlemen* for the type of advertising he wanted *Pathfinder* to carry.

"WHAT'S BOOZE GOT TO DO WITH NEWS?"

Hurja also reshaped editorial policies to reflect, as he told a potential advertiser, General Motors, an "editorial formula" that "is 55% Readers Digest (informative material and background news); 30% Time (without smart alecky writing) and geared to the small town; and 10 to 15% Christian Herald. Just enough religion to fix a firm moral tone to the whole, non-sectarian, of course." He added, "most of our people own homes, and I would say that 99% are church members."[5] When *Pathfinder* ran some brewery advertising in 1943, it received a hailstorm of complaints, with over 4,000 letters of protest. As one complainant wrote, "What's booze got to do with news?" Hurja decided to accept no more brewery or liquor advertising. The pruning of advertising and the new editorial policy was successful. As Hurja noted the revenue losses experienced "when we threw out the undesirable medical and mail order advertising" turned into a plus. Circulation began to climb in large part through renewals made directly to the magazine. "Our renewals are almost sufficient to balance the budget." Hurja took pride in continuing to carry ads for General Electric, Ford, Standard Brands, Arm & Hammer, and the like.[6] Emil also took pride in the special readership he was cultivating. His magazine, which he described as the "champion of small-town America," reached the "elite of the small town"—teachers, ministers, doctors, lawyers, and tradesmen—and "is a family medium," appealing alike to women and men of the family circle, who swear by it religiously. He also told politicians that his continuous polling showed that officeholders could get their message across more effectively in *Pathfinder* than elsewhere. One-half of the voters of this country, Hurja noted, "don't know who their congressman is. In cities 500,000 and over, only 23% know who represents them in congress. In towns below 10,000 61% knew who was their congressman. And 67% of the farmers knew who represented them in Washington." "If you want your message to mean anything for the future," Emil added, use *Pathfinder* as the vehicle to "tell it to people in small towns."[7]

THE WINTER WAR

Soon after Hurja took over the *Pathfinder* as publisher and editor, Europe erupted in war. In September 1939, Germany and Russia savagely attacked and carved up Poland in a few weeks. With one conquest under their belts, the Nazi-Soviet pact gave Russia a free hand to do the same to Finland, and on November 30, Soviet forces unleashed a bloody assault on the world's "northernmost democracy." Soviet authorities and some military observers expected that this would be another two-week war, with the Soviet Goliath marching triumphantly into Helsinki before Christmas. But Finnish ski troops, home militia, and a tiny regular army, outnumbered in many battles by a 20 to 1 ratio, put up a stubborn resistance that stopped the Soviet blitzkrieg far short of its objectives. The intended two-week war turned into a bitter and brutal three-and-one-half-month winter war, costing the Soviets hundreds of thousands of casualties and several hundred tanks and planes, and dragging on into March 1940, when the Russians, frustrated by the bloody stalemate, signed a peace treaty.[8] Soviet leader Nikita Krushchev recalled in his memoirs that the Russians believed that all they had to do was to "shout a little at the Finns and they would bow to our orders. . . . If that didn't work, we could fire one shot and the Finns would put up their hands and surrender. Or so we thought." The Germans were "watching with undisguised glee as we took a drubbing from the Finns" and suffered one million casualties. This David-and-Goliath contest pitted tiny Finland against a military behemoth 50 times larger in population.[9]

Given the manpower shortage that tiny Finland was facing against the Soviets, Hurja, covering a press conference in the White House celebrating FDR's 59th birthday, inquired about the possibility of volunteers fighting for Finland. The president made public a legal opinion, which was widely publicized by Hurja's *Pathfinder*, which held that "U.S. citizens can fight for a foreign power without losing their citizenship, provided they do not swear allegiance to a foreign power." Roosevelt added that it "is not illegal for an American to leave the country and enlist elsewhere." This meant, Emil added, "that any American so minded can enlist in the Finnish Army . . . without losing his citizenship; foreign volunteers for the Finnish Army do not have to swear allegiance to Finland, but merely agree to obey Finnish officers." Emil's *Pathfinder* gave Finnish Americans and others the green light to volunteer.[10]

In the context in which numerous small nations in 1939–40 were being attacked by the totalitarian Goliaths, Nazi Germany and Communist Russia, Finland stands out as a glittering exception. Denmark fell in one day; Norway was occupied by Germany in two months; Poland was overrun by the Nazi blitzkrieg in 27 days; Belgium, Luxembourg, and Holland fell in 22 days; France held out only three weeks before German units overran and took control of the nation. Finland, by contrast, held off massive Soviet assaults for 105 days and preserved her independence and was never occupied by Soviet forces. In the gloomy year that began in September 1939, the only nation to withstand the military assaults of totalitarian powers and to be left standing independent by mid-summer 1940 was Finland: the national festival of Mid-Summer's Day or St. John's Day took on a special meaning for Suomi. In northern Europe neutral Sweden and fighting Finland stood as the lone democracies not conquered or occupied

Acknowledging the tactical victories of Finnish ski troops, the U.S. War Department decided to form a ski division for mountain and winter warfare. Thus was formed a Volunteer Winter Defense Committee, which set up a training site at Camp Hale, Colorado. The new unit was christened the 10th Mountain Division and drew hundreds of recruits from Hurja's home region in the Scandinavian-populated upper Great Lakes states and from the snow country of the West and New England. The *Pathfinder* had played a role in publicizing the successes of ski soldiers against modern Russian panzer units, and this doubtless had some influence on the War Department's decision.[11]

During the Winter War, Hurja used the *Pathfinder* to rally support for the Finnish cause and raise funds for war victims. He was joined by legions of public leaders and celebrities. The American public, with the exception of the American Communist Party, overwhelmingly supported Finland. A Gallup poll showed 88 percent of Americans rooting for Finland and only 1 percent cheering for the Russians. President Roosevelt, stung by isolationist

criticism and restrained by the Neutrality Acts from offering military aid, offered Finland only moral support, although by the end of the war a $30 mil-
lion loan for foodstuffs and agricultural credits was approved by the federal
government. The president, as Nathan Miller observed, spoke out strongly
in favor of Finland and "administered a verbal spanking to the Moscow-
leaning American Youth Congress [AYC]," which opposed aid to Finland.
Roosevelt told them that 98 percent of the public favored the Finns and that
the Communist line, that aid to Finland was part of an "imperialist war,"
was "unadulterated twaddle and based on ninety percent ignorance."
Eleanor Roosevelt was equally annoyed with the AYC for their rudeness toward the president and for their subservience to the Moscow line. Their opposition to all and any aid by Americans to democracies under attack in
Europe by the twin giants of totalitarianism, she observed, ended when the
Nazis attacked the Soviet Union.[12]

In the heat of the Winter War, Finland on December 15 made the next
installment payment due on its World War I debt. It was the only nation to
do so. Hurja saluted Ambassador Hjalmar Procope's nation for honoring its
international obligations. The David of democracy, emptying its pockets to
pay its war debts while fighting for its very existence as a nation, won even
more respect and admiration for Fighting Finland. Earlier in the fall Finland
had sought a $60 million loan to buy defensive armaments, but was turned
down because of the Neutrality Laws and President Roosevelt's alleged
geopolitical hopes for an eventual alliance with the Soviets.

Hurja was disappointed with FDR, but sought through *Pathfinder* to
make the point that the defense of Finland was not a hopeless cause, by
printing war stories told in Finland. In one such tale, a Russian soldier ap-
proaches St. Peter at the Gates of Heaven: "So you're dead now," remarks St.
Peter. "Oh no, " retorts the Russian. "According to the official communiqué
I'm still advancing on the Karelian Isthmus" and on the road to Helsinki. It
was a macabre-like joke, since the public knew that the Finnish defense
forces had brought the massive Soviet attack to a bloody halt on the isthmus.
Hurja hoped that such stories would help boost the morale of potential
fundraisers and "Help Finland" groups.[13]

Republican political leaders were the first to stage rallies for moral and material aid to Finland, but they were soon joined by Democrats, socialists,
celebrities, and ordinary people from all walks of life. Independent Republican mayor of New York Fiorello La Guardia arranged for a Help Finland rally
at Madison Square Garden on December 20 and was joined by ex-president
Herbert Hoover, who established a relief fund for war victims and homeless
Finns who had been burned out of their homes by Soviet incendiary bombing of population centers. La Guardia told the public: "Democracy is on the
side of Finland, civilization is on the side of Finland, and Finland is on the

side of God." Hoover at the rally's end met 20 American Federation of Labor (AFL) leaders and clasped hands with them in a salute to "help Finland." Even the sports editor of the communist *Daily Worker,* a newspaper which publicly mouthed the Soviet line, dissented from his master editors and offered to help raise money for Finnish relief.[14]

Celebrities were especially visible in the campaign. Upper-class society already mobilized for aid to Britain "dropped everything to help the Finns," reported the Institute for Propaganda Analysis. New York City's Regency club staged a benefit for Finnish war victims; concerts were held in Newport, Rhode Island; the Everglades Club of Palm Beach, Florida, auctioned off dolls for relief; and the Lake Placid Ski Club showed a film dramatizing ski troops with the proceeds going to Finland. Rockefeller Center put on a fashion show and ice carnival, and actor John Barrymore appeared at a "Help Finland Cabaret" with socialite Mrs. Cornelius Vanderbilt. At the same affair a DeBeers diamond was auctioned off, and "jolly nighter" Tommy Manville bought it for $500. Industrialist Howard Hughes of the Hughes Tool Company sent a check for $2,000 for "assistance to Finland." Stars of stage and screen across the country appeared prominently in the Help Finland campaign: actress Paulette Goddard auctioned off her nightgown for Finnish aid, as did Dorothy Lamour her famous sarong; Jimmy Cagney put three of his ties on the auction block, and Lana Turner parted with a lock of her golden hair for the cause. Gladys Swarthout offered the first hat she had ever worn in a stage appearance as her contribution. Mrs. John Hay Whitney put on a hunt club breakfast "for Finland." Herbert Hoover announced on February 18 that he had raised $1,600,000 for Finnish relief.[15] Hurja praised ex-president Hoover in his newsweekly, writing, the "Russo-Finnish war has placed Hoover in a prominent light as chairman of the Finnish Relief Fund." According to Hurja, Hoover had impressed the nation as well as reminded a new generation of his humanitarian role as a relief administrator in the last war; he "undeniably remains one of the [Republican] party's biggest bigwigs."[16]

Meanwhile thousands of ordinary people who had been "knitting Bundles for Britain" began stitching and sewing for the democracy of the North. Mrs. Robert Keene Tubman, well known for her work in organizing women war workers into knitting and sewing circles in World War I, launched a "knitting offensive for the Finns, with a major stress on chamois shirts," in addition to organizing food aid.

But as one editor noted, "the Finns needed guns, not butter." Mayor La Guardia observed, "You can't fight a war with aspirin." The nation, although deeply sympathetic to heroic Finland, was not yet prepared to offer military aid: a Gallup poll reported that although a majority of Americans favored a direct loan to Finland for war relief and humanitarian aid, some 61 percent still opposed a loan for military purposes. At that time American major general John F. O'Ryan, commander of the 27th Division in World War I, announced on February 2, 1940, the formation of "Fighting Funds for Finland" to provide realistic aid to the embattled Finns. The military aid that did reach Finland came from Europe and Scandinavia, and was composed of howitzers, rifles, anti-aircraft guns, and aircraft, most of which trickled in late in the war. Fighting Funds for Finland had some impact, for the United States sent a few airplanes known as Brewster fighters and some 350 volunteers, including nurses and refugee aids. The largest bulk of the U.S. contribution—some 40 Brewster fighters, and 200 75-millimeter field canons—arrived after the war ended, in March 1940. Sweden sent some 8,000 "volunteers," along with 28 aircraft and dozens of anti-tank and aircraft canons.[17]

Hurja was pleased to hear about the volunteers, which Finland desperately needed. In the *Pathfinder*, he noted that despite brilliant Finnish victories and the enormous casualties suffered by the enemy, the Russians, with their millions of people and endless supply of manpower, presented a real threat in the long run. Finnish machine gunners could pile high dead Russians in front of their nests, but the Soviets could easily replace them. Emil also noted in his column that Russian bombers had "dropped one thousand bombs on Finland's cities" in one day during the week of February 10, 1940. He took heart and noted to this readers that Swedish and Italian volunteer aviators had joined the Finns in the air war to curtail the Russian bombing of civilian population centers.[18]

THE LARGER MEANING OF THE WINTER WAR

The war also had an international impact. Georg A. Gripenberg, the Finnish ambassador to England (1932–1942), who had been following British coverage closely, asserted that "never before in England—at least not since the German invasion of Belgium in 1914—had a small country been showered with such praise and honor in the press, radio, Parliament, the churches and in meetings of all kinds." British prime minister Neville Chamberlain wrote a friend on December 3, 1939, saying that "Stalin's latest performance [attack on Finland] seems to have provoked far more indignation than Hitler's attack on Poland, though it is no worse morally." Not only could "Americans hate Stalin as they hated Hitler; but they could love Finland as they could never love England," noted the American Institute for Propaganda Analysis, for "there was no counter-weight to their emotions equivalent to Neville Chamberlain." (Chamberlain was the umbrella man who returned after the Munich conference with Hitler declaring "peace in our time.") P. J. Philip cabled the New York *Times* on December 2, 1939, saying: "In the Finnish issue there were none of the complications that clouded that between Poland and the Reich. The American reaction has been so prompt and so unequivocally on the side of justice and decency that it is regarded as marking an important step toward United States intervention, not in European quarrels, but in the establishment of governmental morality in the world." In an insightful analysis, the Propaganda Institute (an organization that hoped to prevent the United States from being suckered into another world war) concluded that "The campaign for Finland in America was essentially an attempt to drown isolationist inhibitions in pro-Finnish emotions. . . . few politicians remained off the bandwagon, leftists and rightists competed in heaping praise on Helsinki and scorn on Moscow (the leftists said Stalin had betrayed Bolshevism; the rightists said he was a Bolshevik.)"[19]

The larger meaning of the Winter War in the United States—which Emil Hurja recognized, as did a few perceptive other souls—was that it began a process whereby isolationists and noninterventionists compromised themselves by strong moral support, and even material aid in support of democratic Finland. Once such public commitments had been made it was not possible to retreat to the old insularity. Ex-president Herbert Hoover was among the most prominent of those who had opposed American involvement and moved from the rigid isolationist position of complete neutrality toward the extension of aid to a democracy under attack. Many congressional leaders who had been purist noninterventionists, along with journalists and other isolationists, found that the Finnish cause dragged them toward moral, if not material engagement, in opposing Stalinist aggression and Soviet imperialism. Once having come out for aid to an overseas democracy, they found it was not easy to put the noninterventionists genie back into the bottle. This made it easier for Roosevelt, as 1940 passed into 1941, to slowly lead the United States toward military aid to Europeans under attack.

In his State of the Union address in 1940, the President said we could not stand by neutrally "if all the small nations of the world have their independence snatched from them," for it is "clearer and clearer that the future of the world will be a shabby and dangerous place to live in—yes even for Americans." All of the cheerleading and moral support being offered to Finland left the Finnish ambassador in Washington confused, as he tried to reconcile FDR's rhetoric and the administration's refusal to offer any military aid to a fellow democracy facing a totalitarian giant. Hurja explained to Ambassador Hjalmar Procope the complexities of the neutrality legislation that originated with the 1934 Nye congressional hearings, which blamed British propaganda and the "merchants of death" (businessmen profiteering from war) for suckering the United States into World War I. Americans, Emil explained, were deeply and genuinely sympathetic to Finland, but a tad skeptical about being "propagandized" into another world war.[20]

As one perceptive observer noted, "the Finns could unite those whom the Allies had severed—isolationists and interventionists." As mentioned earlier, Herbert Hoover, who had vigorously championed isolationists heretofore, had become an articulate pleader for aid to a European democracy. He was but one of the many publicly visible leaders to do so. Isolationist stalwart Senator Burton K. Wheeler joined hands with Finnish ambassador Hjalmar Procope and Dorothy Thompson in pledging help to Finland, and praised the Finns for "preferring death to slavery." A leading Progressive senator, George Norris of Nebraska, gave up isolationism after 1939. In addition to Republicans, dozens of Democrats, some of whom had been noninterventionists, found themselves cheering for Finland. Finland sent two well-known Olympic runners, Paavo Nurmi and Taisto Maki, to garner support for their embattled homeland—a reminder that the Soviet attack had forced cancellation of the 1940 summer Olympics scheduled to take place in Finland. Liberal Democratic senator Robert K. Wagner asked, "how can anyone with a drop of sportsmanship in his blood fail to stand up and cheer for this plucky little nation." Conservative Democratic senator Millard Tydings spoke on behalf of "Fighting Funds for Finland." Father Charles E. Coughlin, the famous radio priest who had preached noninterventionism and the need to maintain the arms embargo, "suffered an internationalist deviation" and sent a $1,000 check to Hoover's Help Finland Fund.[21]

American public opinion was perceptively shifting as the Winter War was drawing to a close. On March 10, 1940, the Gallup organization found that the percentage of Americans favoring floating a government bond to aid Finland had grown to an astonishing 73 percent, and as the Institute for Propaganda Analysis noted, it was "a move which the Allies could not have contemplated in the face of isolationist resistance" before the Russo-Finnish War. By mid-March, *Time* reported that "a U.S. Citizen who had neither danced, knitted, orated, played bridge, bingo, banqueted, or just shelled out for Finland, was simply nowhere socially."[22]

The evolution of public opinion from noninvolved isolationism toward some form of help was one of the unnoticed results of the Winter War. By late spring, although 80 percent of Americans continued to oppose declaring war against the Axis powers (which then included the Soviets because of the Ribbontrop-Molotov pact), a majority supported giving humanitarian and military aid to victims of totalitarian attacks. The switch in the public attitude of approving American military aid was something new in the neutrality equation and had come about because of the Winter War. No longer was the American public, as Emil Hurja observed, neutralized by the 1934 Senator Nye committee's warning of the dangers of being drawn into war by helping the victims of aggression. As the Institute study of American public opinion noted of the Soviets, "no other adversary could have united Rabbi

Wise and Father Coughlin," one a Jew and the other a Roman Catholic accused of anti-Semitism. Those who pleaded for neutrality toward Russia were labeled "pro-Russian"; in 1940 the epithet was more inflammatory than "pro-Kaiser," "as libelous as pro-Hitler."[23]

A vehement and vocal supporter of Finland, *Pathfinder* editor Emil Hurja was stunned by some of the leftist Democrats, such as singer Paul Robeson, who apologized for Soviet aggression, and disappointed that FDR would not use the presidency as a "bully pulpit" for military aid to the world's northernmost democracy. Roosevelt, as Professor Robert Divine noted, had "side stepped a Finnish request for a sixty-million dollar loan" for military supplies by sending it on to Congress with a "very ambiguous recommendation." When the Winter War ended the U.S. government had "given the Finns almost no effective aid." Although Roosevelt had severed diplomatic relations with Nazi Germany after it attacked Poland and the Low Countries, he continued diplomatic relations with the Soviet Union, despite its takeover of a part of Poland and the Baltic nations and its unprovoked attack on Finland. He had Cordell Hull begin private talks with the Soviets and eased trade restrictions, permitting the Russians to import machine tools and other strategic materials from the United States during the Winter War. Defenders of President Roosevelt's double-standard argue that he felt constrained by the Neutrality Acts and an isolationist Congress, and that he was secretly hoping for a Russian defection from the Nazi-Soviet alliance.[24]

Roosevelt's seeming double-standard was for Hurja another reason to abandon support for his former boss. In addition, ex-president Herbert Hoover's organization of a nationwide appeal for aid to Finland won from Emil high praise and regard, even though Hurja's work had helped defeat Hoover in 1932. The Winter War ended on March 12, 1940, with Finland ceding some of its eastern and northern territories (Karelia and Petsamo) to the Soviets. Yet the bloody war seemed worth the effort, for Finland was the only nation contiguous to the Soviet Union between the Arctic Ocean and the Black Sea that did not fall under Russian occupation during the hot war or the "Cold War" that followed.

1940 Presidential Election

While the Winter War continued in 1939–40, Hurja was conducting delegate polls among likely Republican and Democratic candidates to the presidential nominating conventions. On the Democratic side Hurja favored Vice President J. Nance Garner, but when it became evident that neither Garner nor Hurja's former Democratic National Committee colleague, James Farley, were likely to win the presidential nomination, Hurja developed a new interest in Republican contenders for the nomination. He had corresponded with Hoover on Finnish aid, met with the ex-president on several occasions, and soon became a supporter of Hoover for the Republican nomination. Emil noted in his news magazine on April 2 that a New York University expert on "platform speaking effectiveness" made public his rankings of current political figures. In report-card fashion Professor Elmer Nyberg graded Herbert Hoover an "A plus" (in 1928 he had rated him as a "D"), adding that the ex-president had "improved as a speaker more than any other politician." The speech expert gave Roosevelt an "A minus." But by May, Hurja's own delegate polls showed that Hoover was trailing both Senator Arthur Vandenberg and Wendell Willkie in the race for the nomination. Hurja showed increasing interest in the Republican Party.[25]

Having acquired *Pathfinder* news magazine in July 1939, Hurja, like Gallup, now had a vehicle for the national circulation of his polls, which he integrated into the newsweekly columns. As a political consultant he had been polling at the state level for private clients, generally congressional and gubernatorial candidates, but also conducting tracking polls at the national level. Public-opinion polls though 1938 and 1939 recorded a slippage in President Roosevelt's approval ratings. Had this gloomy situation prevailed, it is unlikely that FDR would have sought or could have attained reelection. A December 1938 Gallup poll reported that 70 percent of a national cross-section of potential voters opposed a third term. A few months later, in March 1939, Vice President J. Nance "Cactus Jack" Garner was leading in the public-opinion polls as a favorite for Democratic nomination. Attracted to Garner because he had opposed FDR's "court packing" and 1938 "purge" fiascoes, Hurja had become a "Cactus Jack" supporter and predicted that he would win the Democratic nomination for the presidency in 1940. To answer "yes-butters who say, but if Mr. Roosevelt decides to run again . . . ?" *Time* magazine noted that "Mr. Hurja has only to point to the polls; 54 percent of all Democrats are now opposed against a Third Term." Not everyone admired Vice President Garner; labor leader John L. Lewis disparagingly called him a "labor baiting, power-playing, whisky drinking, evil old man."[26]

On May 15, 1940, Hurja's *Pathfinder* poll showed that the Democratic Party was ahead in any hypothetical race, despite the fact that the party had not yet picked a candidate, nor had Roosevelt made his position on renomination clear. As Hurja noted, the big "imponderable" was "Herr Hitler's forays abroad" and their possible impact upon the U.S. presidential election. "More than ever before, the big question is, will President Roosevelt run again?" After Hitler invaded Denmark and Norway in April and overran France in June, the public mood against a third term lessened, and FDR's interest in renomination grew. After the Democrats nominated Roosevelt and the Republicans Wendell Willkie, Hurja continued polling through the fall in what he called a *Pathfinder* "family poll," which initially was limited to the magazine's subscribers. As he explained to readers: "We want to make it clear that today's poll is a family poll, taken only among Pathfinder's own subscribers and open to anyone who chooses to mark and clip a coupon and send it in. There is no scientific basis for it, such as governs other Pathfinder polls. If the spirit moves you, send in the ballot." Hurja noted that "more Republican Pathfinder readers are tallied than Democratic Pathfinder readers," and then made some effort to weight and balance the skewed results. Mail-in ballots showed that of the 1,000 *Pathfinder* readers who had voted for FDR in 1936, 468 now declared themselves for Willkie, and out of 1,000 *Pathfinder* readers who did not vote for one reason or another, now some 798 declared themselves for Republican candidate Wendell Willkie. The mail-in ballot had been sent to readers on August 10, and by late September some 30,000 had responded.[27]

In mid-September, Hurja published his views: "If the implications of this poll are borne out in the November election—and it might again be said that this is only a voluntary poll of readers and not a scientific, balanced ballot— Wendell Willkie will become president by a landslide vote. He will carry 35 states." Concerned during the last month of the campaign that his family poll might not be fully representative of the national voting population, even after weighting, Hurja sent out a few poll workers "to make a special survey into working-class homes in towns in the battleground states," and to poll the "lower economic strata of voters." Although FDR came out a strong favorite, some erosion of Roosevelt's support since 1936 persuaded Hurja that this small sample of the national vote would not change the results predicted in his family poll. Some of the qualitative data picked up by the interviewers should have given Hurja pause: As a few said, "Don't want to change horses now," "Too dangerous to make a change right now." All reflected the increasing influence of the war on public sentiment that Gallup's preelection and other post-election polling would indicate were operative in how people choose to vote in 1940. The voters were uneasy about changing horses in the midst of a stream of events that seemed to be enlarging into a war.[28]

Did Hurja's personal politics, his switch from Democrat Garner, who was not nominated, to Republican Willkie, shape his interpretation of the poll results? The evidence in the Hurja papers indicates that was not the case. What happened is that Emil was using his polls as circulation boosters with a readership that was heavily small town and middle-American Republican or composed of conservative Democrats who were critical of FDR's "collectivistic rhetoric," his breaking of the third term tradition, and his pro-war push. In addition Hurja, as one of the principal authors of trend analysis, had been observing the consistent Roosevelt drop in popularity since 1937 and overpredicted the downward trend for the incumbent president. In a speech to a group of political "junkies" Hurja asserted: "Trends are great things. Don't fight a trend, accelerate it." Thus, although he understood and publicly warned of the limitations of his "family poll," he became convinced that he had latched onto a larger political upheaval in the making. On November 2, only three days before the election, Hurja wrote in *Pathfinder* the following headline: MIGHTY CLOSE, BUT THE RACE IS STILL WILLKIE'S.[29]

But he was wrong. Roosevelt won an unprecedented third term in 1940, pulling 55 percent of the popular vote, carrying 38 states with 449 electoral votes to Willkie's 10 states and 82 electoral votes. The election was closer than the electoral vote would suggest, for this was Roosevelt's smallest plurality and the smallest plurality since 1916 in a presidential election. Meanwhile, the big three professional pollsters had done reasonably well in their preelection predictions. George Gallup, Archibald Crossley, and *Fortune's* Elmo Roper all pointed to an FDR victory, although Gallup hedged his bets in the end by refusing to make a definitive prediction. On the other hand, Gallup had "the lowest state-by-state error in polling history," observed polling expert Daniel Katz. Although Elmo Roper did not do a state-by-state poll, his *Fortune* poll predicted almost the exact popular vote received by FDR, a repeating of his 1936 best preelection prediction. All of the big three had switched or were in the process of switching to personal interviews or a mix of personal interviews and mail-ballot polls, a strategy that won the high praise of the leading journal in the field, *The Public Opinion Quarterly*. Editor Daniel Katz chided Archibald Crossely for tinkering too much with the poll results and trying to weight them to adjust for turnout, saying if Crossley had not tried to "weight" his sample for turnout, his results would have been even more accurate. On the other hand "tinkering" could sometimes pay dividends, for as Katz noted, if Gallup's American Institute "had not weighted its cross section according to turnout estimated on the basis of past elections," its final poll "would have been less accurate in 1940." The *Quarterly's* editor was harsh on the *Pathfinder*, writing, although "Hurja's capability in the polling field is well known . . . the difficulties of the mail ballot raise some question concerning the seriousness of *Pathfinder* research." Katz labeled the *Pathfinder's* Willkie prediction the "conspicuous failure" in the 1940 polling sweepstakes.[30]

Hurja was embarrassed. It was the first time he had miscalled an election, having been right in 1932, 1934, 1936, and 1938. His editorial mea culpa began, "No Alibis But, Yes we were wrong," and then sought to ferret out the reasons for his miscall. He noted the *Pathfinder* poll had given Roosevelt 25.4 million votes, whereas Roosevelt had actually drawn 26.2 million. He also noted that his organization had stopped polling on October 25 and that there must have been a small but critical shift in voter sentiment in the last ten days before election, when FDR made most of his formal campaign speeches. That seemed plausible, for as Professor Harold Gosnell pointed out the president had been preoccupied with military preparedness and foreign policy issues, and thus did not campaign until October 23 and made only five formal campaign talks in the waning week-and-a-half of the campaign. Hurja pointed out that if 4 out of every 100 voters in the cities of Chicago, New York, Manchester, Philadelphia, St. Louis, Minneapolis, Cleveland, and Jersey City had voted for Willkie instead of Roosevelt, the results would have been different; a switch of 500,000 votes in key states would have carried the electoral college for Republican Willkie. In a typescript post-mortem Hurja identified FDR's last-minute campaigning in Ohio, Pennsylvania, New York, and New England, and the fact that he had run no polls in the last ten days as being critical in not picking up the shift in voter sentiment. A second problem for pollsters was using "secret ballots" with big-city voters. As Archibald Crossley explained, the use of secret ballots, by which the interviewer handed the ballot to a potential voter, asking him to fill it out and then drop it into a box held by the interviewer, "threw us off in large cities." In such areas some of the voters "who were unable to write easily" refused the secret ballot in large numbers; most of them were low-income voters and likely Democrats. The *Pathfinder* poll had also clearly underpolled the low-income silent majority in big cities.[31]

Another factor that Hurja and several pollsters said helped account for FDR's win was the looming threat of war. As Hurja had said in private communications, he feared that "Herr Hitler" could drive the election outcome. George Gallup noted that his and other public-opinion polls detected that "only the events of World War II motivated Roosevelt to seek re-election and made a third term palatable to the American public." Gallup found in an election-eve poll in October 1940 that 53 percent of a national cross-section claimed they would vote for Republican Wendell Willkie over Roosevelt "if there were no war in Europe today."[32]

Other post-election analyses focused on the urban and class vote. Hurja enumerated how the urban vote in critical states had helped swing the balance to Roosevelt: "Roosevelt got all of his New York state majority in four out of 63 assembly districts in greater New York: that he got his entire Illinois state majority in 7 out of 50 wards in the city of Chicago; that he got his entire Wisconsin state majority in five out of 25 wards in the city of Milwaukee; that he got his entire Minnesota state majority in 7 out of 13 wards in the city of Minneapolis; that he got his entire Ohio majority in the cities of Cleveland and Youngstown; that he got his entire Pennsylvania majority in Philadelphia and Pittsburgh" etc. Poll analyst Samuel Lubell, in his "Post-Mortem," would publicize the "Urban Revolution" in voting theory, asserting that FDR owed his election "to a great measure to teeming cities" and arguing that 1940 "was a class conscious vote for the first time in history." Gallup also noted the "increasing stratification of voting on an income basis," whereby FDR overwhelmingly carried the labor and low-income vote. Gallup added that "President Roosevelt lost strength—as compared to 1936—in every major political and social group." Gallup then listed all of the voter occupation and income categories, revealing that the smallest losses occurred with "lower income," which fell from 76 to 69 percent, and "Relief, WPA and Old-Age Assistance," which fell only slightly, from 84 to 80 percent. This could be explained, Gallup continued, "by the third-term factor and by the basic Republican trend shown in the 1938 Congressional elections." Hurja had obviously overinterpreted the downward trend line for FDR.[33]

Meanwhile, back at the *Pathfinder* headquarters, editor-publisher Emil Hurja got raspberries from many readers for his miscall. Some readers threatened to drop their subscriptions, and others sent in Hurja's Willkie prediction column with critical commentary scribbled over the copy. One wrote: "I assume you will follow the path of the late lamented Literary Digest and fold up," referring to the fact that the *Literary Digest* collapsed after its wrong 1936 preelection prediction of a Landon victory over Roosevelt. Another annoyed reader told the editor, "As the Literary Digest went so goes the Pathfinder." Hurja admitted to some of his friends that he had gotten too involved in partisan politics, giving a speech for Willkie at Yale University and helping design a committee called "One Million Votes for Willkie," a repeat of what he had done for FDR one election earlier. Roosevelt appeared displeased with Hurja's switch of political loyalty, for the administration's Federal Bureau of Investigation in December 1940 conducted a secret investigation into Hurja's role in setting up the "One Million Votes for Willkie" committee, the report of which just recently became available to scholars under the Freedom of Information Act. Completely unaware of the investigation, Hurja in the late fall circulated a memo to close friends that read, "I would like to approach this election business on a non-partisan basis. . . . Now that I am out of politics I like to think I have recovered my objective equilibrium."[34]

In the post-election years Hurja's magazine suffered no subscription losses, and actually began to rebuild its subscriber base as a result of a number of new ideas that Emil operationalized. He continued to struggle to keep *Pathfinder* afloat during a time of wartime paper and manpower shortages, both of which hampered efforts to rebuild circulation. Even so, publisher Hurja was able to increase the number of direct subscriptions, which helped on the revenue side. To increase circulation he launched a number of new ideas and programs: He sponsored a history photo identification contest, publishing images of bygone historical figures and offering prizes to those readers or new subscribers who correctly identified them. *Pathfinder* also sponsored a contest offering a $500 war bond prize for the person who could provide the answer to the question, "When Is Germany Going to Surrender?" In an appeal to educators and schools, the magazine launched a book club, offering a bonus book to new subscribers entitled *The Story of the American Constitution.* Hurja also ran a "Know America" contest, which ran 11 weeks and brought in 20,000 entries. Entrants paid $2.50 apiece "just to learn something about American history and democracy." He also invited business and political leaders to write "guest editorials" in hopes of increasing advertising revenue as well as circulation. Several congressmen wrote editorials, which resulted in *Pathfinder's* publishing thousands of extra copies for a single issue. Businessman J. C. Penney appeared on the cover and wrote an editorial, and Hurja circulated an extra 100,000 copies of that issue. Others, such as industrialist Cyrus Eaton, Supreme Court Justice Robert Jackson, and Congressman Karl Mundt, appeared in print as guest editors.[35]

Hurja sought out a subscription deal with *Reader's Digest* whereby the publications offered a joint subscription at reduced prices, and the various efforts began to pay off with some upward movement. *Pathfinder* had nudged up its subscription numbers, from 517,000 to 550,000 by late 1942. Those numbers compared favorably with other national news magazines and placed *Pathfinder* in second place behind *Time,* but ahead of *U.S. News and World Report* and *Newsweek.*[36]

By 1943, however, other problems arose when Hurja canceled his contract with the National Circulation Company, explaining he was dropping the drive to get more subscriptions because the federal "rationing of paper" prevented expansion of circulation. "We are in a fix," he added, "with the current list 20 percent behind our paper capacity to print: we'll have to pare down subs." Meanwhile the accumulated debt and the short-term notes, along with first and second mortgages on the physical plant, imperiled the *Pathfinder.* Several note holders threatened to sue and force the company into bankruptcy and liquidation to pay off at least a part of their overdue notes. "We have come to the end of the trail," Hurja wrote an unhappy investor, "unless I can find new capital willing to venture into the Pathfinder picture. . . . We have outstanding mortgages with unpaid interest amounting in all to something over $111,000. We have unpaid taxes with penalties for non payment, social security taxes, etc., totaling another $16,000. We have other debts of about $20,000, and in addition we have bank loans of over $20,000, partly secured by accounts receivable." "I am borrowing from Peter to pay Paul," Hurja noted, and in the last 44 weeks the magazine lost $11,411 in operating costs. He continued: "I always breathe a sigh of relief when the banks close for the day," and "I am seeking outside aid." Stress had gotten to Hurja, and he had lost some 43 pounds and had elevated blood sugar. He lamented, "I cannot go on with things as they are."[37]

Hurja sought an outside investor to take part ownership of the magazine and pay off some of the threatening debt. Graham Patterson and the Pew interests of the *Farm Journal* moved in. By July 1943 the Pew interests had taken over part of the company, and by early 1944 they had begun paying off its debt and assuming even more control of the editorial office. Hurja's shrinking financial interest was also reflected in his demotion from publisher-editor to associate publisher with no clearly defined editorial duties, even though he continued to write copy for the *Pathfinder* through the summer and fall of 1944.[38]

Hurja had continued his polling operations, conducting and publishing preelection polls for the 1942 congressional campaigns that correctly forecast a Republican victory for the midterm elections. Emil was correct in that 46 of the 53 districts he picked as going GOP went Republican. That took some of the sting out of his 1940 miscall. In 1944 he ran delegate polls to determine who would win the Republican nomination for presidential candidate. His surveys correctly predicted that New York governor Thomas E. Dewey would win the nomination. He did not run delegate polls for the Democrats, since the wartime climate kept serious Democratic challengers in the closet, afraid to face the charge of being unpatriotic in opposing a wartime president.[39]

Lacking funding that he had enjoyed in his polling days for the Democratic National Committee in the New Deal years, Hurja moved away from more expensive national random sampling and state-by-state sampling, and began instead to take cost-saving shortcuts for polling the 1944 presidential election campaign. He sought out a limited number of "banner" and "bellwether" counties from the nation's more than 3,000 counties. Hurja conferred with Claude Robinson, one of the pioneer experts and founding fathers of polling pedagogy, and decided to expand Robinson's suggested use of 10 bellwether counties to 28. Hurja in his preelection press release stated that "Twenty-eight key counties out of the 3,069 in the United States furnish a prediction that Thomas E. Dewey, Republican candidate for the presidency, will win the election on Tuesday, November 7. These 28 counties in 15 states are the only counties which have had perfect records on presidential elections for 11 consecutive elections, since November, 1900. . . . In these 11 elections, the competitive box scores of the 28 counties does not vary but little from the national presidential percentages, amounting to a difference of but 92 votes out of every 10,000 cast." The press release continued: "On the basis of a current poll of the counties conducted by him, Mr. Hurja says that Dewey should get a minimum of 2,000,000 majority in the country as a whole," carrying an electoral vote of 364 compared to 167 for FDR. Hurja assured publisher Graham Patterson that nine of the counties "have the best correlation with the 1932–1936–1940 swing. . . . Each county shows a swing to Dewey . . . sufficient to bring Dewey to the Presidency. Mind you none of these counties went for Willkie in 1940, all were for Roosevelt."[40]

In the *Pathfinder* editorial office, the new boss, Graham Patterson, became increasingly annoyed and impatient with Hurja's preelection polling and asked Emil to make it clear that his preelection polls represented his personal views and not those of *Pathfinder* magazine. Hurja had also worked up press releases on trend analysis, as had other pollsters and pundits, all of which showed a slow but steady deterioration in support for FDR since 1938. Since then the Democrats had lost two congressional midterm elections, 1938 and 1942, even though they retained control of Congress with smaller majorities. President Roosevelt's portion of the popular vote, which had been 62 percent in 1936, had slipped to 55 percent in 1940. (As the later results would show, it would slip even further in 1944, to 53.5 percent.)

These national trends were even more exaggerated in the 28 bellwether counties, as Emil would later discover when the elections returns came in. Hurja sent out several press releases the day before the election, predicting a Dewey victory over FDR. These were widely distributed. The Associated Press dispatch read, HURJA PREDICTS DEWEY VICTORY, and like the banner Chicago *Tribune* headline a presidential election later, this dispatch would come back to haunt Hurja. The "Dewey wins" prediction was overturned by the incumbent Roosevelt, who won 36 out of the 48 states in the electoral college with a college vote of 432 to 99 and a popular vote of 25.6 million to Dewey's 22 million. (Some 2.6 million "soldier ballots" were also cast and appear to have supported the Democratic incumbent, unlike the 2,000 election.)

FDR's unprecedented reelection for a fourth term proved Hurja wrong. Publisher Patterson was furious, as negative letters and editorial commentary flowed in, ridiculing *Pathfinder's* prediction. Patterson removed the associate publisher's name from the masthead and fired Hurja. Shocked and shaken, Emil saw his publishing days come to an end in December 1944.[41]

Emil Hurja's five-year tenure as publisher and editor of *Pathfinder* had not been in vain. Emil rescued a newsweekly that was on the verge of collapse, and the magazine survived only because of the energy, hard work, and new ideas that Hurja brought to it. He turned it into a specialty magazine with a niche market that covered rural America and towns and cities with fewer than 100,000 residents. Reflecting on these demographics, Emil picked a homespun title for his lead editorial column, "Between You, Me and the Gatepost." His 1940 articles on the coming war and the U.S. naval buildup attracted military service readers in some of the world's key trouble spots, such as Guam, Wake Island, and Midway and on shipboard. He also turned *Pathfinder* into one of the nation's most perceptive "insider" news magazines covering Washington, D.C., and national politics. His years of working for FDR as a pollster and political analyst had given him insights into the political scene that few rival newsweeklies could match. For such achievements, Emil won the praise of hundreds of political aficionados and dozens of U.S. congressmen. Senator Arthur Capper of Missouri wrote that the "Pathfinder has steadily improved" under Emil's management and become a "well-edited magazine." Congressman Leslie Arends of Illinois, the new Republican "whip" in 1943, asserted that "the publicity Pathfinder is giving to the membership of Congress in its Family Album is helpful. The more people get acquainted with their representatives in Washington, the more interest we shall find in government and this will likewise result in better men being elected to office." "The Pathfinder is truly a people's magazine," Indiana's U.S. senator Raymond Willis observed, stating, "I believe the sterling character of the great body of people in America has been nurtured by the wide circulation of the Pathfinder."[42]

POST-*PATHFINDER* HURJA

During the war, Hurja and several prominent Finnish Americans had also been active in lobbying Congress and the administration not to declare war on Finland, as America's ally England had. Finland had become an active cobelligerent with the Axis in recovering the territories she had lost to Soviet aggression in 1939–40. The Finnish military quickly recaptured their lost territories and then settled down into a trench war from 1942 to 1944 that was primarily defensive. Although it was easily within reach of the Finns, and despite German urgings, General Carl Gustav Mannerheim refused to cut the narrow link of the Murmansk supply line, the main artery carrying Allied aid to besieged Leningrad. The Finns explained that their objective was not to help defeat Russia, but to recapture their lost territories and gain territorial depth for the defensive war they knew was coming. This was the message conveyed in publications, news articles, and letters to congressmen and the administration, and to the larger public in radio broadcasts generated by a group of Finnish Americans that included the Finnish-American League for Democracy; Dr. V. K. Nikander, president of Suomi College in Michigan; the Reverend Alfred Haapanen, president of the Suomi Synod Lutheran Church; the leaders of the Apostolic Lutheran Church; Congressmen Oscar Larson and Frank Hook; and Emil Hurja. They asked the Roosevelt administration to pressure Stalin to ease up on the oppressive Soviet demands on Finland that threatened to wipe out its independence. The result was that the United States did not declare war on Finland, but it did sever diplomatic relations.[43]

Part of the drive to help Finland was ethnically linked, but part of it was also a matter of political prescience. Already in 1943, Hurja displayed a political foresight about the post-war world that few other editors or policy-makers did. Perhaps that is not surprising, since a pollster's occupation was to foresee and forecast the future. Like a few Finland counterparts and the head of the U.S. Office of Strategic Services, Emil had no illusions about the prospects for a lasting peaceful cooperation between the United States and the U.S.S.R. In September 1943, Hurja in his *Pathfinder* column wrote: "Apropos of the bitter conflict of ideologies in Europe between Fascism and Communism, history warns us that after such conflicts are fought to the finish . . . there is a danger that the war will go right on" with new "words or names." Emil cited several historical examples, including the three-century conflict in Italy between the Guelfs and the Ghibelins, "the first supporting the Popes and the latter the Emperors." The new words describing the post-1945 conflict would be "Communism" versus "Capitalism" in what became labeled the "Cold War." The "Crystal Gazer" from Crystal Falls had again foreseen the future four years before it happened. Unfortunately President Roosevelt no longer employed Emil Hurja to advise him.[44]

Recognizing the dangers the Russian bear presented, and uncertain whether Finland would survive the war as an independent nation, the Finns offered to share top-secret intelligence materials with the United States. In 1944 several Finnish officials and the perceptive American leader of the Office of Strategic Services, William Donovan, realized that the Soviets were likely to be the future threat to Western democracies, even though at the time the Russians were still brothers-in-arms against Germany. Finnish military intelligence, which had broken the Soviets' secret codes, offered and gave to the American OSS chief a code book of 1,500 pages that included the cipher keys to Soviet intelligence agencies, NKVD and GRU. Donovan offered them to Roosevelt, who, strangely enough, ordered the OSS chief to return the secret Russian codes to the Soviets. Why? The likely explanation is that the president was suffering from his great hubris—the illusion that he and Stalin, as great personal friends, could run the postwar world. However, FDR's former postmaster general and Democratic National Committee chairman attributed Roosevelt's mistakes in judgment to his failing health, saying: the "sick man at Yalta . . . should not have been called upon to make decisions affecting this country and the world. Physical illness, as we know, taxed the mind and left him in no shape to bargain with such hard bargainers as the Russians and such astute diplomats as the British." Fortunately the nation's OSS chief, against Roosevelt's bad order, made copies before returning the 1,500-page codebook to the Soviets. Donovan's bold insubordination would later prove the valuable key to the FBI and Army Intelligence's unlocking and deciphering of the Venona papers, which in the 1990s would reveal the depth of Soviet spying on the United States during the Roosevelt administration years. Without the Donovan copies of the Finnish code breakers, the Venona transmissions would have remained unclear as to the extent of Soviet spying.[45]

Finland's debt repayment throughout the war had won it respect from American people and in the postwar period revelations of how Finland and her Scandinavian neighbors had refused to surrender Jews to the Nazis further contributed to the region's humanitarian reputation. With the European war over, Hurja in July 1945 lobbied the State Department and strongly urged President Harry Truman to resume diplomatic relations with Finland. A few weeks later in August, the United States re-established diplomatic relations with Finland. Emil also successfully sought the release of Finnish merchant ships that had been impounded during the war, arguing they were desperately needed to increase the flow of humanitarian aid and foodstuffs to war-devastated Europe.[46] Much of Hurja's work for Finland, such as his lobbying against a war declaration or the resumption of diplomatic relations, was pro bono; he was, however, on a consulting payroll when he secured the release of impounded Finnish ships.

POSTWAR HURJA

By mid-1945, Hurja was back full time in the consulting and public relations business. His main client was the kingdom of Egypt, for which he attended meetings of the United Nations and wrote the addresses delivered by the Egyptian foreign minister at the plenary sessions. During the summer of 1947 he spent much time commuting to Lake Success, New York, where the United Nations was then meeting, hopeful that this new international body would smooth over the irritants that triggered wars. He also conducted polls for his Egyptian client, to measure press views of the Egypt-Israeli conflict in the postwar period. In addition to producing publications with titles such as "News From Egypt" and "Egypt's Case Before the World," Emil was actively lobbying with the public and the United Nations to get Britain to give up Sudan to Egypt. His public relations work resulted in another Federal Bureau of Investigation and State Department surveillance, presumably because his client, Egypt, was considered a threat to the establishment of a Jewish nation.[47]

In May 1946, Hurja returned temporarily to his youthful hometown of Crystal Falls, in Michigan's Upper Peninsula, and entered the Republican primary election for the 12th district congressional seat. He ran twice, in 1946 and 1948, but was defeated by Republican John Bennett, who accused him of being a "carpetbagger," absent from the area for 35 years. Undeterred by his primary defeat, Hurja engaged himself in state-level polling in congressional races and offered consulting advice to several winning Republicans who helped carry the GOP landslide in 1946 for Congress. FDR had died in

April 1945, a month later Germany surrendered, and in September Japan gave up. Peacetime America had gone heavily Republican in 1946, and the public was anxious to demobilize and liquidate price, wage, and production controls, which had proved a burden during "Dr. Win the War's" war. The GOP resurgence, which Hurja had been predicting, and which had been delayed by a two-front war, manifested itself in the first postwar election.[48]

At the same time Hurja continued to be an active proponent and promoter of Alaskan statehood, appearing as an expert witness in congressional hearings. Alaska was the territory in which he had spent his late adolescence and early manhood as a newspaper reporter and editor, and it was there that he had his break into paying journalism. He told President Truman in private communications that bringing about statehood "could be the crowning achievement of your administration." At the same time he continued his low-profile campaign to be appointed governor of the Alaska territory.[49]

Then, in 1952, when the Republicans nominated Dwight D. Eisenhower for the presidency, Hurja began polling again on his own. The hot issues in the campaign were the Korean War, Communist spying, administrative corruption, the national economy, and the fact that the Soviets had matched the United States with an atomic and a hydrogen bomb, presumably from secrets stolen under Democratic administrations. The issues were hurtful to Truman, who left the presidency with the lowest public-approval ratings of any president since polling began. Hurja's New Deal reputation as the "Wizard of Washington" had been tarnished somewhat by his miscalls of the 1940 and 1944 presidential elections. Even so, he reminded critics that he had been "right" in 1932, 1934, 1936, 1938, 1942, and 1946, and "wrong" only in 1940 and 1944. Hurja's preelection polls garnered national publicity when he boldly predicted an Eisenhower victory of "landslide" proportions. Hurja's bold prognostication stood out even more because, as Professor Harold Gosnell observed, "Frightened by their errors in 1948, the pollsters were cautious in predicting the outcome of the election of 1952. Their raw figures indicated an Eisenhower victory, but they were afraid to say so." Hurja was not intimidated and boldly predicted an Ike victory. General Eisenhower took 55 percent of the popular vote to Adlai Stevenson's 44 percent and carried the electoral college by 442 to 89. Hurja took some pleasure in his correct prediction and told an inquiring correspondent, "my polls were right on the button and the 'big shots' didn't see it." The "most accurate of all the pollsters in this election was Emil Hurja . . . who predicted 411 electoral votes for Eisenhower," wrote the Washington staff writers of the Pittsburgh *Post-Gazette*.[50] Unfortunately for Emil, the president-elect was not an avid poll follower and consumer.

Hurja launched a strong effort with President-elect Dwight D. Eisenhower to get an appointment with his administration, preferably as minister to Finland. As Emil explained to Ike's administrative assistants, he had been promised the job back in 1933 by FDR, but it never came through. Hurja's fluency in Finnish, ability to read Swedish, and knowledge of the history and politics of Scandinavia made him an ideal candidate. As Hurja put it, Finland was an ideal "listening post on Russian affairs" that could enable American intelligence penetration through the Iron Curtain. With his extensive personal contacts with officials in Finland and Sweden he could help the United States and the West. Although Hurja was enthusiastically endorsed by more than a dozen representatives and a half-dozen Republican senators including Michigan's Homer Ferguson and Charles Potter, and a friend of Eisenhower's from his Columbia University presidency days, Professor John Wuorinen, the nomination was held up. Unfortunately, Congressman John Bennett from Michigan's 12th district, whom Hurja had challenged for the nomination, opposed the appointment.[51] Before the Eisenhower administration could make a final decision, Hurja died on May 30, 1953, of a heart attack at the age of 61.

The passing of the "Crystal Gazer from Crystal Falls" was widely noted among pundits, pollsters, politicians, and the press. As the New York Times put it, Emil Hurja "was widely known as the man who put mathematics into politics." Hurja was the first presidential pollster and political consultant to apply the newly unfolding science of polling to running political campaigns and to guiding governance during the presidency. At a time when no one had yet field-tested scientific polling for politics, Emil, with his engineering and mineral analysis background, understood probability theory, sampling statistics, and how to use quotas to get representative samples, and perhaps even more important, how to correct biased mega–straw-polls, such as those of the Literary Digest, to make political sense of them. He also contributed to the technical development of polling in that his own experiments convinced him and he tried to persuade his friend George Gallup that smaller sample sizes, correctly apportioned and weighted, could produce the same results as massive 300,000 sized mega polls that Gallup ran in 1936. Hurja also fathered "Trend analysis," which reporters by 1935 were calling the "Hurja method:" trend analysis enabled political consultants to track the public response to their candidate's campaign speeches and policy announcements and use poll numbers to correct rhetorical mis-steps or enlarge upon policy issues that were attracting public approval. Hurja also began the development of another modern-day political technique known as "priming,"—that is, the use of polls to "prime" the electorate by setting the agenda for public discussion and focusing on certain selected topics which the presidential candidate could handle and which would reflect favorably on the candidate. As a capital reporter noted in 1935 when FDR was gearing up to run for reelection the next year, Hurja's job was "to steer conversation or what people were talking about" in reference to Roosevelt and the New Deal.[52]

In addition to being the first presidential consultant who taught presidents how to campaign for office as well as attune policy to poll findings, Emil Hurja also played a key role in helping Roosevelt alter political party management by restructuring the patronage system. Before Roosevelt the majority of patronage jobs were decided locally by state and county chairmen, and members of Congress. Hurja with new management techniques called FRBC ("For Roosevelt Before the Chicago" 1932 convention.) changed the traditional system. Emil installed a bookkeeping system that established more precisely to what extent congressmen were voting for administration measures and kept a record of every congressional district. Through Hurja, Roosevelt undermined the traditional patronage system, changed the makeup of government employees and through this new system guaranteed loyalty to Roosevelt and the executive branch.

Hurja also polled secretly and compiled editorial opinion and press reports on public views in key congressional districts and gave the information to the president. This greatly enlarged the power of the presidency for as presidential aide Stanley High noted, when senators and representatives were called to the president's office, "they were seldom asked what was the state of the public mind in their area. They were told what the state of the public mind in those areas was. Word soon got around Capitol Hill that the President knows more about our constituents than we do."[53] This kind of political knowledge was power and greatly enlarged executive authority of the White House over congress. Whether one wishes to call this an enlarged executive authority or the "Imperial Presidency," the process clearly began when Roosevelt accepted Hurja's ideas and methods on enhancing executive power and put Emil to work liberating the president from much of the state and local and congressional control that had prevailed in past presidencies.

Emil Hurja's reputation soared after successfully directing Democratic campaigns and accurately predicting in advance the 1932, 1934, and 1936 elections. His work as the master strategist in the 1934 congressional elections was noteworthy: normally the presidential party loses seats in congress in the mid-term elections. The Democrats in 1934 won the House election and reduced the Republican majority in the Senate to one vote, an unprecedented and unmatched event in twentieth century Democratic Party politics. The national press corp was stunned. Even President Roosevelt expressed amazement saying it was the "darnest thing he had ever seen in politics." When Democratic boss James Farley revealed after the election who the party's "magic forecaster" was, Emil Hurja soared from backroom obscurity to national attention. By early 1935 the Washington press corps was beginning its political forecasts with bylines such as "as Hurja says" and hung a series of monikers on the "Democratic guess man," including the "soothsayer," the "magic forecaster," and the "Wizard of Washington." In March of 1936 came the ultimate accolade when the "Crystal Gazer" from Crystal Falls, Michigan, made the cover of *Time* magazine, the first American public opinion pollster to be so honored. Hurja by then was the toast of the town and was believed to have the powers of a delphic oracle—despite his protestations that what he was doing had a scientific mathematical basis to it. *Fortune* magazine (which later employed Elmo Roper and whose pre-election polls in 1936 won the popular vote sweepstakes) declared in April, 1935 that Emil Hurja "ought to be in a book."

But for the next two-thirds of a century there was no book and few articles on the "Democratic guess man." Hurja is not well known to historians or political scientists or political writers as is George Gallup or Louis Harris and others. Why? The reasons are several: The White House was not inclined to advertise the fact that Hurja was working for them because they did not want it to be widely known that President Roosevelt was "flying by the polls" instead of by deeply held and principled convictions. (A fact that would tarnish somewhat the reputations of John F. Kennedy and Lyndon Johnson when it became known they were poll-dependent and even more the reputation of the most poll-dependent president in history, Bill Clinton.) Another reason was that George Gallup was such a masterful self-publicist that his name became synonymous with polling in the 1930s. Finally, there was a break in presidential reliance on polling from 1945 to 1961, by presidents Harry Truman and Dwight Eisenhower, who made little use of polling and shied away from employing pollsters in the hustings or in the White House Because of this break in historical continuity, political writers, with a few exceptions, have not searched back for the origins of presidential polling. Finally, the fact that Hurja turned against Roosevelt after his 1937 court packing, and 1938 purge fiascoes, and called FDR a tyrant for breaking the Jefferson two-term tradition in 1940, transformed Hurja in the minds of some writers into a Roosevelt hater and thus easy to dismiss. On a personal basis Emil remained friendly and continued to correspond with FDR through 1944. It was politics they disagreed upon. The fact that Emil became a Republican and a strong Herbert Hoover supporter in 1940, and the only preelection forecaster to correctly predict Republican candidate Dwight Eisenhower's landslide victory in 1952 obviously did not endear Emil to a generation of historical admirers of Roosevelt and the New Deal. (Thus no book from that generation.)

Foreign policy issues also account for Hurja's low profile among scholars. Most textbooks skip over the Russo-Finnish War, as do studies of American isolationism, and move directly from the Nazi-Soviet September 1939 crushing of Poland to the overrun of Norway and the fall of France in June

1940. The intervening period, in which Hurja was active in public debate, was in past textbooks often dismissed as the "phony war," or the "sitzkrieg." But as we have seen in this study, the Winter War was more than a "phony" war and had a significant influence in modifying American isolationism and winning public support for the extension of military aid to European victims of totalitarian aggression. However, those events had a downward impact on Hurja's reputation. Emil and *Pathfinder's* support of Finland during the Winter War, 1939–40, and the Continuation War, 1941–44, against Russia did not endear Hurja to a generation of wartime and postwar pro-Soviets sympathizers or writers on the academic left. The only praise that Hurja garnered during this period came from Republicans like ex-president Herbert Hoover, who wrote, "When all the good Finns are collected in Heaven, they will remember what you did for them and will insist upon your being admitted." Thus despite *Fortune* magazine's peroration in 1935, it would take two-thirds of a century before the appearance of a book on "the Wizard of Washington," Emil Hurja.

NOTES

CHAPTER 1

1. *A Collection of Recollections: Crystal Falls, Michigan, 1880–1980* (Crystal Falls, MI: Centennial Committee, 1980), 56, 58; James H. Ojala, "Emil Hurja: The Years before Roosevelt, 1892–1932," unpublished manuscript, 4 f.
2. W. William Hoglund, "No Land for the Finns: Critics and Reformers View the Rural Exodus from Finland to American 1880s to World War I," in *Migration Studies* C3, eds. Michael G. Karni, Matti E. Kaups, and Douglas J. Ollila, Jr. (Turku, Finland: Institute for Migration, 1975), 23, 38; Amanda Wiljanen Larson, *Finnish Heritage in America* (Marquette, MI: Delta Kappa Gamma Society, 1976), 9.
3. Hoglund, "No Land for Finns," 15, 16; John Kolehmainen, "The Finnish Immigrant Experience in the United States," in *Finnish Diaspora II: The United States,* ed. Michael Karni (Toronto: Multicultural History Society of Ontario, 1981), 9.
4. Kolehmainen, The Finnish Immigrant Experience in the United States," 3; Larson, *Finnish Heritage,* 14.
5. Ojala, "Emil Hurja," 13; *Diamond Drill,* 1 May 1931.
6. William Hoglund, *Finnish Immigrants in America, 1880–1920* (Madison: University of Wisconsin Press, 1965) 11; Hoglund "No Land for Finns," 14; Larson, *Finnish Heritage,* 13.
7. Ojala, "Emil Hurja," 9f; Hoglund, *Finnish Immigrants,* 8–9; Larson, *Finnish Heritage,* 14, 18–19.
8. Hoglund, *Finnish Immigrants,* 20; Ojala, "Emil Hurja," 19.
9. Karni, Kaups, and Ollila, *Migration Studies,* 25; *Collection of Recollections, Crystal Falls,* 56; "Immigration Literacy, 1899–1910," in *Harvard Encyclopedia of American Ethnic Groups* eds. Stephen Thernstrom and Ann Orlov (Cambridge, MA: Harvard University Press, 1980), 478.
10. Jack Hill, *A History of Iron County, Michigan* (Norway, MI: Norway Current, 1976), 4, 13, 14,15, 36; F. Clever Bald, *Michigan in Four Centuries* (New York: Harper Brothers, 1954), 200–202.
11. Hill, *History of Iron County,* 69; Burton Boyum, "Boys Look Around and See What You Can Find," *Michigan History,* 78, no. 4 (November-December 1994), 5, 14.

12. Hill, *History of Iron County*, 19, 36; Russell Magnaghi, *The Way It Happened: Settling Michigan's Upper Peninsula* (Iron Mountain, MI: Mid-Peninsula Library Cooperative, 1982).

13. Harlan Hatcher, *A Century of Iron and Men* (New York: Bobbs-Merrill, Inc., 1950), 208.

14. Burton Boyum, *The Saga of Iron Mining in Michigan's Upper Peninsula* (Marquette, MI: J. Longyear Research Library, 1977), 5–11; Hatcher, *Century of Iron and Men,* 62; 78, 79.

15. Marcia Bernhardt, *Iron County Historical Sites and Landmarks* (Caspian, MI: Iron County Museum, 1985), 14; Hatcher, *Century of Iron and Men,* 62, 108, 281.

16. Hill, *History of Iron County,* 31, 32.

17. Hatcher, *Century of Iron and Men,* 214; Milo M. Quaife and Sidney Glazer, *Michigan: From Primitive Wilderness to Industrial Commonwealth* (New York: Prentice-Hall, 1948), 219.

18. *Recollections of Crystal Falls,* 6, 96; Walter Nursey, *The Menominee Iron Range: Its Cities, their Industries and Resource* (Iron River, MI: Swain and Tate Printers, 1891, reissued 1972), 128.

19. Bernhardt, *They Came,* 77, 158; Nursey, *Menominee Iron Range,* 129, 130.

20. Bernhardt, *Iron County Historical Sites,* 5; Boyum, *Saga of Iron Mining,* 19.

21. Bernhardt, *They Came,* 158; *Recollections of Crystal Falls,* 7; Bernhardt, *Iron County Historical Sites,* 5.

22. *Recollections of Crystal Falls,* 96, 97; *The Diamond Drill,* August 9, 1890; "The Iron Ores of Lake Superior, 1911," Iron County Historical Museum.

23. Hatcher, *Century of Iron and Men* 128; Debra Bernhardt, *Black Rock and Roses: A Play of Iron County* (Norway, MI: Norway Current, 1976), 11.

24. Matti Kaups, "The Finns in the Copper and Iron Ore Mines of the Western Great Lakes Region, 1864–1905," *Migration Studies* C 3 eds. Karni, Kaups, Ollila, 55, 63, 64.

25. Boyum, *Saga of Iron Mining,* 24.

26. Bernhardt, *Black Rock,* 12, 13; Leevi Etelamaki, *The Blue Collar Aristocracy* (Escanaba, MI: Richards Printing, 1996), 38.

27. Paula Stofer, "Shared Beds, Shared Bread," *Michigan History* 38, no. 6 (November-December 1994), 37, 38, 44.

28. Kaups, "The Finns in the Copper and Iron Ore Mines," 55; Terry Reynolds, "We Were Satisfied With It," *Michigan History* 78, no. 6 (November-December 1994), 25, 30.

29. Ojala, "Emil Hurja," 26.

30. *Recollections of Crystal Falls,* 97. Interview with Matti Holli, 7 May 1958.

31. *The Diamond Drill,* 2 February 1940; Keijo Virtanen, "Disaffection: Finns Leave America," *Migration Studies* C3, 121.

32. Kaups, "The Finns in the Copper and Irons Mines," 67; *Recollections of Crystal Falls,* 57, 97; *The Diamond Drill,* 1 May 1931.

33. Kaups, "The Finns in the Copper and Iron Ore Mines," 67; Carl Ross, *The Finn Factor in American Labor, Culture and Society* (New York Mills, MN: Parta Publishing, 1977), 12; Bernhardt, *Iron County Historical Sites,* 91

34. *Recollections of Crystal Falls,* 18, 57; Etelamaki, *Blue Collar Aristocracy,* 10; Bernhardt, *They Came,* 29.
35. Larson, *Finnish Heritage,* 23, 27; Bernhardt, *They Came,* 2.
36. Ibid.
37. Interviews with Arthur and Theodore Siikaniva, 4 July 1975.
38. Raymond Wargelin, "The Suomi Synod Tradition and Its Early Leaders," in *The Faith of the Finns: Historical Perspectives on the Finnish Lutheran Church in America,* ed. Ralph Jalkanen (East Lansing: Michigan State University Press, 1972), 334.
39. *Recollections of Crystal Falls,* 58; *The Diamond Drill,* 17 June 1905; 1 May 1931.
40. Ross, *The Finn Factor,* 28, 29; *Fiftieth Anniversary Publication of Suomi College and Theological Seminary,* 1896–1946 (Hancock, MI: Finnish Lutheran Book concern, 1946).
41. Bernhardt, *They Came,* 2; Larson, *Finnish Heritage,* 1, 9, 41; Marianne Wargelin Brown, "The Legacy of Mummu's Granddaughters," *Women Who Dared: The History of Finnish- American Women,* eds. Carl Ross and Marianne Wargelin Brown (St. Paul: University of Minnesota Press, 1986), 4.
42. *Recollections of Crystal Falls,* 57.
43. Larson, *Finnish Heritage,* 40; Ross, *Finn Factor,* 24–26; Leo Utter, "Western Finn Halls: Scenes of Activity," in *Tyomies Eteenpain,1903–1988* (Superior, WI: Tyomies Society, 1988); *The Diamond Drill,* 31 May 1890. See also Sakari Sariola, "The Finnish Temperance Movement in the Great Lakes Area of the Midwest," special reprint of paper presented at Conference on Social History, 2 January 1984, Berkeley, California.
44. Ojala, "Emil Hurja," 30–31.
45. *Recollections of Crystal Falls,* 223; Arnold Alanen, "Finns and the Corporate Mining Environment of the Lake Superior Region," *Finnish Diaspora* II, 35; Ojala, "Emil Hurja," 18 f. Hurja quoted in Emil Hurja to John Foster Dulles, Box 195 Eisenhower Papers, Eisenhower Presidential Library, Abilene, Kansas. See also "The Home: Center of Activity for Early Finns," in Rudolph Kempainen, *Central Upper Peninsula Finnish American Bicentennial, 1776–1976* (Ishpeming, MI: Finnish American Bicentennial Steering Committee, 1976), 14, 15.
46. Aino Malberg, "The Protected Sex in Wartime," *Harpers Weekly,* 8 May 1915, 436–438; Ross, *The Finn Factor,* 139–148.
47. Etelamaki, *Blue Collar Aristocracy,* 15–18; Viola Hilma Taisto, "The Sauna: Finland's Gift to the World," in *Central Upper Peninsula Finnish American Bicentennial,* 35; Larson, *Finnish Heritage,* 31.
48. Utter, "Western Finn Halls," 3; Larson, *Finnish Heritage,* 42; Kolehmainen, "Finnish Immigrant Experience," 11.
49. Hurja Papers, Box 2, Tennessee State Library and Archives (hereafter Tennessee State Archives).
50. Ibid., Box 2, A Hamilton Scrapbook, Tennessee State Archives.
51. *The Diamond Drill,* 9 January, 2, 27 February, 20 August, 3 December 1904.

52. Hoglund, "No Land for Finns," 43; *The Diamond Drill,* 1 May 1931; *Recollections of Crystal Falls,* 223.
53. Emil Hurja radio talk, 17 June 1946, WDMJ-AM, Marquette, MI., Hurja Papers, Box 2 Tennessee State Archives; Larson, *Finnish Heritage,* 37, 38.
54. Ibid.

CHAPTER 2

1. Richard Seelye Jones, "The Story of a Michigan Boy," 1946; Lemuel F. Parton, "Emil Hurja Charts Trends of Votes for Democrats," New York *Sun,* 29 February 1936, both articles in Box 67, Hurja Papers, Frankin D. Roosevelt Library (hereafter FDRL).
2. Paul Mallon, "Right Hand Man," *Today, An Independent Journal of Public Affairs* 5, no. 3, 3 November 1934; Box 139, Hurja Papers, FDRL.
3. A. W. Greeley, *Handbook of Alaska* (New York: Charles Scribner's Sons, 1925), 49–51.
4. Amanda Hamilton Scrapbook, Hurja Papers, Box 2, Tennessee State Archives; Box 139, Hurja Papers, FDRL.
5. Henry Clark, *History of Alaska* (New York: Macmillan, 1930), 144–145; Jones, "Story of a Michigan Boy."
6. Box 2, Hurja Papers, Tennessee State Archives; *Tyee,* XVII 1916 (University of Washington Yearbook.)
7. Jones, "Story of a Michigan Boy;" Box 139, Hurja Papers, FDRL; James Ojala, "Emil Hurja: the Years before Roosevelt, 1892–1932," manuscript in possession of author.
8. *Tyee* 1915 and 1916 (University of Washington yearbooks); Hurja Scrapbook, Box 2 Hurja Papers, Tennessee State Archives.
9. Hurja Scrapbook, Box 2, Tennessee State Archives.
10. *Ibid.*
11. Hurja Scrapbook, Box 3, Tennessee State Archives.
12. *Ibid.*
13. Box 139, Hurja Papers, FDRL.
14. *Ibid.*
15. "Through Europe with Henry Ford's Peace Expedition," Hurja Scrapbook, Box 3, Hurja Papers, Tennessee State Archives; Frank Kane, "Sourdough Emil," University of Washington *Daily,* 30 November 1915.
16. Telegrams, Frank Kane article and *Chicago American,* 2 December 1915, in "Ford's Peace Expedition" Scrapbook, Box 3, Hurja Papers, Tennessee State Archives.
17. Barbara S. Kraft, *The Peace Ship: Henry Ford's Pacifist Adventure in the First World War* (New York: Macmillan, 1978), 124; "Outline of Plan of the Henry Ford Peace Expedition," manuscript [1915] by Louis H. Lochner, in Box 4, Hurja Papers, Tennessee State Archives.
18. "Ford's Peace Expedition" Scrapbook.
19. Emil Hurja manuscript, "The Fjord Press: A Glimpse of Scandinavian Journalism from the Running Board of a Jitney," Box 4, Hurja Papers, Tennessee State Archives.

20. Emil Hurja, "Stories of the Ford Peace Ship," Fairbanks *Daily News,* January 6, 1916, "Ford's Peace Expedition" Scrapbook; Louis H. Lochner, *"America's Don Quixote: Henry Ford's Attempt to Save Europe* (London: Kegan Paul, 1924), 93.

21. Lochner, *America's Don Quixote,* 97; Hurja letter to Fairbanks *Daily News,* 23 December 1915 in "Ford Peace Expedition" Scrapbook.

22. Emil Hurja, "How the Ford Peace Party Saw Germany," *Caduceus of Kappa Sigma,* 31 March 1916; Ford news clipping, 3 January 1916 in Box 4, Hurja Papers, Tennessee State Archives.

23. HerndonBooton *Ford: An Unconventional Biography of the Man and the Times* (New York: Weybright & Talley, 1969), 321.

24. "Peace Delegate Says Trip Has Done Much Good," January 1916 news clipping in "Ford Peace Expedition" Scrapbook.

25. Box 139, Hurja Papers, FDRL.

26. Hurja manuscript [1952], Box 139, Hurja Papers, FDRL.

27. Emil Hurja to Colonel P. W. Davidson, 6 December 1917, Lillian Ojala Papers, Port Angeles, Washington.

28. Robert Ferrell, *Woodrow Wilson and World War I, 1917–1921* (New York: Harper, 1985), 111; Hurja and Spruce Division, Box 139, Hurja Papers, FDRL.

29. "University Girl Takes Fight . . . ," Seattle *Post Intelligencer,* 12 June 1917, Hurja Scrapbook, Box 4, Tennessee State Archives.

30. *Tyee* 1917; Box 4, Hurja Papers, Tennessee State Archives.

31. Amanda Hamilton Scrapbook news clips, Box 2, Hurja Papers, Tennessee State Archives; Emil Hurja Memo, 22 August 1921; Emil Hurja to Stacey V. Jones, 21 February 1921; to C. Caldwell, 22 May 1922; to Ben Dean, 29 April 1922; and to G. R. McManis, 1 February 1922 in Box 22, Hurja Papers, FDRL.

32. William Rowson to Emil Hurja, 24 July 1926, Box 22, Hurja Papers, FDRL.

33. Box 2, Hurja Papers, Tennessee State Archives; Lemuel F. Parton, "Emil Hurja Charts Trend of Votes," New York *Sun,* 2 February 1936, Box 67, Hurja Papers, FDRL; Michelsen letter 21 August 1939, in possession of Emil Hurja's sister, Lillian Ojala, Port Angeles, Washington; James Ojala, "Emil Hurja: The Years Before Roosevelt, 1892–1932," unpublished manuscript, 1990, 7.

CHAPTER 3

1. David W. Moore, *The Superpollsters: How they Measure and Manipulate Public Opinion in America* (New York: Four Walls Eight Windows, 1995), 77, 79, 89, 243; Susan Herbst, *Numbered Voices: How Opinion Polling Has Shaped American Politics* Chicago: University of Chicago Press, 1993), 159; Larry J. Sabato, *The Rise of Political Consultants: New Ways to Win Elections* (New York: Basic Books, 1981), 70,73. For Clinton see Dick Morris, *Behind the Oval Office: Winning the Presidency in the Nineties* (New York: Random House, 1997) and *The New Prince: Machiavelli Updated for the 21st Century* (Los Angeles:

Renaissance Books, 1999); Diane J. Heith, "Polling for Defense: The White House Public Opinion Apparatus and the Clinton Impeachment," *Presidential Studies Quarterly* 30, no. 4 (December 2000), 784, 789.

2. James Ojala, "Emil Hurja: The Years before Roosevelt, 1892–1932" (unpublished manuscript, 1990), 61–80; Emil Hurja radio address, 1 May 1946, WDMJ, Marquette, MI.

3. Ibid., Frederick Jackson Turner, *The Significance of Sections in American History* (New York: Henry Holt, 1912, 1932), 111.

4. Thomas Sugrue, "Hurja: Farley's Guess Man," *The American Magazine* 71 (1936), 87. There is no evidence that Hurja or political pollsters were aware of the pioneering work of statistician Jerzy Neyman. Jean Converse, *Survey Research in the United States* (Berkeley: University of California Press, 1987), 43f.

5. Claude E. Robinson, "Recent Developments in the Straw Poll Field, *Public Opinion Quarterly* I (1937), 46–49; Archibald Crossley, "Straw Polls in 1936 *Public Opinion Quarterly* I (1937), 32.

6. Alva Johnson, "Professor Hurja, The New Deal's Political Doctor, *Saturday Evening Post* 208 (13 June 1936), 9.

7. Ray Tucker, "Chart and Graph Man," *Colliers* 95, 12 January 1935, 28.

8. Claude E. Robinson, *Straw Votes: A Study of Political Prediction* (New York: Columbia University Press, 1932), 59.

9. "Memorandum and Outline, Poll, 1932," 1, 3, Box 121, Hurja Papers, Franklin D. Roosevelt Library (hereafter FDRL).

10. Ibid., 2, 4.

11. Sugrue, "Hurja: Farley's Guess Man, 87.

12. Special Memo on *Literary Digest* poll, October 10, 1932, Box 69, Hurja Papers, FDRL. See also Mark Sullivan, "Distinct Trend to Hoover Shown," New York *Herald Tribune* 26 October 1932.

13. Louis H. Bean, *How to Predict Elections* (New York: Knopf, 1948), 5.

14. "Trends of the Polls," 11 September 1932, Box 69, Hurja Papers, FDRL.

15. "Straus Poll," Democratic National Committee Papers, containers 151, 831, FDRL

16. Thomas C. Donnelly and Roy Peel, *The 1932 Campaign: An Analysis* (New York: Farrar, Rinehart, 1935), 61.

17. Ibid., 101–02.

18. James A. Farley, *Behind the Ballot: The Personal Story of a Politician* (New York: Harcourt Brace, 1938), 322–23.

19. Lela Stiles, *The Man Behind Roosevelt: The Story of Louis McHenry Howe* (Cleveland, OH: World Publishing, 1954), 197.

20. "Analysis and Conclusions of 1932 Election Statistics," Box 77, Hurja Papers, FDRL.

21. Emil Hurja to John Troy, 30 September and 8 October 1932, Lillian Hurja Ojala Collection, Seattle, Washington.

22. Ibid.

23. Memo, Hearst Polls, September, 1932, Box 69, Hurja Papers, FDRL.

24. "Supplementary Memorandum on Interpretation of the Hearst Poll," Box 69; and "Analysis and Conclusion of 1932 Election Statistics," 3 November 1932, Box 120, Hurja Papers, FDRL.

25. "Review of Colorado Election Statistics" and "Trend of the Polls," 11 September 1932, Hurja Papers, FDRL.

26. "Farm Belt Poll Shows Hoover Gains Among Women," 9 September 1932; and "South Dakota Special Reports," 10 September 1932, Box 69, Hurja Papers, FDRL. For female vote see also Harold F. Gosnell and Norman N. Gill, "An Analysis of the 1932 Presidential Vote," *American Political Science Review* XXIX, (December 1935), 972.

27. "Gains in PA among New Voters: Losses Among Women," Box 69, Hurja Papers, FDRL.

28. Charles Michelson, *The Ghost Talks* (New York: G.P. Putnam, 1944), 39.

29. "Trends in New York and Pennsylvania," Box 69, Hurja Papers, FDRL.

30. Stiles, *The Man Behind Roosevelt, Howe,* 184; Samuel I. Rosenman, *Working With Roosevelt* (New York: Harper, 1952), 85. Democratic National Committeeman Arthur F. Mullen concurred, fearing that if Governor Roosevelt "removed Walker, though, he'd probably lose the New York state electoral vote," adding later, "We didn't know then that we could pull through without New York." Mullen, *Western Democrat* (New York: Wilfred Funk, 1940), 286. See also Herbert Mitgang, *Once Upon a Time in New York: Jimmy Walker, Franklin Roosevelt and the Last Great Battle of the Jazz Age* (New York: Free Press, 2000), 162–63, 200–204.

31. "Memo," 23 September 1932, Box 69, Hurja Papers, FDRL.

32. "Farm Belt Poll Shows Hoover Gains Among Women," 10 September 1932, Box 69, Hurja Papers, FDRL.

33. "State Reports," 11 October 1932, and "Lake Belt Shows Trend Mixed," Box 69, Hurja Papers, FDRL.

34. Frances Perkins, *The Roosevelt I Knew* (New York: Viking, 1946), 120–21. Mary "Molly" Dewson was the energetic head of the Democratic Women's Division. Susan Ware, *Partner and I: Molly Dewson, Feminism and New Deal Politics* (New Haven: Yale University Press, 1981), 168. Seymour M. Lipset and Carolyn H. Bowman, "Clinton: Assessing the 42nd President," *Public Perspective,* 11 no. 1 (January -February 2000), 7.

35. *Public Perspective,* 10 January-February, 1999, 5.

36. Peel and Donnelly, *The 1932 Campaign,* 45.

37. "Memorandum on the Nature and Location of Smith Defectors," Box 77, Hurja Papers, FDRL; Raymond Moley, *After Seven Years* (New York: Harper, 1939), 64, 65.

38. Tucker, "Chart and Graph Man," 28; Farley, *Behind the Ballots,* 323.

39. "Poll Story," press release, 12 October 1932, Box 69, Hurja Papers FDRL. Hurja identified urban voting trends that Samuel Lubell would later publicize in his study *The Future of American Politics* (New York: Harper, 1951,1951), 43 f.

40. "Franklin D. Roosevelt Is as Good as Elected President," press release, 14 October 1932, Box 75, Hurja Papers FDRL; Emil Hurja to Bernard M. Baruch, 9 July 1932, Box 13, Hurja Papers FDRL.

41. Press Release, 4 November 1932, Box 70, E. Hurja Papers, FDRL. Tucker, "Chart and Graph Man," 28; Thomas Sugrue, "Farley's Guess Man, *American Magazine* CXXI, no. 5 (May 1936) 22.

42. Simon Michelet, "The Presidential Election 1932," manuscript report, Box 69, Hurja Papers FDRL.

43. Robert M. Eisinger and Jeremy Brown, "Polling as a Means toward Presidential Autonomy: Emil Hurja, Hadley Cantril and the Roosevelt Administration," *International Journal of Public Opinion Research* 10, no. 3 (1998), 12.

44. "The Machine that Walks Like a Man, *Fortune* XI, no. 4 (April 1935), 133,.135, 136; "Political Notes, *Time* XXVI, no. 9, (2 March 1936), 18.

45. Hadley Cantril, *The Human Dimension: Experiences in Policy Research* (New Brunswick, NJ: Rutgers University Press, 1967), 53–54.

46. Scholars have probably missed this point because the Hurja political papers, running more than 70 linear feet in the Roosevelt Library, are such a confused jumble that 1932, 1934, and 1936 campaign materials are scattered in 30 to 40 different file cases and often turn up in unrelated files. In addition the Hurja political materials turn up in several different archives, including the Tennessee State Library and Archive, Finlandia College's Heritage Center, and in lesser amounts in the James Farley, Herbert Hoover, and DNC collections. Another reason is that DNC chairman James A. Farley appeared envious of Hurja's political skills and barely mentions Hurja in his two books, except to denigrate him for his 1936 call on the electoral college and to insist that Farley's old-fashioned methods of talking to state committeemen was superior to public-opinion polling. In the second edition Farley air brushes Hurja out of existence, not even mentioning him once. James A. Farley, *Behind the Ballots: The Personal History of a Politician* (New York: Harcourt Brace, 1938); *Jim Farley's Story: The Roosevelt Years* (New York: McGraw Hill, 1948).

1. Emil Hurja to James A. Farley, 16 September 1933, Box 33, Hurja Papers FDRL; Harold Brayman, "Roosevelt and the Spoilsmen," *Current History* XLV (October 1934, 21; Roger W. Babson, *Washington and the Revolutionists: A Characterization of Recovery Policies and the People Who are Giving Them Effect* (Freeport, NY: Books for Libraries Press, 1934), 136–37.

2. James A. Farley, "Passing Out Patronage.,"*American Magazine* CXVI, no. 2 (August 1933), 20–21; James A. Farley, *Behind the Ballots*, 223; Paul Mallon, *Current History* XLIII (July 1935), 339.

3. Farley, *Behind the Ballots*, 226; James A. Farley, *Jim Farley's Story: The Roosevelt Years* (New York: McGraw-Hill, 1948), 33.

4. Ray Tucker, "Guardians of the Cupboard," *Colliers* 92 (23 September 1933), 32.

5. Tucker, "Chart and Graph Man," Political Notes, *Time* XXVI, no. 2 (2 March 1936) 16,17; Brayman, "Roosevelt and the Spoilsmen," 20, 21.

6. "Political Notes," 16, 17; Franklin D. Roosevelt to Emil Hurja, 23 August 1935, Hurja Papers, Tennessee State Library and Archives, Nashville, TN; Horatio Abbott to Emil Hurja, 23 November 1933, and 6 March 1934; Murray Van Wagoner to Emil Hurja, 29 November 1933; and Dewey Hanson to Emil Hurja, 24 May 1935, Select Documents from the Hurja Papers, microfilm, Bentley Library, Ann Arbor, Michigan. "The Machine that Walks Like a Man, *Fortune* XI, no. 4 (April 1935), 133, 135, 136.

7. Brayman, "Roosevelt and the Spoilsmen," 21. For patronage charts see Box 35, Hurja Papers, FDRL; Raymond Moley, *After Seven Years* (New York: Harper, 1939), 128.

8. Tucker, "Chart and Graph Man," 41.

9. Gavin Wright, "The Political Economy of New Deal Spending: An Econometric Analysis," *Review of Economics and Statistics* LVI, no. 1 (February 1974), 30, 34, 35, 37.

10. Robert M. Eisinger and Jeremy Brown, "Polling as a Means toward Presidential Autonomy: Emil Hurja, Hadley Cantril, and the Roosevelt Administration," *International Journal of Public Research* 10, no. 1 (1998), 240.

11. Press release, 17 March 1934, James A. Farley Papers, Box 37, Library of Congress.

12. James A. Farley, *Jim Farley's Story,* 46–47.

13. Thomas Sugrue, "Farley's Guess Man, *American Magazine* CXXI, no. 5 (May 1936), 87.

14. Hurja quoted in Alva Johnson, "Professor Hurja, The New Deal's Political Doctor," *Saturday Evening Post* 208, no. 6 (June 1936), 8. DNC Special Notices Showing Appropriations for Your State," 17 September 1934, Box 34, Hurja Papers FDRL.

15. "Memorandum for Col. Louis M. Howe," 1934, Box 70, Hurja Papers FDRL. See also G. Donald Kennedy to Louis M. Howe, 21 October 1934, re: Hurja strategy for carrying Michigan for the Democrats, Box 14, Frank Murphy Papers, Bentley Library, Ann Arbor MI.

16. FDR quoted in William E. Leuchtenburg, *The FDR Years: On Roosevelt and His Legacy* (New York: Columbia University Press, 1995), 29. Arthur M. Schlesinger, Jr., *The Imperial Presidency* (Boston: Houghton Mifflin, 1989).

17. Sugrue, "Farley's Guess Man," 87; James A. Farley to FDR, 3 November 1934, Box 34, Farley Papers, Library of Congress. For midterm elections see Norman Ornstein et al., eds., *Vital Statistics on Congress* (Washington, DC: Congressional Quarterly, 1987), 51f.

18. Memo on FDR response to James A. Farley to FDR letter, 3 November 1934, Box 34,Farley Papers, Library of Congress; Paul Kleppner, *Who Votes? The Dynamics of electoral Turnout, 1870–1980* (New York: Praeger, 1982), 85, 89; "Mid-Terms: President's Party Suffers," New York *Times* 10 October 1998.

19. Ray Tucker, "Chart and Graph Man," *Colliers* 95 (12 January 1935), 41; Sugrue, "Hurja," 87.

20. Hurja memo on using WPA, 23 January, and 18 March 1935, Letterbox; James Twohey to Emil Hurja, 23 January 1936, Box 58, Hurja Papers, FDRL. Richard Jensen wrote, "when Neyman invented modern sampling techniques, virtually the entire array of statistical techniques that would be used through the 1970s was in place." "Six Sciences of American Politics," *Historical Methods* 17, no. 3 (summer 1984), 114.

21. American Institute of Public Opinion poll, 24 November 1936, Hurja Letterbox, Hurja Papers, FDRL.

22. Stanley High, *Roosevelt Then and Now* (New York: Harper, 1937), 14, 88, 116.

23. See Gallup polls, Box 80, Hurja Papers, FDRL. For *Literary Digest* polls see Johnson, "Professor Hurja," 74.

24. "Memo and Questionnaire," 1935, Box 61, Hurja Papers, FDRL; Special Correspondence, Box 35, Farley Papers, Library of Congress.

25. George Gallup and Saul Rae, *The Pulse of Democracy* (New York: Simon & Shuster, 1940), 34–35. See also Tom W. Smith, "The First Straw: A Study in the Origins of Election Polls," *Public Opinion Quarterly* 54, no. 4 1(990), 21.

26. Script for "Radio Talk by Dr. George Gallup and Interlocutor," 1935, Box 91, Eugene Meyer Papers, Library of Congress.

27. Tucker, "Chart and Graph Man," 41; Johnson, "New Deal's Political Doctor," 74.

28. Michael Barone, "The Power of the President's Pollsters," *Public Opinion* 11, no. 3 (September-October 1988), 2. David Kennedy in his book doubts that Longism pushed FDR leftward in 1935. *Freedom From Fear: The American People in Depression and War, 1929–1945* (New York: Oxford, 1999), 242.

29. James A. Farley memo, 18 June 1935, Box 38, Farley Papers, Library of Congress.

30. Farley, *Jim Farley's Story,* 51, 52.

31. *Ibid.,* 54. For polls see "Secret Ballot," National Inquirer, Boxes 70 and 121, Hurja Papers, FDRL.

32. *Jim Farley's Story,* 54.

33. Box 58, Hurja Papers, FDRL.

34. Johnson, "Professor Hurja," 72.

35. Farley, *Behind The Ballots,* 291.

36. William E. Leuchtenburg, cited in *History of American Presidential Elections, 1789–1968,* eds. A. M. Schlesinger, Jr. and Fred L. Israel (New York: McGraw-Hill, 1971), 2809.

37. Harold Ickes, *The Secret Diary of Harold Ickes I* (New York: Simon & Shuster, 1954), 6, 603.

38. Tucker, "Chart and Graph Man," 28; Johnson, "Professor Hurja," 8; "Political Notes," *Time,* 27 March 1936, 16f.

39. Ibid.

40. Claude E. Robinson, "Recent Developments in the Straw-Poll Field–Part 2, *Public Opinion Quarterly* II (October, 1937), 48; Daniel Katz and Hadley

Cantril, "Public Opinion Polls," *Public Opinion Quarterly* I (July-August 1937), 155.

41. James A. Farley to Emil Hurja, 17 September 1936, re: Richfield Oil Poll, Box 70; "Country vs. City," Box 121, Hurja Papers, FDRL. For a study that asserts that the New Deal voter coalition grew mostly from new voters and not "conversion," see Kristi Anderson, *Creation of a Democratic Majority, 1928–1936* (Chicago: University of Chicago Press, 1979). Hurja's on-the-scene polling indicates that both factors were operative, although he also finds that a larger percentage of "new" voters than "old" voters were going Democratic in 1936.

42. Tucker, "Chart and Graph Man," 28; Johnson, "Professor Hurja," 8; *Review of Reviews* 92 (1936), 23.

43. Emil Hurja to Edward Johnson, 22 July 1936, Box 60, Hurja Papers, FDRL.

44. R.H. Tatlow to Emil Hurja, 2 March 1936, Box 80, Hurja Papers, FDRL. See also Emil Hurja to Frank Murphy, 29 May 1936, Box 14, Frank Murphy Papers, Bentley Library.

45. G.D. Kennedy to Frank Murphy, 1 June 1936, "Poll of the Voters of the State of Michigan taken in Spring 1936," Box 81, Hurja Papers, FDRL.

46. Schlesinger, *History of American Presidential Elections,* 2833; Alan Brinkley, *Voices of Protest: Huey Long, Father Coughlin and the Great Depression* (New York: Random House, 1983), 284. Hurja in October predicted: "The left wing has no leadership. The only place it can go in the next election is with President Roosevelt," Memo, 17 October 1935, Box 67, Hurja Papers, FDRL.

47. James S. Twohey to Emil Hurja, memo 1936, Box 58, Hurja Papers, FDRL.

48. "Experiment Operation" 4–6, Box 58, Hurja Papers, FDRL. Robert Eisinger has found some evidence in the Hoover papers that President Herbert Hoover was the "first president to gauge public opinion systematically by creating confidential quantifiable measurement" of newspaper editorials. Robert M. Eisinger, "Gauging Public Opinion in the Hoover White House," *Presidential Studies Quarterly* 30, no. 4 (December 2000), 656. Hurja's measurement of newspaper opinion went beyond editorials and included any press stories on New Deal programs, positive or negative, and details on where the articles were positioned in the paper and the size of the story and the accompanying headline.

49. Harold J. Gross to Emil Hurja, 28 March 1936, Documents Selected from the Emil Hurja Papers Pertaining to Michigan Politics, 1932–1937," microfilm, Bentley Library.

50. "Preliminary Report on Election Situation," 25 September 1936, Box 81, Hurja Papers, FDRL.

51. Sugrue, "Farley's Guess Man," 90; Political Notes, *Time* XXXVII, no. 9 (2 March 1936), 17.

52. Hurja "Memorandum for the President," 24 October 1936, Box 70, Hurja Papers, FDRL.

53. Emil Hurja to Aiken, 27 September 1936, Letterbox, Hurja Papers, FDRL.

54. Tucker, "Chart and Graph Man," 41.

55. Lawrence R. Jacobs and Robert Shapiro, "Issues, Candidate Image and Priming: The Use of Private Polls in Kennedy's 1960 Presidential Campaign, *American Political Science Review* 88 (994), 527–540; same authors, "The Rise of Presidential Polling: The Nixon White House in Historical Perspective, *Public Opinion Quarterly* 59 (1999), 163–195; same authors, "The Presidential Manipulation of Polls and Public Opinion: The Nixon Administration and the Pollsters," *Political Science Quarterly* 110 (winter 1995–96), 72f; Alva Johnson, "Professor Hurja," *Saturday Evening Post*, 13 June 1936, 72.

56. R. H. Tatlow to Emil Hurja, 21 October 1936, Box 81; "Crum Adjusted Poll," 24 October 1936, Box 72, Hurja Papers, FDRL.

57. R.H. Tatlow to Emil Hurja, 19 October 1936, Box 81, Hurja Papers, FDRL.

58. Charles Smith, Jr., *Public Opinion in a Democracy: A Study in American Politics* (New York: Prentice Hall, 1939), 407.

59. Memorandum, 2 November 1936, Box 40, Farley Papers, Library of Congress.

60. Farley quoted in *Behind the Ballots*, 223. Nathaniel Boynton, "James Farley: A Study in Practical Politics" (B.A. Thesis, Princeton University, 1939), 104, Box 40, Farley Papers, Library of Congress.

61. Katz and Cantril, "Public Opinion Polls," 155.

62. Archibald Crossley, "Straw Polls in 1936," *Public Opinion Quarterly* I (January 1937), 32. Crossley's qualifier was "publicly," since Hurja had been using quotas and weighting samples "privately" for the DNC since 1932.

63. Harold Gosnell, "How Accurate Were the Polls?" *Public Opinion Quarterly* I (January 1937), 103; Jean Converse, *Survey Research in the United States, 1890–1960* (Berkeley: University of California Press, 1987), 121.

64. Charles Smith, *Public Opinion in a Democracy*, 400.

65. Katz and Cantril, "Public Opinion Polls," 155.

66. "How a Presidential Election is Won," Box 82, Hurja Papers, FDRL.

67. Speech transcript "Country vs. City," 1940, Box 121, Hurja Papers, FDRL.

68. Samuel Lubell, *The Future of American Politics* (New York: Harper Row, 1951), 43–63. See also John Allswang, *The New Deal and American Politics* (New York: Wiley & Son, 1978), 88.

69. Robert M. Eisinger and Jeremy Brown, "Polling as a Means Toward Presidential Autonomy: Emil Hurja, Hadley Cantril and the Roosevelt Administration," *International Journal of Public Opinion Research* 10, no. 1 (1998), 237, 240, 247.

70. Joseph P. Lasch, *Dealers and Dreamers: A New Look at the New Deal* (New York: Doubleday, 1988), 207–208. For a description of Hurja by a contemporary see File 3, Box 6, Hurja Papers, Tennessee State Archives.

71. Hurja Papers, Box 18; FDR Personal File, 2080–2110 in 2099, FDR papers, FDRL.

72. Washington *Herald,* 26 December 1936 and Washington *Post,* 19 December 1936, Box 67, Hurja Papers, FDRL.

73. Washington *Post,* 19 February 1937, Box 67, Hurja Papers, FDRL.

74. Ibid.

75. Washington *Post,* 7 June 1950, Box 67, Hurja Papers, FDRL.

76. Washington *Post,* 28 June 1937, Box 67, Hurja Papers, FDRL.

CHAPTER 5

1. Nathan Miller, *FDR: An Intimate History* (New York: Doubleday, 1983), 395–98. Senator Wheeler, quoted in David M. Kennedy, *Freedom From Fear: The American People in Depression and War, 1929–1945* (New York: Oxford University Press, 1999), 331.

2. Kennedy, *Freedom From Fear,* 331, 334.

3. Otis Graham, *An Encore For Reform: The Old Progressives and the New Deal* (New York: Oxford University Press, 1967), 48, 49.

4. Raymond Moley, *After Seven Years* (New York: Harper Bros., 1939), 368; Miller, *FDR* 414–415; Kennedy, *Freedom From Fear,* 338; Richard Polenberg, "Franklin D. Roosevelt and the Purge of John O'Connor," *New York History* XLIX, no. 3 (July 1968), 306f. For poll results see American Institute of Public Opinion, 31 July 1938, Box 89, Hurja Papers, FDRL. Hurja quoted in Joseph P. Lash, *Dealers and Dreamers: A New Look at the New Deal* (New York: Doubleday, 1988), 281.

5. "Emil Hurja Returns from European Trip," Washington *Herald,* 16 December 1936; "Alaska Has Lost Potential Governor," Johnstown [PA] *Tribune,* 8 MARCH 1937; "News Behind the News," Washington D.C. *Star,* 11 March 1937, newsclips in Box 67, Hurja Papers, FDRL. See also Amanda Hamilton Scrapbook, Hurja Papers, Tennessee State Archives.

6. Erwin C. Hargrove, *The President as Leader: Appealing to the Better Angels of our Nature* (Lawrence: University Press of Kansas, 1998), 99; H. H. Remers, *Introduction to Opinion and Attitude Measurement* (New York: Harper Bros., 1954), 295.

7. Arthur Schlesinger, Jr., *The Imperial Presidency* (Boston: Houghton Mifflin, 1989), 187, 206–07, 441; Robert M. Eisinger and Jeremy Brown, "Polling as a Means toward Presidential Autonomy: Emil Hurja, Hadley Cantril and the Roosevelt Administration," *International Journal of Public Opinion Research* 10, no. 1 (1998), 237f; Richard W. Steele, "American Popular Opinion and the War Against Germany: The Issue of Negotiated Peace, 1942," *Journal of American History* LLLXV, no. 3 (December 1978), 704f.

8. William E. Leuchtenburg, *The FDR Years: On Roosevelt and his Legacy* (New York: Columbia University Press, 1995), 28, 29. Also see Joan Biskupic, "Gaveling Back the Imperial Presidency," *Washington Post Weekly Edition,* 9 June 1997, 21.

9. David M. Kennedy, *Freedom From Fear,* 338.

10. Emil Hurja to Saul Haas, 23 September 1937, Box 43, Saul Haas Papers, Manuscripts Division, University of Washington Library; Emil Hurja to Bernard Baruch, 18 February 1937 and Bernard Baruch to Emil Hurja, 20 February 1937, Box 13, Hurja Papers, FDRL.

11. "Fairbanksian on Noted Tour of the Orient," 16 December 1935, "Japanese Expansion," 8 January 1935, and "Colorful Shanghai," Juneau *Empire,* 20 January 1936, in Scrapbook, Hurja Papers, Tennessee State Archives.

12. "Merrill-Lambie flight from New York to London and Return," Box 26, Hurja Papers, FDRL.

13. George Gallup to Emil Hurja, 20 and 29 November 1937; polls, 14 and 21 September 1938, Box 88; Special Ohio Survey, 20 September 1938; "Essential Information for Interviewers," Box 14, Hurja Papers, FDRL. See also Box 88 for Ohio polls.

14. Olavi Koivukangas, "The Beginnings of Finnish Migration to the New World," exhibition catalog (Turku, Finland: Migration Institute, 1988).

15. "First Permanent Settlement in the Delaware River Valley, " Report no. 1391, 1–5, 75th Congress, U.S. House of Representatives; "Finnish Aspects of the Delaware Tercentenary," Box 3, Delaware Tercentenary Collection, Finnish-American Heritage Center, Finlandia University.

16. *American Swedish Monthly* 32, no. 3 (June 1938).

17. John Wuorinen, *The Finns on the Delaware* (New York: Columbia University Press, 1938).

18. Emil Hurja to Rudolph Holsti, May 1938, Box 137, Hurja Papers, FDRL.

19. Pehr Holmes, quoted in U.S. Congressional Record, 21 August 1937, 12309, 12312.

20. Frank Hook speech transcript, Box 3, Delaware Tercentenary Collection, Finnish American Heritage Center.

21. Thomas and Speaker of the House, quoted in Ibid., 149–151. Representative Allen's Report to Committee on Foreign Affairs, no. 1391, House of Representatives, 75th Congress, 1–5.

22. Eero Djerf to Arne Suominen, 14 February 1938, Box 3, Delaware Tercentenary Collection, Finnish-American Heritage.

23. Emil Hurja to R. Holsti, May 1938, Box 137, Hurja Papers, FDRL.

24. Emil Hurja to Eliel Saarinen, 27 January 1938, Box 138, Hurja Papers, FDRL.

25. Ray North memo and FDR response, 8 April 1938, President's Personal File 2099, FDR Papers.

26. Franklin D. Roosevelt to Rudolph Holsti, 14 June 1938, Box 3, Delaware Tercentenary Collection; Max Engman, "The Tug of War Over 'Nya Sverige' 1938," *Swedish American Historical Quarterly* XLV, no. 2 (April 1994), 106.

27. FDR "Acceptance Speech: Swedish Monument," 27 June 1938, Delaware Tercentenary, FDR Speech File 1139, FDRL; William A. Degregorio, *The Complete Book of U.S. Presidents* (New York: Wings Books Random House, 1993), 480.

28. Eero Djerf to Ernest Knuti, 4 January 1938; Press releases from Emil Hurja, Box 3, Delaware Tercentenary Collection, Finnish Heritage Center; Mayor William Ward to Arthur Hurja, 15 June 1938, Box 138, Hurja Papers, FDRL; "Finnish American Monument Presented," Chester [PA] *Times,* 29 June 1938. For FDR message see FDR to Rudolph Holsti, 24 June 1938, Box 4, Hurja Papers, Finlandia University.

29. Eero Djerf to Amos Anderson, 5 July 1938; Eero Djerf to Emil Backman (Order of Runeberg), 5 February 1938; Eero Djerf to Ernest Knuti, 11 December 1937; Rev. Reino Hiironen to Eero Djerf, 24 January 1939; Emil Hurja press releases, June 1938; George Halonen (Central Cooperative Wholesale) to Eero Djerf, 25 April 1938, Box 3, Delaware Tercentenary Collection, Finlandia University.

30. Remarks of Eero Jarnfelt, minister from Finland to the United States, at Forefathers dinner, Philadelphia, 6 April 1938, Box 3, Delaware Tercentenary, Finlandia University.

CHAPTER 6

1. Emil Hurja to J. J. Broderick, 2 January 1941, Box 104; Sevellon Brown to Emil Hurja, 5 July 1939, Box 16; *Newsweek* 17 July 1939, XIV, 39; Emil Hurja to J. K. Furnace [1939], Box 104, Hurja Papers, Franklin D. Roosevelt Library (hereafter, FDRL).

2. Sevellon Brown to Emil Hurja, 3 October 1939, Box 16; "Pathfinder Announces New Circulation Guarantees and Rate Reductions," April 1940, Box 110, Hurja Papers, FDRL.

3. Announcement to Advertisers, 1939, Box 100, Hurja Papers, FDRL.

4. Sevellon Brown to Emil Hurja, 5 July 1939, Box 16, Hurja Papers, FDRL.

5. "Resume: Pathfinder Progress in Advertising," 1940, Box 99, Emil Hurja to D. H. Bangs, 1 August 1940 Box 99, Hurja Papers, FDRL.

6. Emil Hurja to Gerard Johnson of General Motors Corporation, 30 April 1943; Emil Hurja to F. J. Solon (Illinois Glass Company), 26 May 1943, Box 97; Emil Hurja to Stuart D. Cowan of Cowan, Inc., 4 March 1941, Box 14, Hurja Papers, FDRL.

7. Emil Hurja to Harold Boeschenstin, 16 April 1942, Box 99, Hurja Papers, FDRL.

8. Eloise Engle and Lauri Paananen, *The Winter War: The Soviet Attack on Finland, 1939–1940* (Mechanicsburg, PA: Stackpole Books, 1973), vii, 270.

9. Nikita Kruschev, *Kruschev Remembers* (Boston: Little Brown, 1970), 152–153.

10. "The National Scene," *Pathfinder,* 10 February 1940, 4.

11. "Winter War" files, National Ski Hall of Fame, Ishpeming, Michigan.

12. FDR quoted in Nathan Miller, *FDR: An Intimate History* (New York: Meridian Books, 1983), 443; and in *Propaganda Analysis* (New York: Institute for Propaganda Analysis, Inc., April, 1940), 15.

14. *Propaganda Analysis,* 2.

15. Ibid., 6, 7. Herbert Hoover memo, 18 February 1940, Box 141; Albert Lodwick to Herbert Hoover, 18 January 1940, Box 5, Hurja Papers, FDRL. Later during the Continuation War Cordell Hull put pressure on to end humanitarian relief to Finland. Preston Davie, president of For Finland, Inc., to Emil Hurja, 23 December 1941, Ambassador Hjalmar Procope Papers, National Archives of Finland.

16. *Pathfinder,* 10 Feb. 1940, 1,4.

17. La Guardia, quoted in *Propaganda Analysis* 7; Engle and Paananen, *Winter War*, 153–157; Thomas P. Morgan, chairman of Fighting Funds for Finland, to Emil Hurja, 5 April 1940, Box 141, Hurja Papers, FDRL.

18. "Between You, Me and the Gatepost," *Pathfinder*, 10 February. 1940, 10.

19. Georg A. Gripenberg, *Finland and the Great Powers: Memoirs of a Diplomat* (Lincoln: University of Nebraska Press, 1965), 91; Chamberlain, quoted in Keith G. Feiling, *The Life of Neville Chamberlain* (London: MacMillan, 1946), 427; *Propaganda Analysis*, 1, 3, 5.

20. FDR, quoted in Miller, *FDR* 442; Emil Hurja notes on Winter War, Hurja Papers, FDRL.

21. Wheeler and Wagner, quoted in *Propaganda Analysis*, 5.

22. *Propaganda Analysis*, 15, 16, Box 139, Hurja Papers, FDRL. Manfred Jonas, *Isolationism in America, 1935–1941* (Ithaca, NY: Cornell University Press, 1966), 274; Wayne S. Cole, *Roosevelt and the Isolationists* (Lincoln: University of Nebraska Press, 1983), 364.

23. Ibid.

24. Robert A. Divine, *Roosevelt and World War II* (Baltimore, MD: Johns Hopkins Press, 1969), 78; "Robeson Opposes Finn Aid as Help to Reactionaries," NEW YORK *World Telegram*, December 1939, Box 139, Hurja Papers, FDRL. See also Ronald E. Powaski, *The Cold War: The United States and the Soviet Union, 1917–1991* (New York: Oxford University Press, 1998), 45.

25. Emil Hurja to Saul Haas, "Nationwide Poll of Public Opinion Respecting Presidential Candidates, April-May, 1939," Saul Haas Papers, University of Washington Library; "Garner for President," 13 April 1940, Box 23, Hurja Papers, FDRL.

26. George H. Gallup, *The Gallup Poll: Public Opinion, 1935–1971* I (New York: American Institute of Public Opinion, 1971), 129; *Time*, 20 March 1939, 12; *Pathfinder* Polls, 12 and 26 August 1939, Box 29, Hurja Papers, FDRL. Hurja's polls were described as "scientifically weighted and balanced to take proper measure of the natural variation existing among such voters as urban workers, farmers, professional people and manual laborers, employed and unemployed, rich and poor, young and old, and all the other disparate groups that make up small-towns, America's big towns and plain dirt-farm America." 26 August 1939 Hurja Papers, Box 103 FDRL.

27. *Pathfinder* Poll, 25 May 1940, Box 103; *Pathfinder* Family Poll, September 1940, Box 99, Hurja Papers, FDRL.

28. Ibid. Pollees quoted in Special Survey, *Pathfinder* Poll, 3 September 1940, Box 114, Hurja Papers, FDRL.

29. "Mighty Close, But Race is Still Willkie's," *Pathfinder*, 2 November 1940.

30. Daniel Katz, "The Public Opinion Polls and the 1940 Election," *Public Opinion Quarterly* V, (March 1941), 52, 55, 67.

31. "No Alibis But," *Pathfinder*, 16 November 1940; Harold Gosnell, *Champion Campaigner: Franklin D. Roosevelt* (New York: MacMillan, 1952), 183; Archibald Crossley, "Methods Tested During the 1940 Campaign," *Public Opinion Quarterly* V (March 1941), 86.

32. Gallup, *The Gallup Poll*, 247.
33. Hurja, quoted in letter to Jim Sweinhart, 27 November 1940, Box 9. Hurja Papers, FDRL.; Samuel Lubell, "Post-Mortem: Who Elected Roosevelt?" *Saturday Evening Post* CCXIII (25 January 25, 1941), 9; George Gallup, "Post-Election Analysis Reveal Political Trends," Washington *Post*, 8 December 1940, Box 116, Hurja Papers, FDRL. See also Richard Jensen, "The Cities Reelect Roosevelt: Ethnicity, Religion, and Class in 1940," *Ethnicity* VIII, no. 2 (1981), 189–195.
34. See FBI investigation into Hurja role in setting up "Willkie Committee of One Million," 20 December 1940, File Number 624179–Reference Number 62–77367–6: U.S. Department of Justice; FBI Files released under the Freedom of Information Act. Hurja quoted in letter to James Adams, 11 November 1940, Box 118, Hurja Papers, FDRL.
35. Hurja to Stuart Cowan, 4 March 1941, Box 14; J. Fritz Randolph to Emil Hurja 1 May 1942, Box 105; Cyrus Eaton to Emil Hurja, 23 March 1942, Box 3; Karl Mundt to Emil Hurja, 3 August 1942, Box 7, Hurja Papers, FDRL.
36. Emil Hurja to Ted Hurja, 16 May 1942, Box 101; Circulation Statement, 30 June 1942, Box 134, Hurja Papers, FDRL
37. Emil Hurja to National Circulation Company, 12 January 1943, Box 133; Emil Hurja to Estelle Smiley, 10 August 1943, Box 105; Emil Hurja to Norton family, 18 June 1943; Emil Hurja to Fred Hargrove, 18 June 1943, Box 104, Hurja Papers, FDRL.
38. Emil Hurja to James Adams, 31 August 1943, Box 107; Emil Hurja to Joseph Pew, Jr., 20 February 20,1942, Box 105, Hurja Papers, FDRL.
39. *Pathfinder* Polls, 23 May and 14 November 1942 and 1 July 1943, Box 109, Hurja Papers, FDRL.
40. Press release—Prediction Monday a.m., 6 November 1944; Emil Hurja to Graham Patterson, October 1944, Box 98, Hurja Papers, FDRL.
41. Press release, 6 November 1944; Emil Hurja to Graham Patterson, 11 November 1944, Box 131, Hurja Papers, FDRL.
42. "Between You, Me and the Gatepost," *Pathfinder*, 13 July 1943, 15.
43. Reverend Alfred Haapanen Petition, 22 May 1944; Emil Hurja to V.K. Nikander, 17 May 1944; the *Raavaija*, 13 October 1941. Box 139, Hurja Papers, FDRL.
44. "Between You, Me and the Gatepost," *Pathfinder*, 25 September 1943, 5.
45. Allen Weinstein and Alexander Vassiliev, *The Haunted Wood: Soviet Espionage in America-The Stalin Era* (New York: Random House, 1999), 246–247. Farley quoted in *Jim Farley's Story: The Roosevelt Years* (New York: McGraw Hill, 1948), 176. For FDR's hubris see Robert A. Divine, *Roosevelt and World War II*, 72–73 and William Bullitt, "How We Won the War and Lost the Peace," *Life* XXV, 30 August 1948, 94.
46. Emil Hurja to Harry Truman, 5 July 1945, Box 140, Hurja Papers, FDRL; Hannu Rautkallio, *Finland and the Holocaust: The Rescue of Finland's Jews* (New York: Holocaust Library, 987).

47. Emil Hurja to Len Billingsly, 3 July 1948, Box 22; documents on Egypt, Box 144, 145. On his work for the Finnish shipping industry and the Egyptian government see U.S. Department of Justice, Federal Bureau of Investigation files released under the Freedom of Information Act no. 248,563.

48. Emil Hurja to Burton K. Wheeler, 27 March 1945; B. K. Wheeler to Hurja, 9 April 1945, Box 132 Hurja Papers, FDRL. Dewey, quoted in Richard Norton Smith, *Thomas E. Dewey and His Times* (New York: Simon & Shuster, 1982), 438. For the influence of the war in keeping the Democrats in the White House see Gallup's polls in the *Public Opinion Quarterly* 9 (Spring 1945), 65.

49. Emil Hurja to James A. Farley, 18 June 1946, Box 3; Emil Hurja to Harry Truman 26 December 1946, Box 21, Hurja Papers, FDRL; Emil Hurja to Harry Truman, 5 April 1952, PPF file 3070, Truman Papers, President Truman Library.

50. Sherman Adams Papers, Box 24, Eisenhower Library; Press release, Box 155, Hurja Papers, FDRL; Harold Gosnell, *Truman Crises: A Political Biography of Harry Truman* (Westport, CT.: Greenwood Press, 1980), 528. Hurja, quoted in letter to Walter Willis, 1 December 1952, Box 155, Hurja Papers. Pittsburgh *Post-Gazette,* 7 November 1952, Hurja Scrapbook, Tennessee State Archives. Pollster George Gallup admitted that the "national polls of 1952 have been justly criticized for being overly cautious in their approach to the presidential election." George Gallup, "The Future Direction of Election Polling," *Public Opinion Quarterly* 17 (spring 1953), 202. Forecaster Louis Bean developed a theory of election cycles by which he predicted that the 1950 elections were the beginning of a "Fair Deal tide" that would win the White House for the Democrats in 1952 and extend into the 1950s. Bean overlooked the impact of several events, including the Korean War, Communist infiltration and spying, and corruption charges that led to a Republican landslide victory. Bean's reputation as the "lone prophet" of 1948 was quashed by the 1952 election results. Theodore Rosenof, "The Legend of Louis Bean: Political Prophecy and the 1948 Election," *The Historian* 62, no. 1 (fall 1999).

51. Emil Hurja to John Foster Dulles, 6 March 1953, Box 195 and "Finland-Hurja file Endorsements," Box 314, Eisenhower Papers, Eisenhower Library.

52. "Emil Hurja Dead: Political Analyst," New York *Times,* 31 May 1953; *Pathfinder* Weekly Radio Broadcast, 12 August 1939; John Bennett speech, 11 June 1946, Bennett Papers, Bentley Library; Herbert Hoover to Emil Hurja, 16 January 1940, Amanda Hamilton Scrapbook, Hurja papers, Tennessee Archives; Alva Johnson, "Professor Hurja," *Saturday Evening Post,* 13 June 1936, 72.

53. Stanley High, *Roosevelt Then and Now* (New York: Harper, 1937), 88, 116.

PRIMARY SOURCES

The principal collection of Emil Hurja papers, 161 boxes, is located at the President Franklin D. Roosevelt Library at Hyde Park, New York. Hurja materials can also be found in the Franklin D. Roosevelt President's Personal File; in the Democratic National Committee and Women's Division papers; and in collections of other New Deal contemporaries, including Louis Bean, Stanley High, Mary "Molly" Dewson, and Harry Hopkins. The second largest collection of Hurja materials is located in Nashville at the Tennessee State Library and Archives, and it covers the early years, including Hurja's college days at the University of Washington and the Ford Peace Ship scrapbook. The collection appears to have been included, possibly by mistake, when Hurja's widow Gudrun sold the President Andrew Jackson collection to the State Library.

Other presidential libraries also produced Hurja correspondence and policy and poll-related materials. They include the Hoover Library, in West Branch, Iowa; the Truman Library, in Independence, Missouri; and the Eisenhower Library, in Abilene, Kansas. The Library of Congress contains several relevant collections, including the papers of James A. Farley of the Democratic National Committee and Eugene Meyer of the Washington *Post* (the latter contains a small but revelatory George Gallup collection). Under the Freedom of Information Act, I was also able to obtain from the U.S. Justice Department the Federal Bureau of Investigation files on Hurja.

Other repositories of primary sources that helped shed light on Hurja's political, public, and private career include the Congressman John Bennett, and Governor Frank Murphy papers, and a microfilm—"Selected Materials from the Papers of Emil Hurja, 1932–1937"—at the University of Michigan's Bentley Library; the Saul Haas papers at the University of Washington Library Manuscripts Division; patronage correspondence in the Ralph Lozier papers at the University of Missouri Western Historical Manuscript Collection in Columbia; the Hurja and Swedish-Finnish Tercentenary files at Finlandia University's Heritage Center Archive; and the Frank C. Walker papers at University of Notre Dame Archives. The Finnish National Archives (Valtionarkisto) in Helsinki produced Hurja correspondence from the Ambassador Hjalmar Procope papers and the Foreign Minister Rudolph Holsti papers. The Migration Institute, directed by Dr. Olavi Koivukangas in Turku, Finland, has online passport and ship registry records.

Finally local archives at the Harbour House in Hurja's hometown, Crystal Falls, Michigan, and the Iron County Museum in Caspian, Michigan, were helpful in filling out young Hurja's life and getting an accurate picture of fin de siècle life in Michigan's Upper Peninsula.

SELECTED BIBLIOGRAPHY

Altschuler, Bruce. *Keeping A Finger on the Public Pulse: Private Polling and Presidential Elections* (Westport, CT: Greenwood Press, 1982).

Ambrose, Stephen. *Eisenhower: Soldier and President* (New York: Simon Shuster, 1990).

Bald, F. Clever. *Michigan in Four Centuries* (New York: Harper Brothers, 1954).

Barone, Michael. *The Almanac of American Politics, 1990* (Washington, D.C.: National Journal, 1990).

Benson, Allan L. *The New Henry Ford* (New York: Funk & Wagnalls, 1923).

Bernhardt, Marcia. *Iron County Historical Sites and Landmarks, 1885–1985* (Caspian, MI: Iron County Historical Museum, 1985).

————. *They Came: Iron County, Michigan* (Norway, MI: Dickinson Iron County School District, 1975).

Berry, R. Michael. *American Foreign Policy and the Finnish Exception* (Jyvaskyla, Finland: Gummeros Oy. 1987).

Burns, James MacGregor. *Roosevelt: The Lion and the Fox* (New York: Harcourt, Brace, 1956).

Boyum, Burton. *The Saga of Iron Mining in Michigan's Upper Peninsula* (Marquette, MI: Longyear Research Library, 1977).

Brinkley, Alan. *The End of Reform: New Deal Liberalism in Recession and War* (New York: Vintage Books, 1995).

————. *Voices of Protest: Huey Long, Father Coughlin, and the Great Depression* (New York: Random House, 1983).

Brown, Mary Ann Wargelin. *Women Who Dared: A History of Finnish-American Women* (Minneapolis, MN: University of Minnesota Press, 1986).

Clark, Henry W. *History of Alaska* (New York: Macmillan, 1930).

Cole, Wayne S., *Roosevelt and the Isolationists* (Lincoln: University of Nebraska Press, 1983)

Collection of Recollections, Crystal Falls, Michigan, 1880–1980 (Crystal Falls, MI: Centennial Committee, 1980).

Converse, Jean M. *Survey Research in the United States* (Berkeley: University of California Press, 1987).

Crowell, F. and B. Murray. *Chemists and Metallurgists: The Iron Ores of Lake Superior* (Cleveland, OH: Penton Publishing Co., 1911).

Dallek, Robert. *Franklin Roosevelt and American Foreign Policy, 1932–1945* (New York: Oxford University Press, 1992).

Divine, Robert A. *Roosevelt and World War II* (Baltimore: J. Hopkins Press, 1969)

Dorsett, Lyle. *Franklin Roosevelt and the City Bosses* (New York: Kennikat Press, 1977).

Etelemaki, Leevi. *The Blue Collar Aristocracy* (Escanaba, MI: Richards Printing, 1996).

Farley, James A. *Jim Farley's Story: The Roosevelt Years* (New York: McGraw-Hill, 1948).

Ferrell, Robert H. *Woodrow Wilson and World War I, 1917–1921* (New York: Harper & Row, 1985).

Flynn, Edward J. *You're the Boss* (New York: Viking Press, 1947).

Gallup, George. *The Sophisticated Poll Watchers Guide* (Princeton, NJ: Princeton Opinion Press, 1972).

———. *The Pulse of Democracy* (New York: Simon Shuster, 1940).

Greeley, A.W. *Handbook of Alaska* (New York: Scribners's Sons, 1925).

Fine, Sidney, *Frank Murphy* (Ann Arbor: University of Michigan Press, 1984).

Freidel, Frank, *Franklin D. Roosevelt: A Rendezvous with Destiny* (Boston: Little Brown, 1990).

———. *Franklin D. Roosevelt: The Triumph* (Boston: Little Brown, 1956).

Gripenberg, Georg *Finland and the Great Powers* (Lincoln: University of Nebraska Press, 1965).

Gosnell, Harold F. *Champion Campaigner: Franklin D. Roosevelt* (New York: Macmillan, 1952).

Hatcher, Harlan *A Century of Iron and Men* (New York: Bobbs-Merrill, 1950).

Harris, Louis. *Inside America* (New York: Vintage Books, 1987).

Herbst, Susan. *Numbered Voices: How Public Opinion Polling Has Shaped American Politics* (Chicago: University of Chicago Press, 1993).

Hoffman, Bernard. *Reflections of Old Crystal Falls* (Crystal Falls, MI: 1990).

Hill, Jack. *A History of Iron County Michigan* (Norway, MI: Norway Current, 1976).

Hoglund, A. William. *Finnish Immigrants in America, 1880–1920* (Madison: University of Wisconsin Press, 1960).

Honkala, Maxine. *Red Dust 1988* (National Mine, MI: Middle School, 1988).

Jalkanen, Ralph, ed. *Faith of the Finns: Historical Perspectives on the Finnish Lutheran Church in America* (East Lansing: Michigan State University Press, 1972).

Jonas, Manfred. *Isolationism in America: 1935–1941* (Ithaca, NY: Cornell University Press, 1966).

Karni, Michael, Matti Kaups, and Douglas Ollila, Jr., eds. *Migration Studies C3* (Turku, Finland: Institute for Migration, 1975).

Karni, Michael ed. *Finnish Diaspora II: United States* (Toronto: Multicultural History Society of Ontario, 1981).

Kempainen, Rudolph. "The Home: The Center of Activity for Early Finns," in *Central Upper Peninsula Finnish-American Bicentennial, 1776–1976* (Marquette, MI: 1976)

Kennedy, David M. *Freedom From Fear: The American People in Depression and War, 1929–1945* (New York: Oxford University Press, 1999).

Kero, Reino. *Migration From Finland to North America: U.S. Civil War to First World War* (Vamala, Finland: Vamala Publishing, 1974).

Kleppner, Paul. *Who Voted? The Dynamics of Electoral Turnout, 1870–1980* (New York: Praeger, 1982).

Koivukangas, Olavi. *Migration Studies* C1 to C3 (Turku, Finland: Migration Institute, 1974, 1995).

——*Delaware 350* (Turku, Finland: Migration Institute, 1988).

Kostiainen, Auvo, ed. *Finnish Identity in America* (Turku, Finland: Historical Archives, 1990).

Kraft, Barbara S. *The Peace Ship: Henry Ford's Pacifist Adventure in the First World War* (New York: Macmillan, 1978).

Krosby, H. Peter. *Finland, Germany and the Soviet Union, 1940–1941* (Madison: University of Wisconsin Press, 1968).

Larson, Amanda Wiljanen. *Finnish Heritage in America* (Marquette, MI: Delta Kappa Gamma Society, 1976).

Lash, Joseph. *Dealers and Dreamers: A New Look at the New Deal* (New York: Doubleday, 1988).

Leuchtenburg, William E. *The FDR Years: On Roosevelt and His Legacy* (New York: Columbia University Press, 1995)

——. *Franklin Roosevelt and the New Deal* (New York: Harper Collins, 1963)

Lindley, Ernest K. *The Roosevelt Revolution: The First Phase* (New York: Viking, 1933).

Lochner, Louis P. *America's Don Quixote: Henry Ford's Attempt to Save Europe* (London: Kegan Paul, 1924).

Magnaghi, Russell M. *The Way It Happened: Settling Michigan's Upper Peninsula* (Iron Mountain, MI: Mid-Peninsula Library Cooperative, 1982).

McJimsey, George. *The Presidency of Franklin Roosevelt* (Lawrence :University Press of Kansas, 2000).

Michelson, Charles. *The Ghost Talks* (New York: Putnam & Sons, 1944).

Miller, Nathan. *FDR: An Intimate History* (New York: Meridian Books, 1983).

Mitgang, Herbert. *Once Upon a Time: Jimmy Walker, Franklin Roosevelt and the Last Great Battle of the Jazz Age* (New York: Free Press, 2000).

Moley, Raymond. *After Seven Years* (New York: Harper Bros., 1939).

Morgan, Ted. *FDR: A Biography* (New York: Simon Shuster, 1985).

Nichols, Jeannette P. *Alaska* (New York: Russell & Russell, 1963).

Nursey, Walter R. *The Monominee Range: Its Cities, Their Industries and Resources* (Norway, MI: Swain and Tate Printers, 1891, reissued 1972).

Moore, David W. *The Superpollsters: How They Measure and Manipulate Public Opinion in America* (New York: Four Walls Publishing, 1995).

Peel, Roy V., and Thomas C. Donnelly. *The 1932 Campaign: An Analysis* (New York: Farrar & Rinehart, 1935).

Powaski, Ronald E. T. *The Cold War: The United States and the Soviet Union 1917–1991* (New York: Oxford University Press, 1998).

Riccards, Michael P. *The Ferocious Engine of Democracy: A History of the American Presidency* (New York: Madison Books, 1995).

Rosenmann, Samuel I. *Working With Roosevelt* (New York: Harper Bros., 1952)

Ross, Carl. *The Finn Factor in American Labor, Culture, Society* (New York Mills, MN: Parta Publishing, 1977).

Roosevelt, Eleanor. *This I Remember* (New York: Harper Brothers, 1949).

Sabato, Larry J. *The Rise of Political Consultants: New Ways of Winning Elections* (New York: Basic Books, 1981).

Shapiro, Robert Y., Martha J. Kumar, and Lawrence R. Jacobs. *Presidential Power: Forging the Presidency for the Twenty-First Century* (New York: Columbia University Press, 2000).

Schlesinger, Arthur M. Jr. *The Imperial Presidency* (Boston: Houghton Mifflin, 1973, 1989).

——*The Politics of Upheaval* (Boston: Houghton Mifflin, 1960).

Schlesinger, Arthur M. Jr., Fred Isreal, and William Hansen. *History of American Presidential Elections III* (New York: McGraw Hill, 1971).

Schwartz, Andrew. *America and the Russo-Finnish War* (Washington, DC: Public Affairs Press, 1960).

Sherwood, Robert. *Roosevelt and Hopkins: An Intimate History* (New York: Harper, 1948).

Smith, Charles W. *Public Opinion in a Democracy: A Study in American Politics* (New York: Prentice-Hall, 1939).

Smith, Richard Norton. *Thomas Dewey and His Times* (New York: Simon Shuster, 1982).

Sobel, Robert. *The Origins of Interventionism: The United States and the Russo Finnish War* (New York: Bookman Associates, 1960).

Traugott, Michael W. and Paul Lavrakas, *The Voters' Guide to Election Polls* (New York: Chatham House Publishers, 2000).

Tugwell, Rexford G. *The Brains Trust* (New York: Viking Press, 1968).

Utter, Leo. "Western Finn Halls: Scenes of Activity," in *Tyomies-Eteenpain,* anniversary issue (Superior, WI: Tyomies Society, 1988).

Virtanen, Keijo. "Disaffection: Finns Leave America," in *Migration Studies* C3, eds. Michael Karni, Matti Kaups, and Douglas Ollila, Jr. (Turku, Finland: Institute for Migration, 1975).

Ware, Susan. *Partner and I: Molly Dewson, Feminism and New Deal Politics* (New Haven: Yale Press, 1987).

——. *Beyond Suffrage: Women in the New Deal* (Cambridge, MA: Harvard University Press, 1981).

Weed, Clyde, P. *The Nemesis of Reform: The Republican Party During the New Deal* (New York: Columbia University Press, 1994).

White, Edward. *The Constitution and the New Deal* (Cambridge, MA: Harvard University Press, 2000).

INDEX